Unhinged in Ethiopia

Two Thousand Kilometers of Hell and
Heaven on a Bicycle

George Balarezo

Dear Camp,

I hope you enjoy
my book!

All the best!
— George —

ISBN: 978-1-0879-8726-2 (paperback)

ISBN: (ebook)

cover design: Rafael Andres

intrepidglobalcitizen.com

Contents

Chapter 1

Shovel Trouble

"Do try to not fight a lion if you are not a lion yourself."
—Tanzanian proverb

Having been on the road in Ethiopia for two and a half weeks and having covered a thousand kilometers, I was finally acclimating to high-altitude cycling. It was around two in the afternoon, and I'd been pedaling uphill since seven that morning. After a hard-won battle with the switchback roads, I found respite in a straight incline. With my lungs taking a much-needed break, I exhaled in relief. It was the hottest time of day, and my cheeks and nose stung from the relentless onslaught of the Ethiopian sun. At least I was breathing easily again.

Two young men toiled in the distance. Wielding shovels, they strained as they broke and tossed the hard-baked earth. Growing swiftly larger as I approached, they stopped working and glared at me. My eyes darted around, scanning for the Kalashnikovs so many villagers in the Wollo Highlands carried. The only weapons I saw were used for digging, but I knew these men wouldn't simply let me pass.

Suddenly, I was almost upon them. They were both about 180 centimeters tall, perhaps a bit shorter, and appeared to be in their late teens. With their chiseled deltoids and triceps, they looked like anatomy-textbook illustrations. Red capillaries mapped menace in their eyes, and the dark rings beneath those eyes spoke both of toil and long-standing *khat* addiction (green khat leaves protruded from their cracked lips). Furrowed brows signaled emotional duress. They had an aura of tough persistence: no doubt the world of khat, cattle wars, and blistering sun had long-since robbed them of their innocence.

My heart rate shot up, and my neck and shoulders pulsed with tense energy. My breathing shallow and rapid, I felt as if I were pedaling uphill again. The desert landscape disappeared as my vision narrowed to the threat in front of me.

I attempted to cycle around them, but they blocked my path. My front tire brushed one of their knees.

I scanned my surroundings for someone else—a priest or mullah, a village woman, anyone who might support me. I saw no one. Malformed cacti towered nearby, suggesting a way of defending myself. Unfortunately, even if I dashed for their thorns, I wouldn't make it in time to use one as a weapon.

"Money! Money!" they chanted. The teens clutched their shovels with both hands.

"Hi. My name is George. What is your name?" I stuck my hand out and smiled in a desperate attempt to humanize myself and deescalate the situation. Perhaps they would realize I was just a guy who was living his dream by cycling from Addis Ababa to the remote desert highlands during his winter vacation.

"Money! Money!" They ignored my attempt at a handshake.

"Are you students? Where is your school?" I asked. "*Hasta mari.*" *I am a teacher*

"Money! Money!" Their voices rang louder as their eyebrows creased into a V-shape.

Once again, I tried to cycle around them. The boy to my right jammed his shovel into the spokes of my front wheel while the other gripped his as a weapon.

We were at a standstill. Time compressed itself and I found myself in a slow-motion movie. My thoughts and emotions froze. The tips of my fingers pulsed with anticipation. Each inhalation made my stomach tingle. Every exhalation sent adrenaline surging through my body. The feeling was foreign, primal, and unlike anything I'd ever experienced before. I was ready to battle 20 men without giving a thought to the consequences.

Over the course of 20,000 kilometers on a bicycle in Asia and the Middle East, I'd never been mugged. Heck, I'd never even been in a schoolyard fistfight. I thought about my two-workouts-per-day routine leading up to the trip. The sets and reps of cleaning and jerking barbells, the mountain-trail runs in the snow, the ring muscle-up competitions. These men were 20 years my junior, and if they were anything like I was when I was their age, probably willing to take risks without thinking deeply about the consequences.

The wind suddenly picked up, and the shovel-armed teens' shirts flapped in the breeze. The veins on their forearms and biceps bulged underneath their skin as their grip on the shovels tightened.

I was oblivious to the waves of sand that blew in the distance, the desert slowly eroding the nearby mountains into new shapes. I glanced up at the sky: clear blue without a wisp of white. Two brown vultures circled far overhead, cawing across the empty vault of heaven. If God was up there watching, I was in dire need of His help.

Chapter 2

Addis Ababa Awareness Academy

"The heart of a fool is in his mouth and the mouth of a wise man is in his heart."
—Ethiopian proverb

"The most spiritual men, as the strongest, find their happiness where others would find their destruction: in the labyrinth, in hardness against themselves and others."
—Friedrich Nietzsche

I gazed out the airplane window at the land that would change me forever. Curves of erosion shot upward, forming beige mountains whose summits sliced through a smattering of cotton-white clouds. At their feet lay an ocean bottom of yellow, which gradually became dotted with tiny brown homes and paths that swerved around these mountains with jagged peaks. No green trees or bodies of water. The winter, *bega*, of 2019 had sucked the moisture from the soil, leaving it lifeless and burned. Silver lines of desiccated rock snaked along the valleys—dried-up streams that probably meant that most water-dependent life had fled for wetter lands. Intimidated by my glimpse of the uncompromisingly parched terrain I'd be pedaling through for the next month, I let out a nervous sigh as goosebumps formed on my arms. Ethiopia, here I come!

While on the plane, I chatted with a middle-aged man from Addis Ababa, Ethiopia's capital, which was located in the central part of the country. He had three children on three different continents with three different women. Our encounter must've been predestined since my Korean name, *Chunsam*, means "spring three times."

The man chuckled at his lifestyle, which involved flying back and forth between Berlin, Dubai, and Addis Ababa to visit his kids. "I send them money every month, so I work day and night. I also run in the hills around my home to relieve stress. You have fun riding your bike in my country. I want to do this one day but am working too much." He mentioned all this in between bites of spiced spinach, beets, and rice—by far the best airplane food I'd ever tasted.

As we said our goodbyes, I walked into the airport terminal, a sparkling, new building with silver trusses hanging several meters above my head. White-tiled floors reflected the shiny yellow lights hanging from the ceiling, stinging my eyes into a slit-eyed squint. Scrolls of tribal art dangled from the ceiling, its stripes and patterns of pink-, red-, and green-painted fabric giving the newly constructed building a traditional flair. The scent of lemon cleaning solution lingered, the aroma foreign to a guy who keeps his refrigerator filled with kimchi and feels ambitious enough to clean his room about once a month. After living in South Korea for 12 years, I'd grown immune to the pungent odor of bacteria-infused garlic, red pepper, and pear juice—that is, the kimchi, or fermented cabbage, which is the country's staple at every meal. At first whiff, Ethiopia seemed germ-free.

As I heaved my unwieldy cardboard box through customs, the excitement of landing on a different continent with my bike at my side overrode the mild fatigue caused by the six-hour time difference and an entire day in the air.

"Hello, handsome man." The customs officer was a thin woman in her late twenties with a dimpled smile. "Oh, bringing TV to Ethiopia?" She gestured at the box in my luggage cart.

"Hi, pretty lady. Ha! I haven't owned a TV in 15 years. There's never anything good on television. It's a bicycle to ride around your country." My palms moistened in anticipation of what would lie ahead once she had granted me permission to lug my hunk of metal and rubber into her country.

"Oh, 15 years? Bicycle? You very clever, my friend. Your legs very strong." The officer chuckled while clapping her hands.

"Crazy is more like it. And my legs are thin and hairy." I laughed while inhaling the dry mountain air and stretching out my lower back, sore from hours of sitting on the plane.

"Why you doing this? You go car. Much better."

"Cars are so boring and I'll get fat and flabby. Life with no roof is better. I can go fast, slow, stop, eat, sleep whenever I want. Every day is an empty canvas." I focused on her eyes. They had a quality I couldn't quite pinpoint.

"No friend? Will you be lonely?" Her eyes widened with what I took to be curiosity and genuine concern.

I nodded in appreciation of her show of empathy. "No worries. I can always talk to the mountains, animals, and trees."

"Ha! No problem in Ethiopia. You have great time, my friend. My country good place."

"Yes. That's what I've heard." My stomach was still gurgling with pleasure over the inflight meal.

"You being careful hyena and lion. Animals sometimes eating people, you know? Hyena and lion eating my friend in village, okay? Sometimes people gun fighting my country. You careful. People gun fighting, okay?" She handed me back my passport.

Gunfights? Lions? I had heard about wild animals, political instability, and tribal clashes, but her words made the possibility real as I buzzed with nervous energy.

I said goodbye to the pretty customs lady and lugged my big box to a shady spot outside the airport. I ripped it open and assembled my bike piece by piece. Seat, pedals, tires. Ready.

My love affair with Ethiopia began in 2005 when a friend introduced me to the country's cuisine in Ann Arbor, Michigan. Sourdough flatbread, turmeric-infused lentils, spiced spinach, sliced raw beets. As we picked at the same big, round, silver tray, my fingers turned orange. Sweet and spicy flavors slid into my stomach and curry dribbled down my chin. All washed down with a cup of black tea. The colorful murals, the blaring music, and people shimmying on the television screen added to the festive atmosphere. I fell hard for this place even though I was over 7,000 miles away.

I was a middle-class North American, a twentysomething traffic engineer who longed for excitement. My job was timing traffic signals so people could arrive at their destinations a few minutes earlier. It seemed so meaningless. Where, exactly, did everyone have to go? Were they curing cancer or creating something beautiful for the world? Everyone used busyness to claim status, cramming their lives with compulsive activity so they could eventually relax and enjoy a future that wasn't guaranteed.

I searched for ways to deal with my restlessness. My eyes, neck, and back throbbed from sitting in the same chair and staring at the same screen every day. Every morning when the alarm clock rang, my mind screamed, "No! No! Not another day at the office!" Another day, another eight hours looking at spreadsheets and writing reports for clients. The world was so huge and my cubicle so tiny. I needed to inject fresh air into my suffocating lifestyle.

Having taken the high school–university–graduate school–corporate job route, I'd begun to be consumed by wanderlust and a thirst for personal growth as I watched the clock strike 6 p.m. five days a week for three years. That Ethiopian restaurant had been one of my places of escape.

Time seemed to fly by, and every day was the same. I was living on autopilot, lost inside my head instead of being present and aware. Each day the same internal chatter dominated my thoughts. *How much longer will you live like this? You're wasting your youth. There is more to life than sitting at a desk, isn't there?* If I kept this up, I would become at best a wrinkled, bitter man reflecting on his youth with regret. At worst, not even here any longer. William James said it well in *Principles of Psychology*:

> The same space of time seems shorter when we grow older. In youth, we may have an absolutely new experience every hour of the day. Apprehension is vivid, retentiveness strong, and our recollections of that time, like those of a time spent in rapid and interesting travel, are of something intricate, multitudinous, and long-drawn-out. But as each passing year converts some of this experience into automatic routine, that we hardly note at all, the days and the weeks smooth themselves out in recollection to contentless units, and the years grow hollow and collapse.

I searched for anything to disrupt my familiar pattern. It started with simple commutes to work by bicycle through inner-city Detroit. My friends and family warned me about gang violence, drug-addicted thieves, and stray gunshots.

"Stop watching the news," I told them. "All it does is pollute your mind with stereotypes. I'm more likely to get struck by lightning or die in a car accident than fall victim to a gunshot wound. This is exactly why I don't watch TV."

After three years I handed in my resignation letter. No more clock-watching. No more red eyes. No more traffic-signal timing data. Headaches I'd been experiencing disappeared. I stopped grinding my teeth at night and my strides became lighter. I punctuated every sentence with laughs of satisfaction. "I'm free! Woo! Haha! No more desk jockeying! Woo! Haha!" I screamed in the street after my last day of work.

After leaving my job, I spent three months backpacking in Central America. One day I was hiking up volcanoes and dodging lava streams; the next I was sipping hot chocolate while chatting with a guerilla-war hero who was an expert in explosives and mines; the following night I was getting lost in a remote jungle while exotic creatures screeched all around me. The journey slowed time down and snapped me out of a life in fast-forward. Every day was an adventure, and the child in me was ready to explore the world.

When I returned to Detroit, I learned there was a demand for English teachers in South Korea and started applying for jobs. Within a few weeks, I found myself at Detroit Metro airport with a backpack and a one-way ticket to Seoul.

I fell in love on day one. First, it was the spicy vegetables, fermented in pepper and bean pastes, doused with garlic and ginger. Then it was the language. Every spare minute I filled my head with abstract grammar concepts that, to a native speaker of English, defied logic. I mirrored dialogues and wrapped my tongue into shapes that tickled the roof of my mouth. Next, it was my girlfriend: a woman who wore skirts and black stockings and had a voice that made my mouth water. Her sweet personality and warm touch had my heart pounding every time we were together. But mostly it was the teaching that I loved—a job I would've done for free. I couldn't believe I was getting paid to have fun in the classroom with teenage students. My soul needed Seoul.

The best thing about living in Seoul was cycling around town. My rusty, third-hand bicycle went everywhere with me. I pedaled to work every day with a smile. I pedaled in sharp clothes to barbecue restaurants for dates. I pedaled home from my free Korean classes while reciting vocabulary out loud.

Within a few months I had graduated from commuting by bike in Seoul to week-long cycling trips around the country. Speaking Korean became my passion, and tour cycling was the best way to slow down and use what I had learned in the classroom. No maps, no GPS, and no plan other than pedaling and practicing. After memorizing a few survival phrases (*left, right, straight, sleep, eat, drink*) I hit the road.

Whenever I mentioned my cross-country South Korean adventure, people dropped their jaws out of genuine concern for my well-being. I laughed off their doubts and pedaled alongside 1,000-year-old Buddhist temples, sniffed moist mountain air, and listened in wonder as insects sang their choruses while resting in lush trees. Sweat dripped from my chin, wrists, and elbows as the unrelenting humidity only a peninsula can produce left me soaking wet. I was comfortable being uncomfortable in a faraway land with a bicycle.

After three years in Seoul, I hit the jackpot: a university teaching job that included four months of paid vacation per year. I jumped at every opportunity to pedal.

During summer and winter vacations, I searched for more challenging destinations beyond Korea. Every journey was a master course in global knowledge and self-discovery. Self-conquest became my joy and onerous tasks a privilege, a recreation. Extremes shattered my limiting beliefs, and I repeatedly shocked myself.

Mongolia piqued my interest as a landlocked country of steppe, desert, and mountains inhabited by nomadic tribes whose ancestors had launched worldwide wars. During almost three centuries of China's Qing Dynasty rule, Buddhism reigned supreme in Mongolia. Nearly half the men were monks who couldn't have children. The harsh terrain was unfit for raising crops. This, combined with war deaths and Lamaism, gave Mongolia the world's lowest population density and an unrivaled amount of open space to explore.

Cycling in the land of Genghis Khan, where there are more horses than people and punishing winds had my ears ringing and nearly knocked me off my bicycle, was a dream come true. Tajikistan's Pamir Highway, dubbed "the roof of the world" since the Tian Shan, Himalayas, and Hindu Kush mountain ranges meet here, was an unforgettable high-altitude adventure. While pedaling through the remnants of a pothole-ridden Soviet-era highway, I wheezed for air as summer hail pelted my cheeks and neck. In Xinjiang, China, I patched punctured tires in intersections alongside tanks. Xinjiang, in the country's far west, is a place that makes Beijing and Shanghai residents' voices quiver at the mention of its "dangerous" ethnic minorities (Uyghurs, Kazakhs, Tajiks, and Kyrgyz), a label resulting from the government's propaganda efforts. Han Chinese and Xinjiang's ethnic minorities have been clashing for years. In Bangladesh, one of the world's most densely populated countries, I dodged swerving vehicles and marveled at the rings of black dust around my eyes in the mirror each evening.

Tour cycling became my new addiction.

Fear was my compass, pointing toward the places I needed to explore. I longed to wobble on a tightrope while becoming my own hero, a person who could inspire me during life's hard times. I hoped to look inward amid life's chaos and find a fire of boldness ready to light up the world with positive energy. The fire of true courage would char fear and self-doubt to a crisp.

Tour cycling became a way to combine movement and stillness. After every action-packed day in the saddle, I would sit in my tent and observe my breath and bodily sensations. The next morning, as soon as the sun's rays pierced my tent, I spent another hour watching my body's fleeting state of being. Eight to 10 hours of pedaling—combined with two hours of stillness—had left my mind quiet and clear.

Ever since my first 110-hour, 10-day meditation retreat in India eight years earlier, reaching a state of infinite peace, grace, and bliss had become my passion. My interest in meditation began with an innocent curiosity about Indian culture. Submerging myself in silence was a way of challenging my restless, active nature. I expected to visualize butterflies floating across sunny, blue horizons while listening to audio recordings of flowing streams and chirping birds. I was wrong. At retreats, my days were filled with the excruciating physical pain of sitting in the same position for one-hour intervals. Mental explosions of grief, sorrow, and uncontrollable thoughts took over. Demons and angels from the past surfaced: failed relationships, unresolved conflicts, regrets about the trouble I'd caused others as an adolescent.

These distractions tormented me while I attempted to observe my bodily sensations and breathing. I couldn't focus for more than 10 seconds. After practicing for one to two hours per day for several years, my mind became quiet. The loud voices turned into whispers I could listen to or ignore. The meditation practice carried into my life even while I was not meditating. An invisible shield blocked the surrounding negativity, and I didn't respond to stimuli the way I used to. With heightened awareness came increased self-understanding. My thoughts and their outrageous attempts at self-sabotage became a source of humor. I finally succeeded in taming my mind. The mental clarity was priceless.

Six months before setting off on my Ethiopian adventure, I bought a second-hand mountain bike—my biggest purchase of the previous 10 years. The price: a whopping three hundred dollars, equivalent to one month's rent of my studio apartment in Seoul. My previous bike was too weak to handle the rugged Mongolian steppe, so I splurged. Every time I mounted my bicycle, I felt like a teenager behind the steering wheel of his first car. It was love at first pedal.

On that trip an American traveler gave me my second-most-treasured possession—a tent. While drunk on the Mongolian steppe, the man had tripped over my leaky, rusty, $20 fisherman's tent, snapping the frame in half. He rendered it a plastic tarp whose ceiling flapped against my forehead as the steppe winds sang their nightly melody. That makeshift home had accompanied me on my first journey to Africa six years earlier. Before that trip, it had survived sandstorms in Oman, Turkish snowfalls, Siberian mosquito attacks, and a flood in China. I had no qualms about making do with the broken shelter, but the man insisted on replacing it. A trip to the local market later, I was holding a brand-new set of plastic sheets and poles.

Ethiopia was a place many bicycle-touring veterans had made infamous via internet stories of stone-throwing children. My youth-avoidance response: push myself with life-or-death tenacity. I had to whiz past them, wear them down on their own turf. My two workouts per day in the months leading up to my trip gave me the courage I needed to believe in myself.

I was in Ethiopia. A country whose name derives from the Greek words "burn" and "face" and roughly translates as *burned-face* in noun form and *red-brown* in adjectival form. Ancient Greek historians used the designation to denote regions of Africa west and south of Egypt as habitable. Since the Greeks used the term "dark-faced" they classified Ethiopians into two groups, those in Africa and those from eastern Turkey to India. The name Ethiopian Sea was given to the present-day Atlantic Ocean and the name appeared in maps from ancient times until the mid-19th century. Nowadays the term has become obsolete, as modern Ethiopia is far from its namesake body of water, and much closer to the Red Sea.

I arrived in the capital of Ethiopia, Addis Ababa (which translates to *New Flower* in Amharic, Ethiopia's national language). A city of about five million, it's perched on a plateau at the base of mountains and cliffs in a central region of the country. Its predecessor, Entoto, was in the highlands and deemed unsuitable due to its cold climate and a lack of firewood. (The town ran out of firewood soon after being founded, and Eucalyptus trees were imported from Australia to provide foliage, shade, and fuel.)

Empress Taitu persuaded her husband to move near a cluster of hot springs at the base of a mountain (present-day Addis Ababa). At first, Addis was thought of as a military encampment because its population consisted only of the emperor's palace and army personnel. Moreover, the site was nearly abandoned until trees were shipped in from Australia. Now, Addis Ababa is home to a vibrant cultural and art scene and is referred to as "the political capital of Africa" due to its historic and diplomatic importance.

Outside the airport in Addis Ababa, locals stared at me as they passed. Perhaps they'd never seen a quarter-Finnish, quarter-Scottish, half-Ecuadorian guy with greasy hands assembling a bike at the airport? Some even applauded as I tightened the last screws on my handlebars. My heart nearly burst like a champagne cork.

Improvisation was essential since I would face the unknown every day.

My next task was to cycle to a city campsite. It was one in the afternoon as I pedaled out of the airport on a cloudless sunny day with a slight breeze. My nose hairs tingled during the first few inhalations of Addis Ababa air. As I cruised along a calm street, the faint smell of dust, car exhaust, and incense filled my nostrils. Soon, a woman roasting coffee beans on a sidewalk sabotaged my senses. Three plastic chairs, red and child-sized, surrounded a burning pile of wood as the lady shook the pan of sandy-brown beans from side to side over the flames. The piney aroma permeated the air with flavor. I couldn't wait to try a cup but didn't yet have any local currency.

My bicycle felt light. In Mongolia and Siberia several months before, I had packed thick jackets and sweatshirts into my panniers to prepare for the Altai Mountains. Ethiopia's warm climate meant I only needed the bare minimum: three T-shirts, one pair of shorts, one pair of long pants, three pairs of underwear, a toothbrush, toothpaste, dental floss, three pairs of ankle socks, a sleeping bag, tent, spare tube, pump, tire patch kit, and a pen and pad to record stories while practicing my Korean writing skills.

I continued along the main road, passing shopping mall windows sparkling in the sun next to boxy, half-built, concrete structures. Workers pounded and cut steel with metal tools. *Clang! Clang!* I sped by a construction worker who plopped a sandbag on the ground, kicking up a knee-high cloud of dust. The man jabbed his friend's shoulder and pointed at me while letting out a yelp of laughter. "*Ya! Ya! Ya! Ya!*"

With a smile painted on my face, I waved and greeted people as the sun warmed my skin. I was on a bike in Ethiopia. I couldn't wait to see what the next month would bring.

I cycled through a two-lane roundabout as motorcycles and box-shaped vans overflowing with people cruised by. A rusty-green Toyota Corolla came to a screeching halt to let me pass. The driver smiled and stuck his shaved head out the window as I sped by. "You! You! Welcome Ethiopia!"

"Thank you! Have a wonderful day!" I yelled back. It appeared there weren't many light-skinned guys wearing helmets with bags tied to the backs of their bicycles in Addis. It was refreshing to see people smiling and amused by my presence. I was glad to add a dose of humor and intrigue to their day. Their positive energy and the excitement of being on a bike on a new continent woke me out of my jet lag. I felt alert, aware.

I had memorized the Addis Ababa city street plan by studying a Google Maps printout on the airplane. As a proud minimalist and 2G flip-phone user, the only electronic device I took with me was my secondhand camera. I relied on memorization, instinct, and body language conversations for navigation. Straight for five blocks. Left turn. Straight for three blocks. Left again. Find the Lion of Judah monument and turn left into an alley. Pitch tent at campsite. No time to slow down. No time for paper maps. People seemed friendly and jovial, but avoiding petty crime was paramount. *Stay aware. Stay alert.*

Shaded from the blazing sun by an elevated train track. I passed by an expansive concrete square devoid of people. Cartons full of mangoes, oranges, avocados, and sugar cane filled the streets with color and fruity scents. The sound of honking cars and locals yelling over the noise pollution rang through my ears.

As I waited to cross a busy street, two shaven-headed children wearing tattered sandals and matching green T-shirts stared up at me and held out their hands. "Money." They smiled mischievously.

"What is your name?" I smiled.

"You! Money!" They slapped my bags with their palms.

I waved my index finger in the air and furrowed my eyebrows as cars zoomed by.

"Money," they persisted. One kid shook my left pannier. The other reached for my right pannier's zipper pocket.

"No! No!" I said, raising my voice in frustration. Passersby giggled and pointed in my direction, amused by my predicament.

"You! You! Money!" The youths followed me across the street while digging their hands into my bags. These kids were way more persistent than any I had encountered during my trip through southern Africa six years earlier.

Tatek Abebe, associate professor of childhood studies at the Norwegian University of Science and Technology, states the following about children who beg in Addis Ababa.

> Poverty is a major reason children beg. Family disintegration, abuse and neglect by parents, and the lack of social services were common. Other reasons include the failure of rural livelihoods, including displacement from drought, famine and war; harmful traditional practices (for example, early marriage) or the loss of a parent. There were two categories of child beggars: full-time and part-time child workers. Full-time beggars include children that are born to parents with disabilities. Because there is no social support system for these people, they will often depend on their families for survival. In this scenario, begging is a source of livelihood and children learn how to beg when they accompany their disabled parents.

Some children viewed begging as a job or learned skill. It was referred to as
s'ik'alla or simply *business*. *S'ik'alla* derives from *shigul*, an Arabic word meaning *work*. Activities such as street vending or shoe-shining were formalized and contributed to the national economy via taxes. Begging was outside of "formal" and "informal" economic activities.

Even though there were many children in dire conditions, I'd held a firm stance on begging. Many well-intentioned travelers had argued that we ought to hand out candy or coins to kids who beg but providing handouts may lead to unintentional and detrimental effects. Kids are fast learners. If one interaction led to success, why wouldn't others? Wouldn't parents prefer their children beg rather than go to school?

Also, by giving youths money, the tourist could disrupt family power dynamics. When kids collected pens and other gifts, many sold them and returned home as their family's breadwinner. What child would listen to their parents while knowing they are their family's financial backbone? Instead of giving out pens or school supplies on the street, it is best to donate them to a local teacher to ensure they aren't pawned for cash.

Even worse, tourists could unwittingly finance human trafficking schemes. Starved or mutilated youths were big money earners because of their shocking appearances. Trafficking agents often amputated limbs, scared faces with acid, or cut out eyes. Mob bosses kept kids addicted to opium or other hard drugs in horrific attempts to prevent them from running away. When trafficked children became too old to beg, criminals sold them on the black market for their organs or forced them into lives of prostitution. How could I tell whether a child was involved in the organized begging market?

Instead of rewarding begging children, I had for five years donated money through an organization that supports sustainable development. My money could have up to one thousand times the benefit if allocated to an organization that used funds efficiently. For example, every dollar spent on deworming kids was hundreds of times as effective at increasing school attendance than providing pens and books. Likewise, every euro spent on bed nets was hundreds of times more effective at preventing malaria than funding hospital supplies.[1] After educating myself on effective altruism, this was the way I gave. But for Ethiopian children, it was hard to understand.

I pedaled for less than one hundred meters while children chased me, chuckling and grabbing at my bags. Deep potholes and uneven sidewalks with rebar sticking out of concrete forced me to dismount and slow myself to a walk. The kids pushed

---

1. MacAskill, William. Doing Good Better: How Effective Altruism Can Help You Help Others, Do Work That Matters, and Make Smarter Choices About Giving Back. Penguin Publishing Group, 2016.

my bags and tried to unzip my outer pockets. I'd encountered begging children every day on three prior trips to India, but they weren't anything like this. How was I supposed to stay sane during the next month?

After several more minutes of fending off the children, I found it--there! The sign for my campsite! I turned down a cobblestone alley into the campsite, and the kids scurried away. Perhaps they'd grown bored or thought of a better idea for fun. My chest lightened and the tense energy left my shoulders.

After setting up my tent in a guesthouse yard and taking a quick nap, I hit the streets. A five-minute walk later, I peered at a cluster of slum dwellings. Sandy, gravel foundations supported baseball bat–sized wood scraps that had been nailed together. Dusty-brown plastic sheets draped from the roof protected inhabitants from the elements. Cloth hung from vertical sticks jabbed into the soil, creating walls of privacy. I inched closer. A pot shook back and forth over a fire. A short kid in his early twenties with a curly afro stood next to it with a silver ladle in his hand. Three shadowy figures sat around a circular tin tray and shoved food into their mouths. The one in the middle waved me in and pointed to the plate, insisting I stick my hands into the mess.

"This is called a *shy-beet*. That means cheap place to eat. Do you want something?" the worker with the afro asked in near-perfect English.

"Oh sure. What do you have?"

"Pasta, injera, shiro." He revealed the contents of the tin pot. A red mixture bubbled in it, and the aroma of pepper and garlic made my stomach swoon.

"How did you make that?" I inhaled the spicy scent while fanning the pot's steam in the direction of my nose.

"This is tomato, garlic, onion, and berbere."

"What is berbere?"

"Ethiopian spices."

"Yeah, how much for shiro and injera?"

"Twenty birr."

After a quick mental calculation, I realized that was only the price of a small North American candy bar.

"Okay. Done."

"You like this place? I made it with my family," the kid said proudly while stirring the mixture.

I marveled at the ingenuity and creativity. His food shack was made from recycled scrap materials. Shade and a simple place to sit down. Exactly my style.

As I waited for my meal, a guy sitting next to me signaled to join him and his friends. He was a thin man who appeared to be in his early twenties. He had light brown skin and his veiny forearms stuck out of a blue T-shirt. The noodles and red sauce fused together over a beige piece of injera looked tempting.

"You want eat with us?" He pointed at his dish.

"Thank you, but I ordered something."

"This pasta. Every restaurant have pasta from Italian people coming here," he said while chewing his food. "City center called *piazza* from Italian people. When you coming Ethiopia?"

"This is my first day, actually. I arrived this afternoon."

"Oh! Welcome! You know, our city Addis very high. Third-highest capital in the world. Two thousands, four hundred meters. Many mountains in Ethiopia. How long you in Ethiopia?"

"One month. I'm going to ride my bike around the country."

"Oh! Motorbike?"

"Not by motorbike. By bicycle. No petrol. Only leg power." I pointed to my thighs.

"*Ayy Ayy*! Only bicycle?"

"That's right. I like mountains and am excited to experience Ethiopian culture."

"You going north part? So much history and culture." He continued to chew on the red-and- brown fare.

"Yeah? Go on."

"You seeing Bahir Dahr. Many islands with old churches. Lalibela very special. You seeing spiritual powers there. Aksum so much history. You must see Aksum. Mountain monasteries close to Aksum. Monks climbing rocks there every day. This place so nice. Aksum 1700 kilometers from here. You going with bicycle only?"

"Yeah. Only a bike. That's how I get around. That area is safe, right?"

"Last month gun fighting in north but now finished. You going there no problem."

"Are you *sure* it's okay now?"

"Maybe small gun fighting now. Big gun fighting finished."

My stomach tightened with tense energy, and I clenched my hands together under the table. Hopefully, as an outsider, I'd be spared the violence. "Okay, thanks for the guidance."

"Your food here now. You eating." He nodded toward my plate.

I was so engrossed with the guy's travel recommendations; I didn't notice the round plate of food in front of me. My eyes widened at the sight of my first meal on Ethiopian soil. My taste buds were moist with anticipation. Steam climbed through the air and fogged up my spectacles. Hands washed and ready to be coated with just-cooked grub, I took bite after bite with careful awareness. My stomach let out a bellow of satisfaction. I couldn't wait to have this for every meal.

This was my first time tasting authentic injera. This vitamin-and-mineral-packed, fermented flatbread is the most important component of every Ethiopian meal; it is simultaneously used as a plate, utensil, and main course. Stews, referred to as wat, are placed on top of the injera and its spongy texture soaks up the ingredients to create a sour and spicy treat. The eater tears a piece with the right hand (after washing), soaks up some wat, and places it in their mouth. Traditionally, injera is made of two ingredients: *teff* and water. Teff, a grain found in Ethiopia and Eritrea, is ground into flour and fermented into injera. Gluten-free, it is rich in protein, iron, calcium, zinc, and many essential amino acids. Grown in the highlands at certain elevations, the grain is relatively expensive, so many families harvest their own supply. Teff's origin is a mystery, but some scholars think it was domesticated in 4000 BC. When teff isn't available because of financial or geographical constraints, families make injera using barley, corn flour, or wheat.

After washing my red-stained hands, I said goodbye and returned to the campsite.

That evening, I studied the map in my tent. I took the man's suggestion to head north. With plenty of mountainous roads to tackle, historical spots to discover, and hyenas to chuckle with or get eaten by, I wondered what I was getting myself into.

I'd start from Addis Ababa and cycle up to Bahir Dar and then cut east to Debre Tabor and Lalibela. After passing Woldia, I would head north again to Mekele and Aksum. Two thousand kilometers in a month. During past trips, I had learned that the most important part of every plan was planning on my plan not going according to plan. This one would be the same.

That evening, I went to sleep with a faint buzz in my chest.

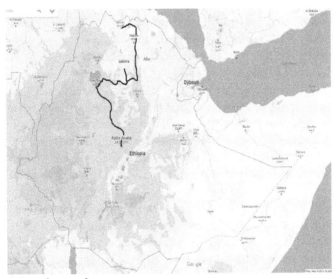

Map of my cycling route

The next morning, I woke up early and cycled to Saint George's Church in the city center. I entered a serene oasis of foliage and purple flowers. Leafy eucalyptus trees shielded the monastery grounds from automobile exhaust, which gave the city a metallic stench. Thin, wrinkled men in jeans and colorful, collared shirts filled the wooden benches on both sides of the church. I plopped myself down, took a seat, and inhaled a deep breath of cool air. Finally, shade and quiet.

While taking a breather, I pondered the importance of Christianity to the country. Overall, Christians comprised nearly two-thirds of the population. Ethiopia was one of the first regions in the world to adopt Christianity in the face of Islamic expansion in the region. Locals followed various denominations. The largest and oldest was the Ethiopian Orthodox Tewahedo Church. The earliest reference to the faith is in the New Testament, which mentions Philip the Evangelist converting an Ethiopian court official in the first century AD.

Saint George's Church has enormous historical significance. The church, built on the ruins of a monastery from the 15th century, was where Emperor Haile Selassie was crowned in 1930 and became a site of pilgrimage for Rastafarians. Rastas currently use the flag Ethiopia flew during the reign of Emperor Selassie as their primary symbol of unity and believe the Bible was first written in stone in Amharic, the national language of Ethiopia. *Ras* means prince and *Tafari Makonen* was the name of Emperor Selassie before he became ruler. Rastafarians view Emperor Selassie as the reincarnation of God on earth and as the Second Coming of Jesus Christ. They also believe the mention of "The Lion of Judah" in Genesis 49:9 and Revelation 5:5 to refer to Selassie. They seek the resettlement of the African diaspora in Ethiopia, referring to it as the Promised Land of Zion.

Ras Tafari was a towering historical figure, ruling Ethiopia from 1930 to 1974. When Tafari was appointed king, he changed his name to Haile Selassie, meaning Power of the Trinity, believing he was ordained by God to be emperor. He claimed the imperial dynasty was descended from King David, making Selassie a relative of Jesus Christ. During his induction as "King of Kings," his throne stood on a slab that had been hewn from the bedrock beneath Solomon's Temple in Jerusalem, a symbol of his divine destiny. Until the end, Selassie remained steadfast in his belief that he was the *Negusa Negast* or Elect of God, affirming his title in the two constitutions he spearheaded in 1931 and 1955. During the first few years of his reign, he instituted programs to build roads, schools, hospitals, public services, and communications. Tax money from coffee exports funded Ethiopia's thriving economy in 1932 and the country gained international attention.

At that time, neighboring Eritrea and Somalia had been Italian possessions since the 1880s. Benito Mussolini took notice of Ethiopia's rising power and sought to enhance Italian national prestige, which was wounded in 1896 after Italy lost the Battle of Adwa in northern Ethiopia. He planned a preemptive strike, worried that, if he didn't act swiftly, Ethiopia would become too strong.

Italians and Ethiopians clashed at the Wal Wal Oasis in 1934, triggering a new conflict. Selassie assumed Ethiopia's inclusion in The League of Nations would lead to collective security, and after learning Italian forces had crossed into Ethiopian territory, ordered an attack. During the seven-month Second Italo-Ethiopian war, the Italian command violated international law by spraying poison gas from airplanes to destroy Selassie's poorly equipped army.

After the defeat, the Conquering Lion of the Tribe of Judah, Elect of God, King of the Kings of Ethiopia, went into exile in England. During his absence, the Italians hunted down and executed well-educated Ethiopians and over 2,000 monks, priests, and deacons at holy sites around the country. While abroad, Selassie pleaded with The League of Nations in Geneva for aid and, with British assistance, regained his country's security. He returned to power in 1945 and ruled until members of a rebel force strangled him to death in his bed in 1975.

I couldn't believe I sat in the Saint George's Church where this iconic figure had been crowned. In *A Long Walk to Freedom,* Nelson Mandela wrote: "Ethiopia has always held a special place in my imagination. The prospect of visiting Ethiopia attracted me more than a trip to France, America, and England combined. I felt I'd be unearthing my own Genesis, unearthing the root of what made me an African. Meeting the emperor himself would be like shaking hands with history."

According to his memoirs, Mandela was in shock when he boarded a plane from Khartoum to Addis Ababa and found an Ethiopian pilot under control. "I had never seen a black pilot before," he wrote, "and the instant I did I had to quell my panic. How could a black man fly an airplane? But a moment later I caught myself: I had fallen into the apartheid mindset, thinking Africans were inferior, and that flying was a white man's job. I sat back in my seat and chided myself for such thoughts."

While relaxing on a bench, a young man interrupted my reflections on Ethiopian history. Ready to make a new friend, I motioned for him to sit next to me. He was a short, wiry guy with an afro that shot up about five centimeters in the air. A thin layer of dark-brown dust covered his clothing, and it appeared he hadn't showered in a few weeks. Much to my surprise, he spoke perfect English, with the cadence and speed of a standup comedian. He could have been from New Jersey or Queens.

"I graduated from university and don't have work." He threw his hands up in frustration. "I came to Addis to find a job, but there is nothing. Now I sleep on the streets. People stare at me like I'm a bum and I can't stand it."

After some small talk, he accompanied me for a walk to the church entrance. While sharing several Wikipedia-quality facts about the church's history, he made a brash request.

"I explained a little about the church. Now give me money," he insisted, pushing himself into my personal space. I could feel his warm, coffee-scented breath against my cheeks.

His behavior caught me off guard. I clenched my fists, ready to defend myself.

The man moved in closer, a few nose lengths from my face. "Give me something. Come on!"

My lizard brain told me to shut this guy up with an uppercut to the jaw, but the meditator in me regained control of my temper. He could have been armed. *Stay aware of your emotions.*

"Okay. Take this," I said while handing him a one-birr coin.

"This is one birr. I can't buy anything with one birr." He sounded insulted.

"That's all I have for you. If you don't want it, I'll keep it for myself," I said.

"Why are you smiling like that? *Go fuck yourself!*" he said with furrowed eyebrows.

"Okay. I'll do that," I responded in a sly tone as he stomped away. I don't know whether I was more shocked by his explosive reaction or his perfect English expletive.

I felt sorry for the man. If he'd had a job and been earning a living wage, I'm sure our conversation would have been different. Was it desperation that had caused him to lose his cool? Maybe he was hungry. He'd viewed our interaction as labor, while I'd been looking for friendship.

There was nothing I could do to control his actions; I could only strive to improve myself. A fistfight on my first day in Ethiopia would have resulted in bad karma for the next month. I stopped and reminded myself what my trip was about: I longed to learn about Ethiopian culture and listen to stories about life in the only African nation to survive the threat of imperialism. I wanted to inhale her thin mountain air and sweat in her deserts under a relentless sun. Travel has always made me aware of my own deficiencies and strengths. This was a spiritual quest to connect with the world and myself at a deeper level.

During my travels, people had approached me hundreds of times for money, but this was my first time getting cussed out. I had wanted to see how I would react to unpredictability and danger, so in a sense I had asked for it—and he had delivered.

By my personal tape-measure, I had failed my first test on the Horn of Africa. My ego had grown out of control. I had spent three to four hours per day over the last month heaving barbells and jumping over knee-high boxes. The confidence I'd gained from rigorous physical training turned into arrogance, which led me to answer with sarcasm. I should've had more compassion and understanding toward a man fighting for survival. If we ever meet again, I'll buy him a meal. That way at least I could actively listen to his story and turn him into a friend.

That first day was an eye-opener. Yes, there was a failure on my part, but I had at least gained more self-knowledge. *Stay aware.*

Chapter 3

First-Love Cup

"Coffee and love are best when served hot."
—Ethiopian proverb

I launched myself on the bike the next morning. I was a bird in flight. With each pedal pump, my heart jumped a few centimeters closer to my throat. My arms tingled with exhilaration as I left the capital city. I was doing it! Tour cycling in Ethiopia!

I was alive and in alignment with nature. The joy of movement and fresh air, fused with the rush of exploring the unknown, replenished my spirit. For me, the essence of being human lies in my connection with the natural world—no more fluorescent lights, dreary buildings, fans, electric heat, or air conditioning. A vagabond by choice, I was submerged in an ocean of liberation. Tour cycling was my life force.

Despite snowstorms in Turkey, torrential rainfalls in South Korea, traffic-clogged cities in Bangladesh, confrontations with corrupt police officers in Tajikistan, and an absence of running water for days in rural Uzbekistan, I had always returned from my tour cycling trips with newfound energy and a desire for challenge. While on the road, survival was my full-time job. Restaurants and shops sprouted up after hours of pedaling through grasslands, windy mountain pathways, and scorched desert plains. Thirst, hunger, sweat, frost-bitten and sunburned skin became normal. Upon returning to South Korea, life with a roof turned alien and unnatural. I had trouble sleeping in my apartment with a shower, sink, and flushable toilet only steps away. Familiar comforts had become foreign.

While on the road, I'd enter a flow state. No time to fret over a breakup. No time to contemplate the digital numbers in my bank account. I escaped to a simple if challenging reality. I adapted to everything the world heaved at me. Pedal, eat, drink; pedal, eat, drink; pedal, sleep. Repeat. Survive.

Leaving Addis Ababa, I reflected on past adventures. My tent had been surrounded by darkness and rifle-carrying Chinese police officers. Mirages of nonexistent towns tormented me after I'd depleted my water ration in a sun-scorched Uzbekistan desert. In Peshawar, a Pakistani town near the border of Afghanistan, barbershop customers had accused me of being a CIA spy. What surprises lay ahead in Ethiopia?

These expeditions have put everything into perspective and reframed my daily routines. Negotiating with my boss was a simple task after using my hands and preschool-level Pashto to convince 30 locals from Peshawar I wasn't plotting a drone strike. There were plenty of jobs, but I only had one life. Heaving weights above my head and flinging myself over pull-up bars was easy—a cooler full of distilled water was an arm's length away.

After each journey, I returned home with a newfound zest for life. My trips became metaphors for every routine task. Every book read was a kilometer traveled on the road to knowledge and wisdom. Each hour of meditation was a kilometer traversed on the route to self-understanding, mental clarity, and enlightenment. Every barbell press was a kilometer completed on the trail to an increased lifespan and better brain health. Each minute spent with others was a kilometer traveled on the path of sharing positive energy. Tour cycling gifted me the tools to attack life with vigor 12 months a year. I cherished every second. Day by day. Kilometer by kilometer.

I thought of my girlfriend Ina in South Korea, the big-hearted girl who had changed my socks when I had sports injuries. The lady I could talk to for hours without tiring. She was my hiking and meditation partner, a friend who helped me understand the intricacies of Korean culture. The woman who lugged backpacks of home-fermented vegetables across the city on her one-hundred-pound (forty-five kilogram) frame. "I made this for you," she'd say, plopping down her backpack and stretching out on my apartment floor to let her back and shoulders recover from bearing that load for an hour. Ina did so much for me. I owed it to her to return stronger, more unwavering in the face of everyday challenges.

I tumbled back to reality. Heads turned, teenagers whistled, and ladies with braided hair and colorful dresses smiled and waved. Suddenly, I heard the phrases that became etched in my nightmares, daydreams, and waking reality: "*Faranji* (white guy). China! China! You! You! Money!"

A group of men hollered, grinning from cheek to cheek while each man held out one hand and thrust themselves in my path. Their spotless jeans, clean T-shirts, and fresh haircuts told me they were begging out of playfulness, not desperation. These were not the rail-thin, dust-covered, frowning faces of apathy I had encountered in Bangladesh, India, and Nicaragua. I waved and smiled. As I sped by, muffled laughter filled the air, as if our brief interaction was entertainment.

Their reaction surprised me. During my other journeys, people had hardly begged outside of tourist destinations. The charm of tour cycling was getting off the beaten path and having sincere interactions with locals. It had been a few hours since leaving the capital, but I wondered what made Ethiopians' behavior different from people in other parts of the world.

Newly paved roads waited for me. Ethiopia planned to double its highway network, from 100,000 to 200,000 kilometers, between 2015 and 2020. Chinese construction companies were often awarded the projects, resulting in an influx of Chinese workers. No wonder everyone yelled "China!" The roads were a pleasure to ride on and I was happy to test them. The flawless pavement extended to the mountain-clad horizon.

Knee-deep ditches of brown mud lined both sides of the tarmac. Makeshift balance beams bridged the ditches, allowing people to access tin shacks where used electronics, snacks, coffee, and home-cooked meals were sold. Each shop blasted its own pop tunes. Together, they smashed various songs into a mesh of lively rhythms and computerized vocals.

Men carrying chest-high sticks chased donkeys and goats as animals gradually replaced motorized vehicles. Shepherds yelled and swung their sticks while livestock jumped in pain. Manure stains dotted the pavement, tainting the dry air with putrid fumes peculiar to life. Men were barefoot or wearing sandals. I wondered whether their feet hurt from chasing their animals. Or maybe their soles were so callused they were numb to the stones strewn over the terrain. I wanted to give them a South Korean bathhouse tour. I was sure they would've appreciated a soak in tubs of warm water infused with liquid ginseng.

People were everywhere. They walked in groups. They stood in circles, laughing and socializing. Squads of teenagers huddled around outdoor pool tables. Posses of wrinkled men squatted on wooden stools while sipping coffee out of white-and-red espresso cups. Gangs of children crouched in front of plates of injera and wat.

"*Salam!*" I howled as distracted heads turned away from their group banter.

The sheer number of people in the streets was overwhelming. After Nigeria, this was Africa's second-most densely populated country. Crowds of 20 formed around me when I stopped for water. Twenty sets of open palms. Twenty sets of glaring eyes. Twenty voices shouting the same four words: "You! China! Money! *Faranji!*" Stopping when every person yelled for money was a terrible idea. I wouldn't have moved 10 meters.

Being the center of attention was intimidating. Several years ago in Bangladesh, hundreds of faces had surrounded me as I pushed through crowds during water stops. If one person decided I was there for the wrong reason, they'd have stomped me into oblivion. After a few weeks, I became used to the spotlight and discovered locals were the friendliest and most hospitable people in the world. I hoped the same was true for Ethiopians.

There was only one thing more intimidating than being the center of attention—Kalashnikovs. After a few more kilometers, they were everywhere. Strapped around the arms of villagers casually strolling in the street with their livestock. On the ground next to men sipping cups of coffee. Resting against the walls of convenience stores. My chest pounded at the sight of so many weapons. What if there was a dispute and I got caught in the crossfire? Worse, what if someone decided they should become the new owner of a funny-looking mountain bike from North America? I'd vowed never to handle a gun and hoped the killing machines would stay out of my way over the next month.

As I coasted along, a class of elementary school kids ran out to catch a glimpse. They wore beige, long-sleeved shirts and green pants. I wondered whether their gap-toothed smiles resulted in visits from the tooth fairy. Perhaps she had left them a coin or two. Maybe she waved her magic wand and gifted them mangoes instead of Snickers bars and sugar cane instead of chocolate chip cookies. Or did they preserve their baby teeth in jars at home, staring proudly at them every evening?

"Ay! Ay! Ay! You! You! You! Money! Money!" The yells became rowdier and more difficult to tune out. I picked up my pace, and the shouting turned into a faint hubbub. Speed was the key to maintaining sanity. By the time the villagers reacted to my presence, I was several meters in front of them.

Finally, I escaped to a quiet path. Bronze-colored grass and waist-high desert bushes lay all around me. The air was fresh and dry, allowing me to take deep breaths with a smile. I slowed my pace while appreciating the abstract shapes created by the clouds. They glided over the hills, shrinking with each passing second.

After a few hours of pedaling, the combination of sun and altitude caught up with me. The uphill trek had my legs burning. The afternoon wind jabbed away until I became a weary, droopy-eyed sloth. The equatorial sun shone through the cracks of my helmet, and linear braids of sunburned skin on my shaved head pleaded for relief. I needed a break.

A high-pitched sound caught my attention from behind a wooden shack.

"Coffee! I make you coffee. You like?" said a short woman in a multicolored dress.

"Sure! Make me a cup."

Coffee time! I ordered my first cup in the land where drinking the beverage had originated. In the sixth century AD, in the Kaffa region, a Sufi goat herder named Kaldi found his goats prancing near a group of trees. He noticed the goats eating red berries, so he tried them. Moments later, he joined his dancing goats in blissful celebration. A monk observed Kaldi and his animals. When Kaldi told him about the berries, the monk thought they might be the answer to his prayers—literally, since he often fell asleep during religious ceremonies. The monk ate the berries to stay awake and focus. Then he dried, crushed, and boiled the berries to make a beverage. His fellow monks enjoyed the drink because it helped them pray—and it tasted good too. The rest was history. Now I was ready to dance in delight while following in Kaldi's footsteps.

I parked my bike along a wall of blue plastic sheets and thick tree branches. Two pieces of white cloth with green, yellow, and red stripes hung from a clothesline, adorning the entrance with a hint of national pride. The coffee shop's interior was three times the length of my bicycle and three paces wide. Knee-high seats of red plastic surrounded two white tables. Wooden benches lined the shop's perimeter. A bouquet of pink flowers rested on a white bench, infusing the mocha-scented air with a trace of honey. I lumbered over to a seat and gave my body a much-needed break.

A few minutes later, a couple plopped themselves next to me. The girl appeared to be just out of high school. She was tall and slim, her skin reddish-brown with a warm orange undertone. Her cheeks looked as if she'd sprinted a mile: a tinge of pink glowed under the shadow of a ponytail tied above her head. She held hands with a man twice her age. The two giggled in a dubious age gap. He beckoned the server in the local tongue.

Moments later, the chuckles of romance turned more passionate. The couple broke out into a below-the-belt boxing session. They jumped out of their seats, clenching their fists at their waists. Knuckles jammed into crotches. Swiveling hips didn't evade oncoming blows. Each whimper of pain and knuckle-to-cloth strike became louder. They bit their lips and furrowed their brows as jabs connected in the genital area. The man grimaced as the girl landed a right hook to the groin. Tongues clicked as vocal cords cut sharp words in Amharic. They gasped for air mid-syllable while popping their tongues—spoken word artists engaged in battle. To my untrained ear, a conversation in Amharic sounded like asthmatic acquaintances struggling to craft the perfect beatbox rhythm.

I was witnessing what appeared to be a lovers' quarrel. According to my Korean- and Ecuadorian-infused North American values, this was inappropriate coffee-shop behavior. Once again, I reminded myself I was thousands of miles from my comfort zone. Everyone else ignored their exchange of blows. A few minutes later, the couple returned to fondling each other and wobbled out of the cafe, arm in arm, body parts intact.

Maybe one of them had been unfaithful, or they were fighting over money. It was a big mystery to me. Whatever the case, the groin shots must've hurt.

"What happened?" I asked the server.

"They doing that sometimes. That happening sometimes here." She shrugged her shoulders.

"Wow. Is that behavior common?"

"Sometimes this happening in café and restaurant," she said in a screechy voice. "They okay now."

"My name is George, by the way. Nice to meet you."

"My name Moren. You and me be friends, okay? I show you good Ethiopian culture. I make you coffee." She batted her eyelashes.

Moren's white teeth and red lipstick gave a lovely contrast to her flawless skin. Her eyes sparkled with intrigue as they scanned my crusty, salt-caked pants and armpit-stained, navy-blue shirt. She held my glance long enough to make my stomach flutter. Stepping toward me, Moren leaned her chest into my personal space while handing me a plate of peanuts. I caught a hint of her maple syrup–scented perfume. A recovering pancake addict, I was plunging into relapse.

We brushed elbows as I stood up to stretch my legs. She tugged on my hand and gestured toward a plastic chair. My arms moistened with sweat. A pool of drool formed in my mouth, and I couldn't swallow. A gulp would've betrayed weakness. Every cell in my body pulsed with anticipation. My veins were filled with nitroglycerine, and she was dangling a match.

Moren's maple-scented perfume triggered visions of my first date in 1995 ... showered and soaked in the fragrances of a cheap, musky cologne and an aerosol deodorant, I'd smelled like anything but my 15-year-old self. A 16-year-old, tall, hard-bodied girl picked me up in her blue Dodge sports car. We sped off to the movie theater while she chuckled at my horrid attempts at humor.

The lights faded as we took our seats. My youth shone through the dark theater. Brushing her blond hair to the side in flashes of yellow and white, she exposed her creamy neck. It beckoned for my lips, but I failed to answer. She crossed her legs and her calves bulged. The tips of her high-heeled shoes stroked my shin in a perfect clockwise motion. Goosebumps shot up my body, and my legs tingled. As her neck waited for a tickle, I froze, arms pinned to my sides, waist and neck paralyzed. The massage ended as blinding lights snapped me upright in my seat.

We strolled back to her car, and her eyes widened with excitement. "What do you want to do now?"

It was a daunting question.

"Oh ... I don't know. What do you want to do?" I stumbled over my words.

"We can do anything you want."

"Let's go for a drive in the woods and talk." I shriveled up in my seat.

"Sure."

Fifteen minutes later, we were surrounded by forest. Darkness camouflaged the hues of yellow, orange, and brown leaves. Crickets chirped and cool fall air from the cracked windows fanned my moist palms.

She parked the Dodge and turned off the engine. After wetting her lips with her tongue, she ran her fingers through her wavy, yellow hair.

She closed the windows, and I inhaled her maple syrup–scented perfume. The fragrance paralyzed me. One moment my heart had stopped beating, and the next it drummed snarls of evil rhythm. The pounding sent my mind into fast forward, rewind, and fast forward again. She leaned in closer, neck exposed, eyes twinkling with anticipation.

I bit my lip and tucked my hands into a ball on my lap.

After 30 minutes of forced conversation and dissipated sexual tension, our date ended with a handshake of disappointment and a flare of shame. I feared the potential embarrassment that comes with a romantic mishap. She was a gossiper. By Monday my entire class would know what had happened. I hated attention.

Moren's gentle voice transported me from suburban Michigan to Ethiopia. "This give good smell," she said. "Good smell and coffee I make for you."

She sprinkled dried, yellow grass over the floor of her shop. Moren picked up a candleholder laden with incense and wood, dropped a match in it, and placed it next to my feet. My foot odor must've been a shock to her nostrils.

"Hee hee hee!" She giggled and glanced away as her cheeks turned into roses.

She roasted coffee beans with a steel plate over a flame, stirring them with a wooden spoon. A cedar aroma tickled my nostrils. The beans darkened, and the scent changed from medicinal and tarty to smoky and charred.

Drops of perspiration formed on Moren's temple as she hovered over the flame.

"You eating popcorn now. *Blah! Blah* mean *eat* in Amharic. I teach you Amharic." She dashed into her home and fetched a bowl. It was like North American or Korean movie-theater popcorn, except granules of sugar replaced the salt and butter.

"*Blah!* Yeah! *Blah!* Great word! Teach ... me ... Amharic." I paused between words.

"This called khat. You want eat?" she said.

"What ...? Khat? Oh, that tree branch ...? Ah ...thank you, Moren, but I'll stick with coffee. No khat for me. But I'd love to chat with you."

I marveled at the leaves pinned to the roof of Moren's café. There it was, the infamous leaf chewed for thousands of years on the Horn of Africa and in Yemen. The plant that acted as a stimulant, reduced appetite, and made the user euphoric, dangled in front of me. Sufis and ancient Egyptians used the leaf to manifest mystical experiences and bring themselves closer to divinity. In Ethiopia, people often chewed khat and chatted to make peace after a conflict. Locals consumed the leaf during traditional activities, such as weddings or requesting a bride's hand in marriage from her parents. It was illegal in many parts of the world, but the government earned over 10 times as much from khat sales as from coffee, the country's official leading export.

Next, she moved the coffee beans into a steel cylinder and pounded them with a wooden stick.

"You like my coffee-making? Where you from? America? Nice country. I love you. Will you marry me? My husband gone for the day." She slowed her speech and held eye contact.

Husband? I visualized a broad-shouldered man scowling at me with a pickaxe as I begged for mercy. One smack from the ax would thrust me into a world of disfigurement. If I had infuriated the kid at Saint George's Church over a few coins, I could only imagine the havoc an irate spouse could wreak.

"The coffee smells nice."

"You love me?" she asked with a smile.

"I'm too old for you. You're too young for me. I'd like to meet your husband. I'm sure he is a nice man," I answered, breaking eye contact.

"Here my phone number. You calling me? Promise?" Her eyes traveled down my body as she handed me a paper with her number.

"Sure, Moren. You and your husband will be my good friends," I said, emphasizing her marital status.

Next, she transferred the crushed beans into an earthenware kettle and added boiling water.

"This called *jebena*." She pointed to the coffeepot of hardened mud while exposing the side of her neck.

A few minutes later, the jebena gurgled. Moren held the pot over a shot glass–sized cup of white porcelain painted with red and green flowers. Steam rushed upward as the stream of black liquid poured into the cup and formed pebble-sized bubbles around the rim.

A kid in a collared shirt carried a box of peanuts into Moren's cafe and placed a handful of nuts on my plate. He motioned to the snack and flashed a toothless smile.

"He say that gift for you. You enjoy! That called *loas*."

"Hey, Moren. What happens when children lose their teeth? I see he's missing a few."

"Oh! This fun story! Children throwing teeth on house roof. They singing song to bird. Bird picking teeth and bringing child big tooth."

No tooth fairy. Singing and tooth-throwing. What a fun way to enjoy the transition to the next stage of maturity.

"Now you drinking coffee I make for you." She took a seat next to me and leaned in close. Our forearms brushed against each other. Her touch had goosebumps shooting up my shoulders.

"Thanks for your hard work, Moren. Ten birr, right?"

"No money. My gift." She pushed my hand away.

Our hands dangled together for a few seconds. Her touch was cool.

"Take it. I want to pay. That coffee took so much time and energy."

"Okay." Her glance wandered to the floor.

I held the miniature cup close to my nose, shut my eyes, and took in my first hint of Ethiopian coffee. The scent traveled up my nostrils and caressed my brain into a frenzy of anticipation. *Seduced into doing it*, my heart observed. *Scared to do it. Postponed doing it. Now I was doing it! Ethiopia on a bike!*

The first taste stung. The caffeine rushed to my head in an instantaneous electric shock. Time stopped as the liquid swirled around my mouth. A mild bitterness infused with a tinge of salt suffused my palate. A few sips later, I felt energetic, hyperalert, and ready to ride across the entire planet.

I sipped coffee several times per day throughout my stay in Ethiopia, but nothing compared to Moren's love-laden liquid.

I wondered about Moren's past and the details of her relationship with her husband. Child marriage had been around since the beginning of Ethiopian civilization and become normalized in rural society, even encouraged. Four out of 10 women were married before age 18 and Ethiopia had the 14th-highest prevalence of child marriage in the world.

Family members preferred girls to marry while in high school so the husband could protect his bride from rape or violence that sometimes occurred on the way to school. Parents also forced their daughters to wed to prevent sexual promiscuity, believing they wouldn't engage in extramarital sex. A pure daughter guards the family's honor and avoids contracting an STD. Also, by marrying their daughters early, parents hope, in the absence of social security, to have grandchildren who will look after them in their old age.

Sometimes a suitor can't afford the dowry, so he'll gather his friends and ride on horseback to kidnap his future wife as she walks home from grade school. After collecting the girl, he rapes his adolescent wife. Once a girl has lost her virginity, she is tainted in the eyes of other men and has no option but to stay with her abductor. A local council of elders passes judgment on the abduction and has final say in the matter. Most of the time, they agree with kidnapping practices, basing their decisions on tradition. Often, a girl who is not married by late adolescence is a disgrace to the family. A girl's father loses status if his daughter is single by her late teens.

Moren appeared to be in her early 20s, and I hoped she hadn't been forced into a life she didn't choose.

Thoughts of the timid adolescent of my past upset me. My longing to add victory points to the scorecard of my youth rang out loudly. The deep-seated wounds from childhood failures still needed healing. Was that shy teenager gone forever? I played the coffee seduction game to let myself know that I could have had her. It was ego-building instead of playfulness. The narcissist in me roared.

The bumbling teenager had to sort himself out. The intrepid lifestyle, the Ethiopian trip—were they for redemption? Every bold action drove another stake in the heart of that emasculated kid who trembled in front of pretty faces. It should've been about more. My goal was to attain the confidence that comes with doing something hard and to learn about Ethiopia and its people. I was there to show myself that I could do anything with the proper mindset and preparation. Now I questioned my real motives.

My priorities were global knowledge and truth, but I felt more ignorant than ever. The questions overwhelmed me. What was Moren's past like? What had made the couple throw fists? What did Ethiopia have in store for me?

Chapter 4

A Tour-Cycling Tandem

"When the webs of two spiders join, they can trap a lion."
—Ethiopian proverb

I pedaled through pastures surrounded by beige fields. Off-white rays of sunlight provided an energy source to pull from as the midafternoon sun snapped me to attention. The color contrast generated a magnetic aura. The subtle warmth tantalized my skin.

Nature's beauty had me ready to push on and explore. The desert horizon was like an evil clown, juggling its balls of temptation with a goofy smirk—alluring, nonetheless. I chased it until it chucked the round toys in my direction. It rendered me a limp, fatigued mess.

The masochist in me awakened, my thighs pulsated, and I gasped for breath as the sun went down. The pain changed into numbness as I marveled at the peaks that lingered above, safeguarding me from the burning sun.

I'd gone about 80 kilometers on my first day. As I pushed on, Moren's coffee gave me the vigor to defy the odds, reach the velvet clouds, and punch through my hesitation. I had tasted compassion and desire in her coffee. Excited by the unknown, I pedaled.

That first-love cup had me on a rampage until nightfall, immersing me in the grim truth of my mortality. It stopped me in my tracks.

Families on motorcycles zoomed past me as I approached a noisy village center. Wrinkled men with ox carts bowed and waved, and a classroom's worth of energy-charged children in ragged clothes sprinted toward me.

I convinced myself to stop and a crowd of people surrounded me while I attempted to explain myself. Mid gesture, I noticed a scruffy-haired Asian kid in his early twenties. Thirty bicycle lengths away, he was encircled by a group of admirers. His tan lines gave him the appearance of a farmer who tended teff fields and chased livestock wearing the same outfit every day. Panniers dangled off the rear rack as he pushed his bike along the street. Painted-on cycling shorts emphasized the angular outlines of muscular thighs that shook with authority. He became bigger as he stomped in my direction, camouflaged by Ethiopians who came up to my chin.

"Wow ... you are on a bicycle. My name is Tetsuya, from Japan. I cycled here from Cape Town and am going to Cairo." He held eye contact longer than most Japanese men I'd encountered. His eyes peered into mine as he raised his bushy eyebrows. Tetsuya had an energy of enormous action, someone unwavering in the face of their goals. A guy who sings his own song.

"Nice! How has your ride been?" I asked.

"Great. Except a man put a gun to my head and robbed me in South Africa. He only took my phone."

Tetsuya's grin, while he described his brush with death, bewildered me. His tone gave no hint of fear, anger, or worry. If he could speak of a near-death experience so nonchalantly, then I knew we'd get along. He and I were likely to have tales of adventure to share. I leaned in as he continued his trip's highlight reel.

"In Zimbabwe, I had nineteen tire punctures. It was annoying. Here, in Ethiopia, children throw stones at me. Every day it's the same thing— 'You! You! Money, money! Pen, pen!' People mistook me for a girl, so I grew a beard." He laughed at the stereotype of East-Asian men.

Tetsuya's hardships in Ethiopia were no surprise. My counter-stone tactics were kindness and playfulness. A genuine smile and a salute in the local language had never failed to win others over. Show teeth, avoid rocks, and make friends. If that didn't work, I'd press on until they became weary. It was simple math.

My degree of consciousness decides what I see: Every outcome mirrors my internal state. At low levels, the children are social menaces that can be met with negativity or indifference. At the height of never-ending peace and tranquility, they'd be revealed as my inner self. Likewise, the children's responses to strangers with varying degrees of consciousness would change. Some they'd greet with pleasure; others would be dummies for target-practice sessions with stones. I had it figured out.

Tetsuya's tire-patching tale impressed me. On bicycle tours, deflated tires made me fume. This guy had almost as many punctures in one day as years he'd been alive. If my goal was to tame the mind and develop patience, riding across Zimbabwe ought to fix me. Puncture. Patch. Puncture. Patch. Repeat eighteen more times.

He had so many adventures under his belt at the ripe old age of 23. While on college breaks, Tetsuya had pedaled across South America and Europe. If only I'd discovered the magic of cycling around the world decades sooner. Back then, I'd focused on basketball, summer jobs, and little personal growth. I was still proud to be a late starter in my thirties. Traveling by bike had given me the coming-of-age expeditions absent from my university days.

Since we were both heading north, we decided to travel together. Finding a suitable companion was tough since tour cyclists were an eccentric mix with unique quirks. Distance and speed goals motivated some to zoom past stunning mountain terrain without stopping to appreciate the scenery. Others took it slow and hit the street in the late morning after sipping tea and dining on meals of rice and mayonnaise they'd cooked themselves. Some traveled with only the clothes on their backs and slept in hotels while eating in restaurants. Others pushed themselves to their limits, catching shuteye while collapsing on piles of rocks and sand. Tetsuya seemed easygoing, a key quality in a great travel partner. I didn't know it then, but a kid who was young enough to be my student would teach me valuable lessons and test my composure with his boldness.

Chapter 5

Help Me Wash My ...

"You think of water when the well is empty."
—Ethiopian proverb

That evening we crashed at a village hotel owned by Tetsuya's friend, a local named Sai. He was in his mid-twenties, but his short, curly hair had already begun to recede. He wore a collared shirt of red-and-black plaid, and his paunch poked over the waistline of his gray shorts. Sai squinted in the sunlight, exposing crow's feet that turned to horizontal lines of mystery. Semicircular shadows under his eyes intimated weariness despite his enthusiasm upon greeting us. Dimples gleaming with elation, he grabbed my hand to draw me in for a gregarious shoulder bump.

We took selfies with Sai for over 10 minutes. He snatched our helmets and posed with our protective gear until we were perfectly centered in front of his hotel. His excitement was endearing and made me want to help his business by filling my stomach with food and staying the evening in his guest house. Our new friend gave us a great deal—a grand total of $1.60 per night. Tetsuya and I looked at each other in disbelief.

Sai led us across the porch of his restaurant, and we entered a small room with blinking Christmas lights and forest-green walls. The area was comfortably dim, with a ceaselessly revolving fan hanging from the ceiling and a cracked mirror stuck to the wall behind a bar counter.

He opened another door, revealing an open courtyard with a rocky surface. Piled with lanky scraps of wood and used car tires, the place had the vibe of an old junkyard. Leafy green trees outlined the yard's periphery. Concrete walls with coils of barbed wire protected us from intruders. Burning logs gave the yard a faint, musky odor. Five rooms were off to one side, and Sai unlocked two of them.

"You sleep here. Very safe. No problem. Look here." He pointed to the walls and barbed wire.

"Oh yes! This is great," I said.

"You want shower? Ready 30 minutes. Me make water hot for you with fire." Sai gestured to a nearby tin shack with a wooden roof where a red glow smoldered in the room's drab blackness.

Sai showed us to separate rooms. The heavy, rusted door swung into mine and screeched, pleading for oil. The door took up half the floor space, clearing the bed by a few centimeters. There was just enough room for my bike. Yellow blankets covered a single mattress, and a pair of pink, child-sized sandals—waiting to give my sweaty feet some fresh air—lay on the floor next to the bed. Pink cracks laced the windowless walls and ceiling, and chunks of crumbled paint hung limply from the corners. The concrete floor was swept and well-kept. A battered wooden table and creaky-looking chair were the only other pieces of furniture. A single light bulb dangled from the ceiling.

"Electricity working in two hours." Sai pointed proudly to a switch on the wall.

"This is perfect." I smiled and patted Sai on the shoulder.

Moments later he signaled for his worker to bring the water. A chubby-armed woman with thick dreadlocks tied into a ponytail stomped out of a tin shack that lay opposite our rooms.

She rested a bar of soap on one of the spare tires and grasped a pitcher of water while signaling us to come forward.

"Water warm now. You showering and she help!" yelled Sai as he returned to his restaurant to greet a customer.

Tetsuya and I giggled like children getting high off laughing gas in a dentist's office.

I wondered whether Sai's employees had helped other hotel customers bathe. Did Tetsuya and I receive special treatment? Were we the only ones who had requested a shower? Perhaps pouring hot water on others was a sign of hospitality in Ethiopia. In South Korea, people scrub down friends and family members in public bathhouses as displays of affection. I've had Korean girlfriends who washed my feet to show their love. Maybe I was about to experience something deeper.

Outside of major cities, Ethiopian toilets were holes in the ground. Pitchers like the one she held in her hands replaced sinks. Wooden shacks with barely enough room to squat replaced stalls and flushable machines. If you were lucky, doors closed properly. Over the years, I'd learned to treat open fields or green spaces behind trees as business offices. No water, no tissues, no problem.

I stripped to my boxer shorts and stumbled toward the woman. The heels of my feet stuck out of the miniature sandals. I pointed to my head in anticipation of the upcoming bath.

She grabbed the pitcher with a big smile, and the washing began. The warm water trickled down my face until I could taste the acidic tartness of my sweat. I rubbed soap over my forehead, cheeks, and behind my neck until a white film slid into my eyes. A sharp sting had me squinting in pain. The lukewarm cascade massaged my aching shoulders and back into relaxation as it rinsed the salty, earthy crust off my body. Brown muck flushed from my head crept down my thighs and drenched my throbbing feet.

Thank you! Thank you for this water, I thought as I luxuriated in the love and energy that went into making my bath possible. Taking hot water for granted had become commonplace in South Korea and North America, especially in the winter.

Someone had to chop wood, fetch water from afar, and start a fire so I could bathe.

Next up, crotch. I pointed to my boxers and signaled that I'd take over. The woman's face turned beet red as she whooped in laughter. A teenager dashed in my direction and snatched the pitcher. He splashed water down my pants while I scrubbed the dirtiest part of my body. *What a riot!* Cleaning oneself is so personal, but it was great to have helpers. Ethiopian hospitality had me giddy.

My Ethiopian bathing experience had me feeling more connected to water. My body, like everyone else's, is composed of it. It helps me stay germ-free and keeps me hydrated. Plants and animals soak it up to stay alive. Perhaps water should be our new God. With it, we thrive. Without it, we perish. We can float or drown in it. Water moves mountains one particle at a time. My tears of joy and sadness are drops of water.

I learn from water. Water is humble. All streams and rivers strive to make it to the ocean, the point of lowest elevation, which becomes deeper and deeper as water accumulates. It has taught me to seek depth in relationships, knowledge, and self-understanding. Water gives to all free of judgment. It penetrates the earth through unwavering persistence. It finds a solution without force and works in harmony with the environment. It's never in a hurry yet accomplishes everything. Reflecting on water has motivated me to do the heavy lifting to free myself from my default setting of self-centeredness. It has taught me that real freedom comes from sacrificing for the good of humanity.

Water has infinite adaptability. Always open to temperature variation, it reinvents itself, changing states, from solid (ice) in winter to liquid in spring to vapor in the summer sun. To fit in a coffee mug or a flower vase, it is never afraid to change its shape. It has been around for billions of years and is vital for the survival of all earthlings. Every spot along a river is different. Water keeps flowing and changing just as every cell in my body changes as I type these words.

Water has unrivaled clarity. It shows me my reflection with no distortions. The lines on my face appear as they are, without computerized touch-ups. Clarity is priceless. It aids me in decision-making and empowers me to ignore things that contaminate it in an era of information overload. Mental clarity led me to give up fast food and soft drinks, convinced me to stop watching television, and prevented me from buying a smartphone. Just as pollution morphs water into a murky substance that gives humans diarrhea, cholera, and polio, advertising, excessive expectations, and junk foods send us into a whirlwind of prescription drugs, depression, and suicide.

Water is the ultimate teacher and provider. Cleanse me, teach me. Give me life, health, and clarity.

Chapter 6

Filthy Altruism

"One should punish a child the day he comes home with a stolen egg, or else the day he comes home with a stolen ox it will be too late."

—Ethiopian Proverb

We were clean and ready for dinner. Sai ordered us food from his restaurant, and we polished it off the way two guys cycling through the most mountainous country on the African continent should. After the meal, Sai called me over to the bar area.

"Please helping," he said. "You be American."

Here we go! I thought, reminding myself of the times people across the world had asked for US visa-related help. A Bangladeshi man in Oman ambushed my thoughts. This kind soul had invited me to his home for a meal and persuaded me to write a letter stating he was a skilled carpenter ready to work in the United States. When a tall, hairy-armed guy on a bike pops into town and mentions his place of birth, wide-eyed faces full of hope gazed in wonderment. I wished I had a magic wand. They'd appreciate the conveniences of life in the United States in ways I couldn't. Who could blame them for asking?

"Contact these people important. This couple in the United States sending me money every month since I child until graduating university. Love them so much. Me no have mailing

address so money stops. Please help tell them. Because of them, me have business here. Happy to have business," he continued.

Sai's English seemed good enough to contact the couple himself. I wasn't sure what he was trying to ask, but I told him to email me in the future if he needed help.

After making short work of Sai's injera and pasta, Sai's business showed its true colors. Several skimpily dressed women entered his restaurant as the music blared at decibel levels that would have made a tranquil temple of the heaviest of heavy-metal concerts. Only two clients remained. They sat alone at opposite corners of the room, surrounded by empty bottles of beer. Their faces were reddened, and their speech was slurred. One man stumbled over and plopped himself onto the plastic chair next to me.

"I am veterinarian. Love me job. I be help cows and people be so happy. I study hard now. I am writing thesis but have plagiarism problems. I don't know avoid plagiarism. What doing?" he asked.

The man slouched in his seat, neck tilted to the side, and pouted while he pointed his forehead at the bottle. I attempted to give him advice on how to cite research and data from other studies. No reaction. The doctor continued to suck down his drink and drown his sorrows.

The veterinarian changed the subject, and our conversation became a confession session.

"My wife always angry with me. Me drinking too much ... sexing other girls."

That's when it hit me. The alcohol, cheap rooms, and half-naked women added up to bad news. Sai was enabling Ethiopian sex workers to sell their bodies at his bar. The American couple had funded it.

I stomped off to my room in disgust and crashed for the night.

A few hours later, the blaring sounds of computerized male vocalists, snare-drum beats, and shrieks from the courtyard interrupted my dreams. I cracked open my door and glimpsed the action. Sai unloaded punch combinations with all his might.

First a left hook to the temple then an uppercut to the jaw. The victim covered himself with both hands.

Who was that guy? Oh! The veterinarian.

Next, he connected with the midsection, and the doctor hit the ground. The animal healer lay in the fetal position as Sai kicked his head. The veterinarian squirmed in pain and humiliation. Sai had transformed himself from a charismatic young hotel operator into a pimp of the night.

I shut the door and my mind went wild. Was this because of poverty's vicious cycle? On one hand, Sai earned a decent wage and appeared to lead a comfortable life. But there he was, watching others poison themselves with alcohol while promoting sexual promiscuity. His actions could only worsen the HIV epidemic.

I'd researched the topic before setting off on my journey. Prostitution is legal in Ethiopia. While operating a brothel is a breach of law, it is rarely enforced. Ethiopian authorities would probably never crack down on Sai's operation. Although Ethiopia had grown into one of Africa's fastest-growing economies, over a third of the population survived on $1.90 per day. Ethiopian families who couldn't afford to support their children often sold them to human traffickers. The "brokers" forced children, often from rural areas, to work as prostitutes or domestic slaves after promising to send them to major cities for better employment and educational opportunities. Deception, lies, and humiliation were the foundational principles of trafficking. Brokers were often well-respected community members who promised everything and delivered nothing. Many girls, some as young as eight, couldn't return home after becoming sex workers because their families had disowned them. Prostitutes who tried to quit couldn't find a job for years or even decades.

I wondered whether the sex workers at Sai's establishment had been at it since childhood or whether they'd sell their children's bodies for money. Had their families ostracized them? Had they tried to work elsewhere?

The reality of foreign aid left a big knot in my stomach. Wasn't someone from the organization checking up on Sai?

Perhaps he told the agency he was running a bar and hotel while leaving out the sex worker part? Did the American couple know about this? How many people from abroad were aiding the human trafficking industry with their altruistic motivation to "help children in Ethiopia?" Weren't there better things Sai could do with his money?

Then again, there was a lot I didn't know. Prostitution was a social norm in Ethiopia. If the oldest job in the world enabled people to feed themselves and earn a living, then shouldn't sex workers be able to perform their duties? I wondered how they felt and how he treated them. Perhaps Sai thought he was altruistic by letting prostitutes work at his establishment and put injera on their families' tables. I'd never understand what it's like to be an Ethiopian villager. I had so many questions, but the biggest one twisted my mind into a pretzel. Were the altruistic filthy or were the filthy altruistic?

I stayed quiet. No contacting the American family and no preaching about my version of morality.

The next morning, Tetsuya and I tiptoed out of the hotel moments after sunrise. We said our goodbyes to Sai, who was conscious enough to wave.

As the sun rose from the horizon, I filled Tetsuya in on the fight. He'd slept like a guy pedaling from Cape Town and missed the action.

"Oh?" Tetsuya said, barely half-surprised. After cycling through faraway lands on the bike for several months at a time, nothing shocked him. He was still the same calm, collected kid. Perhaps even more so after a rest in a sordid hotel (loud music and shouting notwithstanding).

After chatting about the previous night's antics, a new temptation loomed: a canyon in the distance called and our hearts answered. *Here we go.* Off the beaten path and into lawlessness.

Chapter 7

Ras Tafari's Ghost Speaks

"When the Nile River knows a secret, the desert will soon know it too."
—Ethiopian Proverb

The main road became dull. It provided certainty in an uncertain environment and stability in an unstable land. The rush of cycling in a new country tapered into familiarity. Wild cats, hyenas, and robbers with Kalashnikovs would avoid noisy places with people around, right?

We turned onto a dirt path that had my tailbone bouncing. The rigid seat on my bicycle slammed into my crotch. I grimaced and tightened the grip on my handlebars to maintain balance.

Teff crops swayed back and forth, and rocky sand dotted with thick, ankle-high weeds surrounded us. Dried-up trees that resembled shriveled mushrooms provided evidence that life existed despite the rough conditions. Beyond the yellow mounds of teff lay a brown wall of stratified rocks. Ribbon-like fissures created a raw earthy sculpture. Shadowed grooves on the sloping surface ran several hundred meters down the cliff. The charcoal curves resembled the outline of a face with a sharp jawbone and a steep nose. Perhaps it was the spirit of Ras Tafari, carved into the stone by mystical energy. As we moved closer, a grainy headwind slowed us to a crawl—Ras Tafari's exhalation warning us off, perhaps. I felt like I was entering a gateway charged with supernatural energy.

We turned down an empty thoroughfare as a few coin-sized beetles scattered in the sand. My tires sank into potholes and swerved around fallen rocks. Memories of the rugged Mongolian terrain that snapped my spokes a few months ago paid my brain an unsolicited visit. Another obstacle course.

As we continued onward, I reflected on nature's overwhelming power. Steep drops and inclines put me into a state of ecstasy that lakes, oceans, and forests couldn't compete with. Humility was paramount when observing the grandeur of nature's creations: I was an ant in the face of 5,000-meter-high peaks. Tumbling boulders could pulverize me, and crumbling dirt paths could plummet me into my next life. I did my part by sidestepping insects that others consider filthy pests. I must've resembled a gigantic mountain peak to the tiny creatures that built webs in the crevices of our precious buildings. Respect nature, I thought, and it would respect me.

It was great to have Tetsuya there. His laid-back demeanor had a calming effect that made escaping my comfort zone more tolerable. I felt more secure on the road less traveled, especially in a land of gun-fighting and predatory beasts. Tetsuya wasn't a regular guy. He was well-versed in the art of putting himself on the line and coming out on top while staying humble about his accomplishments and cool under pressure.

"I wouldn't have come here if you weren't with me." His eyes gleamed through his sunglasses.

"Me neither."

Adrenaline charged through me. That canyon's mysticism beckoned us, and the scenery morphed into a more surreal landscape every minute. A tailwind picked up, providing a much-needed speed boost. Mud-walled homes with straw roofs dotted the horizon as villagers tended to their nearby crops and livestock. At last, my friend and I had a few moments to enjoy the surroundings. No cars. No noise pollution and exhaust fumes. The scent of raw nature drifted through the air.

A few minutes later, we stared into a red-and-yellow abyss. The steep drop could've made a seasoned rock climber's knees quiver. I threw my bike aside and inched toward the canyon. The Blue Nile was four hundred meters below us. The Nile River splits into the White Nile and Blue Nile at Khartoum, with the White Nile flowing into Lake Victoria in Uganda and Tanzania, and the Blue Nile emptying into Lake Tana, a two-day bike ride north of us. The winter drought had reduced the river to a silver wire winding between sand and rocks.

The Nile River Tributaries.

Deep along the bottom of the valley, houses on terraced shelves sheltered villagers from the rest of civilization. They must've been skilled rock climbers since only someone with a ripped torso, bowling-ball–sized calves, and diamond-hard palms could scale the rocky walls that surrounded these homes. I wanted to teleport myself there and witness their magic.

This was it! The Great Rift Valley loomed before us. A giant, 35-million-year-old crack that extended from Lebanon to Mozambique. Goosebumps on my arms grew into beige, pea-sized pimples, and my entire body shivered. I tiptoed closer to the edge and marveled at the gorge as my heart pounded in my chest. Nature's skyscraper had me on the brink of life and death.

Voices from the canyon echoed through the dry air, confusing me with their contradictory banter. "Come closer and take a good look!" They screamed. "I dare you! Back off! Danger!"

Drops of sweat trickled down my palms.

Tetsuya strolled toward the point of no return without the slightest hesitation. Watching him stare into the valley's eye made the hair on my arms and legs stand up. *This guy has no fear.*

"Don't go too close, Tetsuya!" I yelled.

"I am okay." He smiled.

Several village children who'd spotted us came and sat next to me on a rock. Their eyes widened as Tetsuya stood at the edge. He must've fallen victim to Ras Tafari's taunts. The kids yelled as my friend inched closer to the point of no return.

"No! Come! You! No!"

One wrong step would've sent him tumbling. It looked as if he was ready for a base-jumping stunt with no parachute. It seemed my companion had a death wish. My intestines growled and churned. Nervous energy must've triggered an involuntary response. I decided I needed a break from Tetsuya's fate-tempting behavior.

I stomped off while cursing Tetsuya under my breath. A hundred meters from Tetsuya and the children, I squatted next to some green bushes. Suddenly, a rustling sound nearly startled me into painting my shorts. Baritone grunts and thumping feet trampled the silence. The beasts halted as dust floated through the air. I could see one of the creature's dark outlines through the plants. Stone-shaped pecs and pipe-hard arms. The curves on its body commanded power. This thing would manhandle me in a physical confrontation. Were those noises growls of hunger? *Please don't be predators.*

A few seconds later, one of the beasts popped out from behind the bushes. Baboons! Massive, greasy-haired, snout-faced baboons! A group of at least 10 followed their leader out of hiding. The second in line flashed its sharp canines, exposing a pronounced underbite and contracted jaw muscle. They had tufts of hair on both sides of their faces and swollen, hemorrhoid-ridden, cherry-red bottoms. Walking on all fours, they appeared much smaller than I, but I never ceased to forget these were animals who could destroy me in a fight while half asleep.

They'd caught me with my pants down. My knees throbbed. I rocked from side to side and gave each knee a momentary break. I fidgeted with used pages from my journal, makeshift toilet paper. The sweat dripping from my fingers rendered them useless. My chest thumped with thunderous force. Vision blurry, I couldn't keep my eyes from darting around, scanning for more wild beasts.

Ahh! Why now?

Reducing myself to their size could've been the best move I'd ever made. The squatting version of myself appeared less threatening.

You're not attacking their babies or stealing their food, I told myself. *Mind your own business and it will be okay*.

I slowed my breath to calm myself while in the squat position. *Inhale. One. Two. Three. Four. Five. Hold. Exhale. Four. Three. Two. One.* After a few minutes of controlled breathing, the tension and day's lunch exited my body.

They kept staring, and I froze. The kids would know how to handle this situation but were too far away to ask for help. The roof of my mouth was sandpaper, and I couldn't swallow. Fear rendered me voiceless. Pressure from the center of my knee pulsated against the surface of my skin. I continued with the breath work and observed my sensations objectively until invisible spikes twisted deeper into my knees. Mind control was hard under pressure. I'd endured the same pain while meditating for hours on end. This, however, was worse. A single slip-up could have dire consequences. I cursed myself for not having been born in Japan or South Korea, where people got used to sitting on the floor while eating and socializing as children.

The baboons scooped up minuscule pieces of something off the ground and shoved them into their mouths while firmly holding eye contact with me.

Several minutes later, the beasts wandered off.

Released from my ordeal of fear, I broke out of my squatting position and fell on all fours, panting for breath. My head was throbbing with a dehydration headache. Thoughts of my water bottle taunted my dry throat. For a moment I forgot about Tetsuya's antics, the baboons, the canyon. It was time to hang up on nature's call and find safety and shade.

As I stomped off to my bicycle, Tetsuya was snapping pictures with his huge Sony camera, marveling at the gigantic fissures of Africa's most mountainous country. The baboons must have gone the other direction and missed him and the children.

I needed some of Ras Tafari's toughness to get through my cycling journey. While in exile in England, the King of Kings broke his collarbone on the way to a BBC interview. Despite the pain, he continued with the broadcast and attended a Christmas party before visiting a doctor about the fracture.

"I'll toughen you up, give you what you need, but nothing you can't handle," Ras Tafari's shadow whispered in a raspy, intimidating voice. "Right now you're weak, a fearful kitten. Leave and stay mediocre. Stick with me and be rewarded."

After I chugged a bottle of water, I sulked over my ignorance. I was ignorant of the proper way to communicate to evade a baboon beat-down. Ignorant of the power of nature's gorges, shadows, and creatures. Ignorant of my limits and capabilities.

The shadow was right. I needed Ethiopia to awaken me, to slap me with confrontations and setbacks. I was grateful to be with Tafari's ghost. He was the mentor who held my hand and guided me to deeper self-understanding, reflection, and growing pains.

Destiny called, and we had answered.

Chapter 8

Tire Inflated, Spirit Deflated

"Do not spend the evening in a house where you cannot spend the night."
—Ethiopian proverb

"The superior man does not seek fulfillment of his appetite nor comfort in his lodging."
—Confucius

Night arrived as Tetsuya and I maneuvered around boisterous children and weaved past cattle. The jagged mountain peaks blocked the sun, and a gray hue surrounded the desiccated trees and village shacks.

Drunk drivers, famished hyenas, random potholes, roadside cliffs—Ethiopia had a mantra: It's too dangerous to cycle after 6 p.m. We needed to call it a day pronto.

Tetsuya had his own ideas about night cycling. "No one's going to see us in the dark, and people will leave us alone. Let's keep going and pitch the tents in a forest," he said.

My companion's logic made sense, but what would happen when we spoke? We'd eventually be exposed as helpless travelers. Leaving Ethiopia without the psychological trauma of getting beat up for my belongings or attacked by a wild animal was imperative.

Unfazed by the impending darkness, Tetsuya continued up the path one soccer field ahead of me. Clearly, my mind was in Cairo and his was in Cape Town. The risk-taking was bound to catch up with him, and I didn't want to be there when it happened.

Villagers walked their goats along the paved road as I plopped myself down in front of them, pleading for aid. "We sleep your house. Sleep?" I convinced myself that others would understand me if my grammar was bad. I closed my eyes, tilted my head to the side, and made obnoxious snoring sounds with my throat.

"No. Go," said several men, pointing at the horizon.

Green space or sand next to a house would do. Pitching alongside locals who could fend off nighttime bandits and scare away beasts would've put me at ease. Sleeping in the forest sounded horrible. My eyes would be stapled open; every rustle in the trees would double my heart rate.

I continued for a few hundred meters and tried with a different group. One of the men was armed with an AK-47. I was hesitant to spend the night in his home next to that killing machine, but perhaps one of his unarmed friends would offer help.

"No," they said, mid step.

I was a polar bear in the steamy Indian sun. A camel in a Siberian snowstorm. A bumble bee in a flowerless Gobi Desert. During my tour-cycling trips in Asia and the Middle East, locals had invited me into their homes without hesitation, but no one here wanted to help.

My bones trembled as I pondered riding at night and pitching a tent in the forest. Calm as ever, Tetsuya appeared intent on pedaling on for a few more hours. Perhaps I would've ridden in the dark in my younger days, but time had changed me into a man who understood his responsibilities. Risks were foolish, especially knowing how devastated my family and friends would be if anything happened to me.

Light-gray landscapes turned deep blue. I couldn't tell a person from a ghost. As the sun disappeared, it took my sense of well-being with it.

As we rode on, I kept up my desperate attempts to find a yard to pitch our tents in. Villagers responded with blank stares and faces of confusion. The more I gestured to my tent and appealed for space, the more people raised their eyebrows and pointed down the road.

We continued pedaling, and I took in the country's natural beauty. Darkness descended on the jagged horizon as nature closed its curtains on the day. Trees changed from figures glowing red with the last of the sun to pencil-sketched outlines in the foreground of a charcoal canvas. Teff fields became strings of burned matches, weak and limp in the crisp evening air.

The night enveloped me in a state of tension and panic. The fatigue from the day's events exited my body. Blood rushed to my head and had me hyper alert.

A bus dropped off a few villagers. I sped up to catch them and began my pleading routine. A man with a white turban held a wooden cross. He stood a few centimeters shorter than I, and scraggly hair covered his cheeks. He was dressed in a light-blue sports coat that gave him a sophisticated look. His inviting smile had me feeling optimistic.

"*Salam.* I pastor," he said with a big-toothed grin.

"Sleeping? Your house?"

"Come, come. Yes. My house here."

"Tetsuya! Come! We have a place to sleep!" I projected my voice over the sound of an oncoming motorcycle.

Tetsuya, now a couple of soccer fields ahead of us, came rolling in a few seconds later.

"Oh, a holy man!" Tetsuya said, after I gave him the good news. "So he's safe."

My intuition spoke: A guy who devoted his life to God had to be kind. His smile seemed pure, like a young boy ready to make new friends. Surely he'd help two travelers stuck in a bind. Part of me hoped he wasn't a member of a cult that chops up tourists and feeds them to hyenas for sin redemption. At least he was armed with a cross instead of a Kalashnikov.

Memories of Zimbabwe six years ago made me feel flustered. Priests had shouted "Hallelujah!" while delivering passionate sermons in bus aisles. At first, I assumed the preacher's blessing would protect me from car accidents. What a wholesome way to start a ride.

"The Zimbabwean preachers are here to keep us safe from Satanists. Around here, people believe anything a holy man tells them. Witch doctors tell followers to feed sharks a white man's ear off the coast of Mozambique. They think it'll cure them of HIV. Crazy things happen here," my friend Tami informed me. Tami called and emailed every day to make sure I was well during my two months of backpacking and hitchhiking in Southern Africa. He also gave me a place to crash in Johannesburg. He knew a lot about the world since he'd lived in South Korea and Thailand for several years. When his parents came to see him, it harrowed his mother to hear we'd taken local buses with potential ear snatchers.

My bus rides in Zimbabwe were uneventful until Tami filled me in on his country's dark side. His explanation infected me with paranoia and my mind played tricks on me 24 hours a day. The dude over there looks suspicious. *Is that guy staring at my ears?*

My imagination entered a steamy hell every time I boarded a bus. If a Satanist found me, they'd have done anything to confiscate a toe, ear, or nose. I didn't see any white people on bus rides in Zimbabwe, so I felt like a baby goat under a swarm of circling vultures. How could anyone have followed such an insane ritual? Watching over myself during waking and sleeping hours on that trip had me fatigued.

I pushed my bike along the Ethiopian road with Tetsuya grinning by my side. No need to inform him about the Satanists in Zimbabwe. He'd cycled through there a few weeks ago and didn't need any extra nightmares en route to Cairo. The country was in his past and he'd made it out unscathed, ignorant of its frightening underworld. This was the same continent, but we were thousands of miles from Zimbabwe. Besides, the Ethiopian pastor's calm demeanor spoke of no malicious intent.

It would've been even riskier to continue in the dark and camp alone.

It will be okay, George, I told myself. *You are in Ethiopia.*

My imagination drifted in the settling dark. It envisioned ghosts and beasts preying on the vulnerable. With the war and famine in Ethiopia's history, the spirits would suffocate me with their paranormal energy. They'd taste the fear seeping through the pores of my dried skin. Camping alone in the Korean mountains and Mongolian steppe had brought eerie emotions since victims of the Korean War or Genghis Khan could've haunted me, but Ethiopia was a different, higher level.

After pushing our bikes for a few minutes, my shoulders dropped, and my eyes stopped darting around. The holy man's cross would protect us from night demons, and, as a local, he must've been adept at fending off wild creatures. If God existed, he had to be on our side.

"My children." The pastor pointed at two boys running in our direction.

I smiled and waved at the kids. Their eyes widened with curiosity while they inspected my bike. I shook their hands and gave them high fives as they giggled in delight.

Knowing the pastor was a father made him seem more trustworthy. I assumed he'd do his best to be a role model for his children—a model that I hoped included helping strangers in need.

We continued along a meandering dirt path and passed the hums of whimpering sheep. After a few more minutes, we arrived at a two-story house with a tin roof. Dark-brown earth covered the wooden frame. Walls of mud had solidified into a material that appeared hard as concrete.

We ducked our heads under a small door and entered the pastor's home. The smell hit me first, a pine-scented draft with a hint of farm-animal ruggedness. Perhaps air escaped through the walls and provided natural ventilation. The dried grass that surrounded our new friend's home put my nostrils at ease as my breathing slowed. The indoor air quality seemed more pristine than a desolate forest in Finland.

Our host gave us a piece of goat hide to use as a seat cushion. His wife, a petite woman with a shaved head who wore a red robe, sat in the corner, busily preparing food for their four children. We had little interaction with her as she stayed quiet and attended to the housework.

The kids chewed on sugar cane as I waved and made faces, sticking out my tongue and crossing my eyes. The children threw their sweet sticks to the side and a game of copycat began. They mimicked my expressions and laughed with one another until their mother called them.

While at the pastor's home, I reflected on my wild behavior during the mini-crisis. Once again, I had ruminated instead of finding a place to stay. As I sifted through memories of Zimbabwe, my head had created a hell that had ceased to exist. Self-induced suffering. At least I was aware of my faults and caught myself during momentary lapses. My mind hadn't come with an instruction manual, and I yearned every day to use it better. Since the pastor had volunteered to help us, I could rest easy. Taming my brain, however, would be a herculean endeavor.

"Sit down." The pastor gestured. "I make this house only my hands."

The pastor was offering us his best seats, which were next to a fire pit with a mud bench. The holy man reached up and switched on a single light bulb. The light was dim but enough to scan his home. The ceiling with its beams of beige wood, several meters over our heads, was reminiscent of an ancient European cathedral.

Amazing. How did he construct this place with his bare hands?

Above the fire pit, a square gap the size of a small refrigerator led to another room. Chickens jumped from the top of the windowsill into the mysterious space. It was like they were plunging into a black hole, vanishing without a sound or losing a feather.

"Eggs very good," our host barked, gesturing at the white-feathered birds while chewing on a thick piece of sugar cane.

I pointed at the chickens and made wing gestures at the kids while bobbing my head forward and back. The children copied my movements and chuckled away at my games.

The pastor handed Tetsuya and me a big plate of injera covered in the spiced bean paste called shiro. What a kind man, offering food and making us feel at home by providing an animal-skin seat cover. I was grateful for his hospitality.

"Cold," our host said, rubbing his hands together and motioning us closer.

The pastor's wife started a fire to ward off the cool of the Ethiopian night. Dried sweat, a byproduct of hours of cycling in the sun, gave my body a pungent odor, and I loathed the idea of stinking myself up further. The last thing a guy from Michigan needed was to sit by the fire on a crisp evening. Our new friend's kindness was about to make me perspire.

"I want coffee. Do you have coffee?" Tetsuya asked our host.

The pastor nodded and spoke to his wife in Amharic. She popped out of her seat and searched for uncooked coffee beans. As in Moren's cafe, bean roasting and crushing, water boiling, and incense preparation was a time-consuming process.

As we waited for the drink, I needed to get something off my chest. At every stop along the way, Tetsuya picked up at least two bottles of Coke or Sprite. Being a health freak who consumes less than a mini-sized Snicker's bar worth of processed sugar per year, I shifted from tour-cycle adventurer to elder university professor. Today's lecture: thin on the outside but fat on the inside.

"You know about processed sugar, right? Animal studies show it's more addictive than cocaine and can lower your intelligence. Tetsuya, you're 23 and a great athlete, so I understand you might think cola isn't harmful, but I taught a 20-year-old student who found out how disgusting her liver looked after a body scan revealed her internal fat. She was the envy of every girl in the class—tall, thin, pleasant personality—but on the inside she made whales look anorexic. All from eating two ice creams per day."

"I didn't know that. I'll stop drinking Coca-Cola after this trip. Yes, sugar please with the coffee," Tetsuya said, requesting his drug of choice mid-sentence.

Despite my regression to teacher mode, Tetsuya continued binging. I understand it's hard to kick old habits. Maybe he needed a few sugarholics anonymous meetings to get clean. Or perhaps I sounded condescending and fatherly. Then again, friends were supposed to watch out for each other. We were both more likely to fall victim to cancer or diabetes than violent crime or a hyena attack while camping. Maybe my biking companion assumed he'd die young from his crazy stunts. Why worry about the 45-year-old version of yourself when you'll perish from a stray shot, wild animal confrontation, or canyon plunge? But from my perspective as a friend, seeing Tetsuya thrive and reach his full potential was paramount.

An hour later, coffee was served even though it was almost time to sleep. My mind was torn. Enjoy coffee, no sleep. Refuse drink, offend host.

Irresistible. I'd pass out no matter what. Inject my jugular with Redbull and I'd turn into a drooling slob, polluting the silence with my snores. So far, I'd said no to coffee after two in the afternoon. Then again, I didn't want to be a boring rule follower—when would I ever return to Ethiopia?

Our host's eyes beamed as we took a sip. Tetsuya grabbed his cup with the unvoiced hysteria of an addict getting his first fix of the day. His pupils were dilated and glossy, and a huge, clown-like smile illuminated his face.

"Mmm good." My Japanese buddy gleamed in excitement as he guzzled the last few drops of the caffeinated beverage.

The pastor leaped out of his seat and dashed over to refill Tetsuya's cup. His zeal for hospitality made me feel guilty. Perhaps he sacrificed sleep to give his guests an extra dose of kindness. Coffee and comfort served with love.

A few minutes later, the pastor cleared away our cups and spread a sheet of fabric across the mud for us. Falling into dreamland on a surface of earth should've been a cinch. I'd been catching shuteye for nine years on the ground of my South Korean apartment. I moved from a mattress to a wooden floor in search of relief from the sweat-soaked summer nights. During winters, the heated floor gave my body the warmth it needed to enjoy snowy nights. After that, mattresses were history. Even when I visited my family in Michigan, I opted for the carpet next to the bed I'd slept in as a child. That evening in Ethiopia, nothing was more inviting than ground space.

But when I sprawled out on the blanket, I felt sharp stones poking my back. The combination of coffee and the rocky surface resulted in tossing and turning. My mind raced with energy. I sat up and focused on my breath and body sensations. The chemicals in my brain were going to duke it out—meditation versus caffeine in a skirmish over my state of consciousness. I perceived the rocks poking at my glutes and the pressure on my shoulders with perfect equanimity. Soon I lost myself in the technique and entered dreamland. Meditation quieted my brain and relaxed my muscles. What a powerful tool to have in my arsenal!

Spirit inflated: that morning, I was high off the novelty of staying in a villager's home.

Tire deflated. No problem. While on tour, a puncture-repair kit, spare tire, and tube were essential. Fixing a flat was part of the routine.

Tetsuya woke up as I poked at the tube.

Once again, our host offered us injera. What a gracious gesture. Injera always provided me with a very welcome nutrient-abundant meal.

After eating, we packed up and Tetsuya ran out the door. He scurried ahead to the main road, eager to put in a few morning kilometers. I took my time exchanging some last words with the family. They deserved a proper goodbye after rescuing us.

"You coming back. Go back Addis Ababa, you coming here."

The man had no email, home address, or telephone number. He expected me to remember where he lived. Face-to-face communication was the only way to stay in touch with the pastor. Heartbreaking.

I thought of the friends who had waltzed out of my life. On the road, fleeting relationships were the norm, but the sorrow when separating from someone I'd never see again persisted.

Back in junior high school, my partner in crime had moved across the country because his father changed jobs. No more basketball games, bike rides, or swimming in the summers. No more stories of my friend's escapades with pre-teen girls. As a shy boy, I needed coaching in the art of capturing the cute neighbor girl's attention, but my mentor's advice flew away on the plane. The guy who was more experienced in the intricacies of life left me a crying mess when we said goodbye. I remember him riding down the street on his blue BMX bike after whipping me in a round of basketball.

The empty feeling and heart-choking tears never fled my memory. I clung to the hope that one day he'd move back, or we'd visit each other. In the early 1990s, letters and expensive, long-distance phone calls were the only way to communicate. Sloppily written letters came for several months, and I cherished them. But the messages became more and more infrequent, and we eventually lost contact forever. When friendship dies of this affliction, it dies a sad, drawn-out death. I've tried to look him up on social media, but his name turns up thousands of search results. Our digital reunion will have to be a result of his efforts. I'm still waiting for that day.

The Ethiopian pastor's generosity touched me. I'd been on the receiving end of hospitality many times. No matter how hard I attempted to pay for meals in Bangladesh, Myanmar, Tajikistan, Uzbekistan, and Oman, people flat out refused. "There's no money in friendship" was a common reply.

I remembered the 85-year-old Buddhist monk whom I'd enjoyed chatting with over tea in my favorite national park in Seoul. "You can eat and sleep in any temple in Korea for free. Many Westerners come here and try to hand me money after I give them a meal. They're always so shocked when I refuse. This is our culture—helping others. No money. It was like that when I was catching snakes for food years ago. We were more generous when we were poor and hungry." He repeated this whenever we talked as if I had forgotten what he'd said during my earlier 10 visits.

I thought back to the time when my best friend, Tony, had visited me in Seoul on his first trip outside the United States. After polishing off an enormous meal of kimchi dumplings and fried-bean pancakes at one of Seoul's most famous markets, he attempted to tip the food-kiosk worker.

"That was way too cheap! I've got to give these guys more money," he said, insisting they were on the wrong end of an unfair exchange.

I grabbed his cash and stuffed it back into his hands, picturing the cooks' faces, confused and red with embarrassment. Seconds later, a wrinkled woman with short, permed hair served us an additional pancake "on the house." It was all out of *jeong*.[1] Offering extra money would have been a cultural blunder.

Who could blame Tony? He'd been trying to say thank you for the excellent service and mouth-watering food. I was the same 12 years earlier. My jaw dropped the first time an elderly woman handed me cash on the street after inquiring about bean-paste soup restaurants in broken Korean.

"Enjoy your meal and take this." She grabbed my hand and slammed enough money into it to pay for three meals. It was her way of showing *jeong*. People in South Korea showed their true selves through actions rather than words. Gestures of kindness without expectations were a big reason I couldn't leave South Korea. The generosity was contagious and motivated me to give back. It made me more patient with my students. It made me want to listen more closely to my friends when they vented their stress in the highest-pressure society in the world.

The pastor's children surrounded me as I walked my bike to the main road. "Money, money, give me money! Give me pen. Pen, pen, pen! Banana, give me banana!" they shouted.

The pastor stood back and watched from a distance. Their playful voices pierced my eardrums and ripped my heart into pieces. They viewed me as another rich tourist. They didn't see my stay as a genuine gift of hospitality from their father. To them it was an economic transaction. I'd done my best to play

---

1. Jeong translates roughly to love and kindness.

with them the night before and fought to humanize myself, but all efforts failed.

Tears of confusion rolled down my cheeks. Who was I? A guy who used his leisure time to roam around a country that has seen famine, drought, war, and internal conflict. I'd paid over a thousand dollars for the plane ticket—more than a year's worth of back-cracking teff and coffee-bean harvesting. I was a rich man traveling in a land where people have confronted the horrors of having their basic needs stripped from them several times during their lives. Indeed, I'd won the lottery of life. I longed for genuine connection with no strings attached. I yearned for curiosity for the sake of curiosity, kindness for the sake of kindness. It broke my heart when tourism was all about money.

Nonetheless, I'd signed up for it. When a storm came, I'd wanted to see how I'd react. Well, I'd opened myself up and it hurt.

To the average Westerner, exchanging money for services might seem the obvious thing to do. The pastor and his family had provided me with food and shelter for the night. I was a beggar, searching for anyone who'd help us out. In the absence of a full stomach and comfortable lodging, I'd shouted, "Sleep, sleep! Home, home!" the previous evening.

I was on a different continent and had grown accustomed to life in Asia over the past 10 years. My former self wouldn't have hesitated to give the family a few pieces of paper. Since moving across the world, I'd changed. I wasn't an average North American, but a hybrid version of myself. It was difficult to identify with my native culture after living abroad for a decade. I viewed this in a positive light; I tried to be a conglomerate of the positivity I've experienced in all corners of the globe. Striving to become a better global citizen every day is my life's goal (admittedly, I have a long way to go).

My emotions caught up with me that day in Ethiopia. The knowledge that I'd never see the pastor again and the children's begging resulted in tears of shock and sadness. The statement "There's no money in friendship" didn't apply. I was far away from South Korea. Far away from Oman, Bangladesh, and Tajikistan.

Spirit deflated but tire inflated, I nursed my wounds and pedaled my way to greet Tetsuya up the road.

Chapter 9

Graduation Day

"A sad face is noticeable but not a sad heart."
—Ethiopian proverb

Tetsuya and I continued along the winding switchback roads until a flat tire at midday forced us to stop. It also hastened a moment we'd known would come, the moment when we'd venture off on our own. We would thrust ourselves into the Ethiopian highlands and pedal solo. It would be a different Ethiopia, one where we could trust only ourselves. We'd be immersed in vulnerability and opportunity, fear and excitement. Alone.

When on a bicycle in a faraway land, there's a unique bond that immediately forms when joining up with another tour cyclist. There is nothing to do but talk, share experiences, and help each other. Hours feel like days, and days feel like weeks. Adventures result in tight bonds and new friends turn into family. Your cycling partner wakes up in the tent beside you, helps you fix your spokes, and cooks you breakfast. They gawk at nature's beauty with you and share the awe when overwhelmed by the world's compassion. Your partner takes care of you when traveler's stomach slows you down and encourages you when you face headwinds and sandstorms.

Tetsuya wanted to coast through Ethiopia at a faster pace and start a new journey toward Sudan. Our speeds clashed. I weighed him down. I kept him from biking on at night and camping in isolated wooded areas. For me, the trip was about focusing on one country and taking it in slowly.

Tetsuya and I had been riding together for over 350 kilometers, 20 stick-and-clay-hut- populated villages of yelling Ethiopians, 15 swallowed flies, a day of staring into the depths of a deserted canyon, and an impromptu stay with a pastor and his family. It was only four days, yet it seemed like four years of shared experience.

By the time Tetsuya had fixed his tire and we'd polished off some injera, it was late afternoon. We were in a town, and Ethiopian pop music trumpeted out of the speakers, making it difficult to speak without risking hoarseness.

"I'm going to sleep here tonight. You're welcome to stay!" I screamed over the tunes. My mind was clear. I needed a night of rest. Days of pedaling up mountain passes lay ahead of me. I knew he wouldn't go for it. Tetsuya had to make it to Cairo.

"Well, I'll keep going and camp in the forest tonight, closer to Bahir Dar. See you in Japan or Korea." He maintained a drawn-out pause.

I wanted to fill that pause with so many words. He was one of the most incredible twentysomethings I'd ever met. That meant a lot coming from someone who spent most of his time with twentysomethings. I wanted to tell Tetsuya I wished I'd been more like him as a university student. I wanted to tell him his fearlessness made my blood boil with envy. I wanted to let it out, but I couldn't.

Expressing myself wasn't the Japanese way. Actions were everything in Japan and people internalized their individualism. He came from an island immersed in collectivism, a culture where people don't bother others with their feelings and dealt with things on their own.

I became Japanese at that moment, letting my sentiments stay bottled up. Despite my North American instincts, I said nothing. The blanket of Afro-beats left my speech muffled and distorted. I snatched his hand, shook it, and saw a gleam of sadness and excitement in his eyes. His eyebrows protruded upwards, a look of happiness to have a partner to ride with, sip coffee with, and scoop chunks of pasta into his mouth with. His micro-expressions spoke, but his voice remained silent. Tetsuya and his mettle had turned into a younger brother somewhere along the way, and he deserved to complete his trip as he'd imagined it.

The bell signaling the end of our time together rang. Tetsuya knew he was ready to continue on his own, and I respected him for that. I was also proud of myself for understanding my own needs. No more compromises. Two adventurers with different goals were splitting up to travel further along the path of self-realization.

On January 30, 2019, Tetsuya and I parted ways in the town of Mota. He pedaled along the dusty road and waved one arm as jean-and-T-shirt-wearing teens yelled and howled in his direction. His helmet gleamed in the sunlight as he wobbled around potholes and rocks.

My heart sank and I sulked regretfully. I should've followed Tetsuya out of town and given him a proper goodbye. The children, screaming adults, mountain passes, blistering sun, and AK-47's had my head pounding. Guns were nonexistent in South Korea, but now they were everywhere. Being around so many weapons made my chest throb. Tools for inflicting death and pain weren't part of my life.

Being outdoors took its toll. My eyes stung from the dry air and bright rays. I longed to retreat to a two-dollar-a-night shack and escape the roadside banter. I couldn't muster up the mental energy to be on the street. The moving clown needed rest.

This was how Tetsuya and I graduated from each other's company. Life had taught me that change was the only constant in the universe. Now we'd switch teachers. The Ethiopian climate, animals, and terrain would educate us in their personalized way. The Ethiopian people would become our new companions. Teach us to grow. Teach us to power through hardships. Teach us to be alone.

Chapter 10

Alone

"He who eats alone dies alone."
　—Ethiopian proverb

Alone. Every day was a blank slate. Internal voices became my talking partners. I could rest anytime, start the journey before sunrise, or throw on my helmet for the first time in the afternoon. Now I could be social or introverted and stop whenever I needed recovery. I could do it my way.

As I rode out of town the next day, I realized I'd forgotten how to be alone. Tetsuya was always there to share a chuckle, stare at canyons, or pedal in silence along mundane roads. Now I'd talk to the goats, camels, mountains, trees, and rivers. I'd fend off threats myself and scream at my inner demons. My mind's wild nature made separating from him an arduous task.

Tetsuya had become both a best friend and little brother. The guy who enjoyed companionship for the sake of companionship. The guy who blasted the same North American pop playlist from the 1980s over and over on his mini speakers in our shared hotel rooms. The guy who snapped pictures with his bazooka-sized camera in anticipation of the perfect angle and lighting. The guy who taped a picture of his girlfriend to his handlebars, only to mention a few short words about her over injera. The guy who believed he was invincible in front of nature's enormity and left his friend's arm hair elevated and eyebrows furrowed. I missed his quirks already.

As I climbed up the first mountain pass of the day, a group of kids in tattered shirts pushed my bike up the steep incline while I pedaled. Three sets of avocado-sized hands shoved my bags with all their might while I zoomed uphill. After doing a soccer field's length of work, they shouted. "Give me the money! Pen! Pen! Give me the money!" The grabbing and shaking caused me to lose my balance. Another one unzipped my outer bag's pocket and held my sunscreen.

My sunscreen! If I lost that bottle, I'd be sentenced to an entire month of red blisters. Take my money. Take my mangoes and water. Just don't take that lotion. I'd never find sunscreen at the village convenience stores. The next major city was a few days away, and my skin could never endure the Ethiopian sun without it. Visions of myself sprawled out on a doctor's examining table as a white-gowned, gray-haired man delivered the news of cancerous tumors on my nose and ears commandeered my mind. Give me the bottle!

I came to a grinding halt and threw my bike to the side. Stomping in their direction, I screamed. "*Yah*! *Yah*!"

The two children froze mid-step and leaped a few centimeters off the ground. My shoulders and chest exploded with aggressive energy as I held out my hands in anger. The kids' mouths dropped, and they glanced at each other as the bottle of sunscreen plopped to the ground. They sprinted down the hill and disappeared around the mountain's curve.

I couldn't believe my reaction. I, George Balarezo, was a guy who yelled at children. While on the road, I'd seen countless interactions between children and adults in which the adults had thrown rocks and yelled to get the youths to obey their commands. The kids modeled their behavior on that of the grown-up's. Now I'd modeled their behavior. My slip-up reduced me to a man-child. How shameful.

I'd regained the sunscreen but was losing my sanity. As I mounted my bike again, I thought of Tetsuya. He had dealt with annoyances admirably. What, I asked myself, was the best way to handle this? Giving the kids money was out of the question. "I just ignore the stones and begging and keep going," Tetsuya had said. That had been my original plan, and it had worked for several days, but the rocks and pestering eventually overwhelmed me. It was easy to talk about staying calm under pressure; being poised when the need arose was another matter. Instead of keeping my cool, I often U-turned, yelled profanities, and taught naughty youngsters lessons in manners and respect. To no avail. I became their educator by adopting a "no child left behind" policy in Ethiopia.

"What are you doing?" Tetsuya had asked at one point. His face was red and he was giggling.

"They'll never mess with another traveler again."

Tetsuya always watched me passively as I took out my rage on the children. If we were in the middle of Tokyo, passersby might've glanced and mentally called me an imbecile for disrupting the local harmony. Venting my anger, I knew, would've been selfish. If we'd been in Detroit, people would've praised me for sticking up for myself. In Ethiopia, I didn't know how to handle the situation.

The truth was that the children dominated me. I allowed myself to become the fool of adolescents young enough to be my offspring. In the end, would chewing them out have had any impact? After observing my behavior, they'd hurl more stones at future tourists. What if they'd been trying to incite my expressions of frustration all along?

Tetsuya had it right: the best reaction was no reaction. Thrown rocks, pitched grenades, tossed gold coins—ignore it all.

Tetsuya realized he couldn't change their actions, so the noblest thing to do was to stay in control. Kudos to him for retaining his equanimity despite his environment! One person's hell can be another's heaven. Tetsuya's heaven emanated from within, and it enabled him, amid the fire, to maintain a peaceful state of mind. There were many things to learn even from someone many years my junior.

He was gone. The locus of evaluation lay inside me. I had to live with myself forever, forgiving my mistakes or allowing them to torment me. I had to accept my entire self, not just my best self. Only then could I change and become harder, more unwavering in the face of stressors.

I needed more time to reflect on my actions while pedaling under the open sky. Alone.

Chapter 11

Ethiopia Unmuzzled

"Examine what is said, not who is speaking."
—Arabic proverb

Bahir Dar, on the bank of Lake Tana, was one of Africa's gems. There was no time to rest. The comforts of big-city life awaited me after over a week of pedaling. I longed to interact with educated, English-speaking locals and discuss the intricacies of an alien culture that had left me bewildered.

So much craving filled my days, and I suffered for it. I yearned for the yellow lentils and spiced spinach that had tickled my palate in Addis Ababa.

"It isn't spinach season," people replied when I asked for *golem*.

The same wooden shacks with the same blue and forest-green paint stocked with the same five inedible, sugar-laced snacks had me longing for the rich peanut butter I'd scarfed by the spoonful in the capital.

It was injera, shiro, and pasta for every meal in the villages. The lack of variety left me craving Korean sweet potatoes, Egyptian dates, Florida oranges, and New Zealand kiwis. What a luxury it had been to enjoy out-of-season fruits and vegetables from remote places!

Outside of major cities, food had been organic, grown in nearby fields. No chemicals and a short distance from field to table. This had been the most environmentally friendly way to eat, but I had turned into a swine that needed stimulation. I was the villain responsible for polluting the earth with fumes from imported goods brought in by diesel-spewing big rigs, ocean-crossing jets, and oil-spilling vessels. Others suffered from my habits.

The more I rode, the more I craved comfort foods. I should have smacked my lips after chomping on the same fermented flatbread and red sauce. One reason for traveling by bicycle was to mimic a local standard of living. People in highland villages dug their fingers into the same mushy injera and shiro three times a day with beaming smiles, but my imagination ran wild with thoughts of luxuries. I needed to stop and scavenge for imported produce once I arrived in Bahir Dar. My inner swine had spoken.

As I pedaled along, the highway widened, and I felt like I was on an airport runway. Empty, unused pavement surrounded me, and the terrain became flat and easy on my throbbing glutes. A white speck with a gleaming halo appeared on the horizon. Within minutes, the dot grew into a crystal Rubik's cube and changed into a box twice as large as my rice cooker. Next, it expanded into a shiny building the size of a baseball stadium with a mammoth concrete parking lot. A sign that read Bahir Dar University Specialized Hospital welcomed me to the big city.

Laying my eyes on the enormous structure put me at ease. It was like an insurance policy in a land where insurance didn't exist. I had a place to heal if struck by a rock or wrestled to the gravel.

I jumped out of my seat as a motorcycle zoomed by. Three-wheeled taxis spat exhaust as passengers stuck their heads into the wind yelling, "*Faranji!*" in cracking voices. Palm trees lined the streets and towered above me, providing welcoming shade. Trimmed shrubbery outlined the median, obscuring oncoming vehicles. Jebenas (coffeepots) rested beside burning incense as youths with braided hair chuckled with steaming cups in their hands.

As I approached the city center, more vehicles crowded the roads. Drivers took out their aggression on horns. I covered my ears with my index fingers as traffic came to a stop. The gridlock had my head jabbing back and forth. Momentum propelled my body forward, and my helmet slid down my forehead.

The city crept up on me, its barefoot heels grinding a few pebbles into the sand. A few minutes later, it was a steel-toed-boot-wearing, whistleblowing army sergeant yelling orders in my ear. "Get out of here, maggot! Roads are for cars!" Anything but an upright stance and a "yes, sir!" would lead to a stay in the shiny new hospital.

Along the way to Bahir Dar, everyone had insisted I try a cup of coffee at Wude Bunna Café. Passing on Wude Bunna would have been like opting for convenience store pizza in Rome.

After weaving through gridlocked traffic for several more kilometers, I reached the city center. It only took a few minutes to find Wude Bunna. The gaudy exterior gave the location away. As I entered the café, I felt a bizarre energy in my chest—a charged sensation of apprehension and trepidation.

It began with a look. That malevolent, overlong stare. This was no random act of eye violence. It was intentional and directed at me. The haunting animosity of an erect posture, downward-slanting neck, and upward-rolling pupils rattled my excitement into shambles of cold energy. The malicious intent intimated by furrowed eyebrows and deep crow's feet sent a shockwave through my body. I clenched my fist in a bout of transferred aggression and held on to the gaze to the point of fear.

My glare had much to communicate. I wasn't a chump *faranji* who allowed a short, shaven-headed guy to win a staring battle. I walked toward his table, and he signaled for me to sit without saying a word or breaking eye contact.

My curiosity got the best of me. I had to know more.

"My name is Matt. Do me a favor. I'm a graduate student studying tourism. Could you please fill out a survey for me? I'll pay for your coffee in return," he offered.

It seemed plausible, and I went along with it. I thought he'd dive headfirst into a story about his financial issues and ask for money, but I had plenty to say about travel.

The drink arrived with much anticipation. It had a bitter, woody flavor but couldn't match the first-love cup I'd enjoyed in Moren's shop a few days earlier. Perhaps my palate wasn't yet in tune with the intricacies of coffee-tasting.

Pen in hand, I took out my frustrations on his form. It felt therapeutic getting my grievances down on paper.

Matt skimmed over my answers and nodded with approval. He seemed to be aware of the stone-throwing. My thoughts boomeranged to the guy in Addis Ababa who had blown up in anger outside of Saint George's Church. I hoped the next chapter in Matt's narrative ended in a different beat, one to which he danced with joy, like Kaldi, the goat herder, after graduation.

After a round of small talk, he invited me to hang out with his friends in a quiet part of town by the Blue Nile River. What a unique chance to connect with Bahir Dar residents! Curiosity overpowered my doubts, and we dropped off my bike and made our way to a khat dealer.

We took a bus a few kilometers from downtown and stomped through a shaded forest with avocado and coffee trees spreading branches above us, into the *khat* fields. No cars. No children. Despite the tranquil atmosphere, my heart raced with anticipation. Matt chewed away on his leaves, and although I kept refusing his offers, he rolled me up a wad to stick in my mouth.

Matt and I reached a deal after I filled out his survey. In return for participating in his study, he'd be an interviewee for my video on Ethiopia. His English skills, confident stare, and outspoken personality resulted in a compelling interview.

He shoved a few more khat leaves in his mouth, and we started recording. Matt introduced his country while describing its people and culture. After warming up, the topic shifted to political struggle, and his eyes teared with pride.

"We gained our freedom of speech a few months ago. Before that they tortured me for speaking my mind. Look at the scars on my back!" He lifted his shirt and exposed a large patch of crisscrossed streaks a few centimeters above his tailbone.

"Snipers killed my friends as punishment for speaking out against the government. The military was everywhere. They came into my high school classroom and beat my classmates and me until our desks were covered in blood.

"I love our new prime minister so much. It feels like a dream. He changed everything for us overnight. He's way better than Barack Obama or anyone else this world has ever seen."

Matt's face became red, and he choked up while praising his country's leader. He was in the zone and gave me the best interview I'd overseen during my travels. Honesty, conviction, emotion. Saliva flew out of his mouth and moistened the dirt in front of him. I felt his passion for the man in power, and goosebumps shot up my arms. His comments had my mind firing off endless questions.

A few seconds later, he insisted we stop the camera so he could put his shirt on and redo the interview. Being clothed was a sign of respect to the head of Ethiopia, and he made me delete the earlier version when he'd bared his chest to the camera.

We did the second take, and Matt flew into an even more fervent version of his description of the prime minister. Expressing himself without fear of repercussions must've been a new adventure.

Ethiopia's prime minister, Abiy Ahmed, was a man in his early forties who was transforming the country at an unprecedented speed after decades of authoritarian rule under which countless Ethiopians had been massacred. Besides guaranteeing freedom of speech for allies of his government as well as detractors and releasing thousands of political prisoners, he forged peace with long-time enemy Eritrea by giving up disputed land near a northern border zone.

Dark moments fill Ethiopia's history. Many elders lived through the Red Terror (1979 to 1989), during which a

Soviet-backed communist regime murdered and tortured its political opponents. The leader of the military junta, also known as The Derg, or *Committee* in the ancient language of Ge'ez, was Mengistu Haile Mariam. In 1977 Mengistu delivered a famous speech in Addis Ababa's Meskel Square, hurling bottles of red dye (representing the blood of enemies) to the ground while yelling "death to counterrevolutionaries!" With the aid of East German agents, he killed nearly half a million intellectuals, professionals, and perceived opponents of socialism during The Red Terror.

The following excerpt from the Human Rights Watch report details the brutality:

> Bodies were left on the roadside to advertise the killings of the previous night—those who inspected the piles of bodies to see if their friends or relatives were among the corpses were targeted for execution or imprisonment themselves. Relatives were forbidden to mourn. In other cases, relatives had to pay one Ethiopian dollar for each "wasted bullet" in order to have the body returned. Simply knowing how to read and write and being aged about 20 or less were enough to define the potential or actual "counter-revolutionary." The authorities were even able to institute a law authorizing the arrest of children between eight and twelve years.

Gruesome atrocities were on display in the Red Terror's Martyrs' Museum, located in the heart of Meskel Square. Since I'd toured the museum halls several weeks earlier, I'd received a first-class education on the inventiveness of torture mechanisms. Who would submerge another human being's head in a bucket of vomit and excrement after tying them upside down? My legs shuddered and my hands went icy while observing the graphic oil paintings on the museum's walls. So much blood had been spilled to punish those who'd spoken out.

Mengistu, also known as the butcher of Addis, came to power after much conflict over famine and drought in Ethiopia. The communist model was designed to provide equality to all Ethiopians and gained mass appeal with the promise of distributing land to peasants. Mengistu accused Haile Selassie, the King of Kings, Elect of God, and Lion of Judah, of hoarding millions of dollars in Swiss bank accounts, of leaving his country during the Italian invasion, and of hosting lavish parties at his palace during a famine in the Wollo Province that killed over 200,000 people.[1] Colonel Mengistu ordered a subordinate to strangle a frail, 80-year-old Haile Selassie in his own bed and hide the emperor's remains beneath the floorboards of a toilet in his palace, denying the Elect of God a proper Christian

---

1. King of Kings: The Triumph and Tragedy of Emperor Haile Selassie I of Ethiopia, written by Selassie's grandson Asfa Wossen Asserate, provides counterarguments to the accusations. The author states that Selassie lived very modestly while in exile in England and bank records prove he never opened a Swiss bank account. The Derg claimed Selassie had accumulated 14 billion dollars, but in 1974 the entire budget of the Ethiopian state amounted to 320 million dollars. During the famine, the imperial government was unprepared, and starvation occurred in the remote Tigray and Wollo provinces, where there were no roads and settlements could only be reached by mule along rocky paths. Outrage over lack of government action mounted when it came to light that the central authorities had exported more than 200,000 tons of grain, the largest surplus in six years, during the height of the famine in 1973. As for the parties, they were never for Selassie himself, but for the Ethiopian Empire.

funeral. After the Derg's fall in 1991, Mengistu flew to Harare, Zimbabwe, where he was offered asylum, and currently lives in an upscale neighborhood. In 2007 Ethiopian courts found him guilty of a genocide that killed between 500,000 and 2,000,000 people.

I'd taken free speech for granted. Expressing opinions, no matter how unpopular, made people in the United States proud. I couldn't fathom ever losing this right. Every time I talked to my family, we'd vehemently criticize the gangster posing as a president in the White House who denied climate change, threatened porn stars with death if they didn't keep quiet about extramarital affairs, and endangered the public during a pandemic.

In conversation with a Michigan pastor, I'd criticized the Bible's claims that humans deserve complete dominion over the earth and its creatures. We were in his office. Air-conditioner vents spouted chilly gusts, and equipment along with books stacked waist-high cluttered every corner. Over the years I'd visited mosques as well as Buddhist, Sikh, and Hindu temples where religious leaders had fasted to seek a deeper version of truth. They claimed that when one commits to a spiritual path, he or she ought to lose their baby fat and pursue non-possession. I questioned that pastor's commitment to spirituality. I spoke out in parks and sidewalks in the Christian nation where I was born without ever casting a single glance over my shoulder in fear of government snitches. The pastor had no ill intentions. It was a systemic issue. How could anyone escape overconsumption when the media's subliminal messages primed us for economic growth?

I was no saint either. He could've called me out for taking fuel-burning airplanes to far-off corners of the world. At least we could acknowledge our faults and find a deeper version of the truth. Wiretaps, snitches, and jail-cell torture would never be a reality. Speaking my mind may be a right in North America, but elsewhere, it seemed, it was a luxury.

Aside from thoughtful discussions with others, expressing myself through creation was something I'd fallen in love with. I've thrust myself on stage in front of crowds to spread messages of peace. I pour my frustrations onto pages. Living in fear of repercussions for speaking out must be horrible since suppressing one's emotions manifests into psychological problems.

How difficult for a nation to prosper without free speech. After all, prosperity came from exploring varying thought processes. Ideas thrived in societies where they could be exchanged. I hoped Ethiopians would profit from their newfound freedom.

Several of Matt's friends joined in the conversation and were a delight. They said they could never have imagined such a colossal metamorphosis would ever take place during their lifetime.

After everyone had emptied three bags of khat, Matt and I left the forest and took a bus downtown. Right before we split up, he popped another question.

"Can you give me 300 birr? I'm going to meet a girl and want to make a good impression."

"Three hundred birr? Really? I'm a guy traveling by bike and sleeping in a tent," I barked. His brash request for ten times what a local meal would cost had my blood boiling, and I stomped off in disbelief.

The begging wore me out. I retreated to my tent and meditated while wondering what Gautama Buddha would have done. The Buddha would've been walking, carrying only the clothes on his back, and knocking on doors for food donations to cultivate humility. No bike. No money. The Buddha would've had compassion for Matt, a guy who'd suffered terribly for voicing his opinions. He'd have told me to meditate my way out of ignorance.

I sulked over the loss. My untamed mind had caused me to lose a new friend. The outside world won again, and my inner self needed discipline.

Chapter 12

Stoned

"Calm seas do not create skillful sailors."
—Ethiopian proverb

Every Ethiopian I'd met insisted I visit Lalibela. The town's rock-hewn churches, which dated from the 12th century, are the country's pride and joy. In Lalibela you can witness ancient spiritual practices and Christianity in its rawest form. I was excited to experience the magic. First, I had to pedal there.

"Road to Lalibela very, very bad!" several men in a coffee shop warned when I mentioned my destination.

So what? I've seen my share of torn-up roads.

From the get-go, the bike bounced along on the pothole-riddled gravel. My thighs chafed from the pants-on-skin friction. My glutes pounded the hard seat, my helmet rattled, and my neck was jolted in a seizure of vibrations. Despite the road conditions, the first 15 kilometers were uneventful. A handful of children threw a handful of stones. Nothing I couldn't handle.

An hour later, it changed. The quiet, rocky trail turned into paths of screaming people—and the ruckus directed at me. Teenagers with afro picks jutting out of their hair hurled themselves into my path yelling, *"Faranji! Faranji!"* Seconds before impact, the youngsters leapt out of the way.

As I continued along the road, their pattering feet and panting became louder. I turned my head and saw five handlebar-high children stomping after me. Bodies erect, arms pumping, and eyes locked on me. Legs springing off the ground in synchronized cycles. Two were wearing sandals and three were barefoot, yet they kept up with me. I smiled and yelled, "Salam! Faranji! Faranji!" in a playful tone. One kid was right next to me, and his fingers were only a few centimeters from my handlebars. The little guy wore a purple T-shirt coated with beige dust, and pebble-sized balls of mucus dangled from the corners of his eyes. They needed shade and a drink. Whatever the case, their pace became swifter as I sped up to shake them.

Seconds later, chanting overpowered the footsteps. "Money, money, banana, banana, mango, mango, trousers!"

I glanced over my shoulder once more, and the group of five had transformed into a mob of 30.

"What the—!" I yelled.

An entire elementary school class was hounding me. Most of the children had weathered feet accustomed to running on rocks and sharp gravel. They kept a good pace and didn't tire. How could they keep up with a guy on a bike? I'd never seen runners like this before. The sheer number of children chasing me was overwhelming, and I chuckled in disbelief. This is why Ethiopia produced the world's best runners.

"George *iballalo. Min addis neger aleh?*" I said, riding alongside the jogging children. *My name is George. What's new?* I added, "*Simeh man no? Hasta mari.*" *What is your name? I am a teacher.*

"Give me the pen! Give me the money! China! China!" Their yelps turned impatient.

"*Kayet ahget net? Iwedi halehu. Bakih!*" I shouted. *Where are you from? I love you. Please!*

"Money! Money!" They held out their palms and shoved my handlebars mid-stride.

My balance became shaky, and it was harder to steer my bike in the right direction. I glanced behind me as small hands grabbed my bags.

"Money, money, money, give me the money!" their voices chorused.

I raised my clenched fist, furrowed my eyebrows, flashed my incisors, and screamed in wild aggression. "YAAAA!"

Keep balance. Grab handlebar.

Squeals of laughter rang through the air.

"Banana! Mango! Money! *Faranji! Faranji!*"

They surrounded me on both sides and from behind. *Come on, give me space.* I swerved in a zigzag motion, forcing several to run into the roadside ditch. *This isn't fun anymore.*

As soon as a kid quit, two more sets of fresh-legged children jumped into the mix, scavenging for money, bananas, and mangoes. The louder I yelled, the harder they pulled and grabbed, and the closer I came to a plunge. Ditch on the left? Steep drop to the right? Injury or death? I sped up and decelerated, swerved, and twisted. My erratic path created space between myself and the troublemakers. Soon I couldn't control the bike. Their pulls and tugs were too much.

I heard a revving engine and thick tires pounding along potholes. An SUV zoomed around the corner, and when I looked up, I found myself a forearm's length from its front bumper. My heart jumped out of my chest as the driver honked. I screamed in fury as my heart pounded in my chest, my lungs heaving in the dusty air. The vehicle had nearly turned me into roadkill.

If it was a power game, the youths were my master. The voices hushed and started again. Each scream and push on the bike wounded me anew. The splinter dug deeper. My instincts told me to wreak havoc on their world. I foamed at the mouth and my muscles were tense enough to pick up one child with each arm and choke-slam them on the rocks. Sacrifice several of the ringleaders to show the rest what happens when you push someone past the point of no return. Time for an education. Today's lesson from the street: if you torment others, be ready to be tormented tenfold. If you endanger someone's life, they'll resort to violence. Life is full of choices and risks.

Amid the chaos, my visions shocked me. My mind ventured to places I never deemed possible. The near head-on collision with the vehicle tattered my sanity. So what if I was a guest in their country? So what if their stomachs were rumbling from hunger? So what if they were children! My mind's dark side had been unleashed.

At least I was aware of my thoughts—a welcoming effect of my meditation practice—and simply observed them until they passed. I reminded myself that I was not my thoughts. I was a peace advocate. That was my core identity. A peace advocate who was having his character flaws exposed. A guy who had a long way before acquiring the coveted qualities of unconditional love for humanity, which included when others put his life at risk. No, I wasn't Jesus.

I channeled the inner rage to my calves and hamstrings as sun-charred bushes and giant boulders flew by at speeds I'd deemed impossible 30 minutes ago. My chain clicked and clamored from the tension. My legs were numb with strength, and blood rushed through my thighs in streams of desperation. The children were right behind me, never letting up. I'd never seen speed and persistence like this before.

Adults roared in laughter at the *faranji* on a bike being chased by a mob of children. No one came to my rescue. I was a clown on display for the village's entertainment. A laughingstock. A guy who lost his bananas while children tormented him.

Boom!

What on earth was that noise? Did a tube explode? Did a spoke snap in half? Did the sound of a rock crashing into my cranium hit my ears before the hammer-pounding sensations wreaked havoc on my head?

I hopped off the bike and did a quick scan. My pannier rack had collapsed onto my rear tire. The jolting and grabbing must've put too much stress on the bottom joints. I turned into a demon. "*Ama say kee na roo!*" I screamed while waving my index finger at the kids in disapproval. *Thank you*! My face was a blast furnace. Beads of sweat stung my eyes and dripped down my chin.

Silence. You could've heard a pin drop on a pile of teff. Children elbowed and pushed to get a closer look. Tiny fingers circled my broken rack. Screams turned to whispers.

Mischievous smiles changed into looks of concern. It was as if a buddy had sprained an ankle during a football game, only this buddy was a chunk of metal. The same hands that had swindled items out of my panniers attempted to mend my rack. Together they hoisted the collapsed joint and rested it on my tire's quick-release bar. A clever temporary solution.

Suddenly, an adult clenching a baseball bat–sized stick popped into the mix. Face red and fists ready to attack, he confronted all 30 children while shouting in Amharic. He raised the club over his shoulders and aimed for the bleachers. *Whoosh!* Screams of fear lit up the air as the youngsters stepped back.

Hallelujah! *Allahu Akbar*! The Ethiopian Barry Bonds!

I wanted to hug the fellow and treat him to an all-you-can-eat injera dinner, but survival trumped everything else. While the enraged man fended off the youths, I crept down the switchback road. The rocks and potholes didn't jibe well with my broken joint. My rack creaked and pleaded for relief.

As my backside bounced over the torn-up road, I tried to sympathize with the youths. *Put yourself in their shoes. Kids want to have fun. They were playing the entire time. If I were born in the same environment, raised by their families, with the same social influences, I would've acted the same way. They're only children in need of love. When do light-skinned guys cruise by on a crazy-looking mountain bike?*

Things could've ended badly. I could've lost my balance and fallen off the bike, resulting in a visit to an Ethiopian hospital. Worse yet, if I'd surrendered to my rage and slammed a kid into a pile of rocks, angry parents might've started a *faranji* manhunt by putting a price on my head. Even if I didn't get caught, I'd have to forever carry harming that kid on my conscience. As a man who cycles around the globe to spread friendship, I'd have been an imposter. Imagine the headline: "World Peace Advocate Body-Slams Children While on Bicycle Tour." Haunting hypocrisy headlines.

As I continued along the road, sounds of horror interrupted the silence. Plop. Plop. Hadn't Barry Bonds' home run swing signified the end of hell's highway? *The kids were long gone, right?*

Like resurrected ghosts, the youths reappeared. One at a time, their thin bodies popped up on the hillside, close enough to continue their onslaught. A chill seeped through my polyester shirt amid the sweltering heat. Their paranormal energy weighed on me. It must have been their phantom palms thrusting my bike to the gravel, rendering it too heavy to escape. My intelligence plummeted as my thoughts became incomprehensible strings of words in several languages. *Nasilsin? Honbeebaeksan. Velesped.*

Rocks landed around me in sets of four or five. Dust kicked up from the road. Mini-grenade explosions. A golf-ball-sized rock struck one meter in front of me; another the size of a tennis ball hit the ground an arm's length to the right of my rear tire. It was hailing rocks, and if a kid hit the bullseye, I'd be left for dead in the desert sun, a snack for the lions at sundown.

They had me outnumbered. I couldn't outrun the youths on their home turf. Should I surrender? *Take me alive as a prisoner of war.* At least I could sneak away during the night. Surely, I could outsmart them.

My plastic helmet became more valuable than any African gem. Compared to what could happen to my head, the sting of a body blow seemed trivial. The pain couldn't be worse than enduring my whale-sized friend's slams while playing tackle football as a teenager—gasping for breath had been a monumental task. I could handle this.

My imagination went on a horrific journey. Streaks of blood streamed down my forehead as stones struck me. I was blindsided by a rock to the jaw. Three teeth flew through the air. The children had a few more pearly whites to toss above their roofs. "Money, money, money, money!" they screamed while scavenging for my bloody molars in the sand. Ten kids jumped on me, pinning me to the ground while two pairs of hands pried the remaining teeth out of my mouth. It was my fate to be reduced to a gap-toothed grin and a diet of soggy injera chunks blended with coffee and berbere.

I snapped out of my waking nightmare and thrust myself back into the one in front of me. A middle-aged villager, chasing after goats, leaped over a bush and stomped toward me. Here was my opportunity to make a clean getaway. I had to convince him to help me.

I waved my arms to get his attention. The man yelped in surprise as his eyes darted in my direction. I tossed stones in the air and pointed at the children. Rocks thrown from above landed on either side of us, kicking up dust.

The guy turned into a shot put champion, hurling rocks and heaving Amharic profanities at the tiny bandits. The kids dispersed and ran out of sight.

"*Ama sek kee na roo.*" *Thank you*. I shook his hand while bowing in desperation.

He smiled and gave me a slight bow.

After our exchange, the villager sprinted after his animals and disappeared into the mountains. Another angel had graced me with his presence and vanished forever.

I could've given up everything to escape the wrath of village children. My bike was my most prized possession, but I was ready to toss it down the canyon and watch it turn into a speck if it meant being transported off this road. What gave them the right to torment another human like a lab rat?

Suddenly, a shiny, new Toyota SUV swerved along the gravel, dodging rocks and potholes. Once again, I threw my hands up and waved. Hopefully, they wouldn't mistake me for a bandit. Sweat-soaked guys wearing helmets and safety gloves while riding loaded-up bicycles don't command that kind of attention.

The truck came to a halt, and the driver appeared concerned. I pleaded by tossing rocks in the air and pointing to the mountains. "Children," I said. "Many, many."

"Okay. We understand. We'll give you a ride," said a heavy-set man in the backseat. He wore a blue-collared shirt, and I caught a whiff of his musky cologne. His English was perfect.

Delirious from the day's events, I must have said *ama sek ee naroo* at least 20 times within the first five minutes of meeting them.

"You don't have to keep thanking us."

Finally, off hell's highway. The metal roof and glass windows made the car seem like an armored vehicle. The truck had a new-car scented interior, a mixture of polyester, plastic, paint, and sealants. My heartbeat slowed to a patter of relief.

The three men were agricultural experts with an alphabet of letters after their names. They'd been around Europe and North America's most prestigious universities. One guy had visited the University of Michigan several times to present at academic conferences.

"Your president, Mr. Trump, doesn't believe in climate change. It's a shame. Here in Ethiopia, climate change has had a large impact on our agriculture sector. We don't have as much coffee as before. It might disappear in the future," said the cologne-scented man.

After the morning's antics, politics weren't my concern. I mentioned the stone-throwing kids again. I longed to understand them. What drove a child to violence? Kenyan children had been so polite during my month in their country, just several hundred kilometers to the south. What made Ethiopian history and culture different?

The men nodded but didn't explain the children's behavior. Were they attempting to save face by glossing over Ethiopia's dark side? We sat in silence for a few minutes. I didn't mean to criticize their country, but I thought it was necessary to raise awareness regarding the issues tour cyclists encounter. I wanted Ethiopia's tourism industry to thrive, but who'd visit with stories circulating about rock-hurling kids?

Eventually, it dawned on me that these men had had little interaction with villagers. "Why do they carry wooden sticks?" one asked another. Perhaps they'd grown up in academic bubbles in the capital city and only interacted with others of similar socioeconomic status. This caught me off guard and, as well-learned as one can be through books, I reminded myself that resilience-training education would pay off. I'd find happiness where others found their destruction.

The men dropped me off at a hotel in Lalibela.

Emotionally drained, I plopped onto the bed. No kids at last. My teeth were in the correct place. There's been no bloodshed. Finally, I could rest in peace. Not for eternity but for a few moments.

I reflected on my violent thoughts. Anyone who thinks they can control their thoughts should try to stop thinking for 10 seconds. We often think we have mind control, but it's an illusion. Perhaps Buddha and Jesus had violent thoughts, or worse, acted on them in ways we don't know about. History tells us they chose love over violence. Compassion over negativity. Wise choices indeed.

Self-realization was unattainable. How was anybody supposed to stay equanimous when harassed by an entire schoolyard? Ethiopia threw more than rocks at me that day; it hurled my mind into a spiral of bewilderment. How could anyone cycle here for more than a week?

I am not my thoughts and can't control them. This was the ultimate lesson my meditation practice had instilled. It was a game changer. Thoughts change every few seconds; actions have dire consequences that can last for a lifetime. At least I let my horrid visions pass instead of reacting in a toxic way. If an eye for an eye makes the entire world blind, then I'd be visionless, crawling on my hands and knees, feeling around with my palms in a deathlike existence of regret and agony. After all, they were children. Had something happened to one of them, even in self-defense, the memory would've inflicted deep wounds on my psyche.

Although I hadn't acted on my worst thoughts, the incident with the youths had left a scab on my unconscious. How could I eradicate the impurities? If my goal on this trip was self-realization, had I taken a giant leap backward and pushed myself too far? I was the fellow who couldn't swim, spitting up saltwater as the undertow overpowered my kicks of panic in an ocean of great white sharks, piranhas, and poisonous jellyfish. I didn't want to become too frightened to step foot in a wading pool.

I thought of the research I'd done to prepare for my trip. Alastair Humphreys, a legendary adventurer who'd cycled from England to South Africa and through the Americas, walked across India, rowed the Atlantic, and trekked across the Empty Quarter desert, wrote extensively on Ethiopia in his memoir. "The children mobbed us, shouting, pulling our bikes, chucking stones ... sometimes shoving sticks into our spokes. Village after village, this went on. I did not feel as though they regarded me as a fellow human being... I have never sworn at so many people in one country."

Another European tour cyclist had mentioned pedaling around Ethiopia with homemade spiked bars surrounding his bicycle frame to fend off youngsters. When I read his tale, I'd thought he was overreacting, but now I considered him a genius.

I had never encountered children like this. Not in India. Not in Bangladesh. Not in Kenya or Venezuela. These were children whose family members had survived a murderous dictatorship, scavenged for food and water during famines and droughts, and endured gruesome vendetta killings over tribal clashes. Maybe their behavior was a side effect of foreign-aid handouts and tourism? I was on my way to Ethiopia's largest tourist attraction: Did tourists hand out coins, pens, and candy to kids, reducing visitors to gift-giving robots? The world was complicated, and I yearned to understand.

That evening I had a great session of metta[1] meditation, wishing all sentient beings love, peace, joy, and freedom from suffering. Starting with myself, my family, my friends, my students and coworkers, I expanded to everybody in the United States and the Americas, moved on to everyone in Asia and every human across all continents, and finished with all living creatures. I focused extra energy on the children who'd harassed me and sent them my positive energy. My heart expanded

---

1. A Pali word from the language used in northern India that roughly translates to kindness and compassion towards others. In the West, the practice of Metta is referred to as loving-kindness meditation.

and contracted with vibrant, pulsing sensations. I replayed the scenes of stone-tossing and bag-grabbing and wished them liberation from the regret they might face when they are adults. I wanted to let them know I forgave them. After a few mouse clicks, I could flee Ethiopia; they couldn't. I wished them a better life. I wanted to teach them metta meditation and help them reap the benefits that I'd encountered only in adulthood. The kids needed love, and I sent it to them.

As I closed my eyes in contemplation, I reminded myself that I came to Ethiopia for a struggle. Perhaps one day I'd thank those kids for testing the limits of my mental and emotional strength, exposing my weaknesses, and keeping me humble and grounded. Those children became the unlikely teachers who helped me move forward on the path to dealing with anger. Tough times create tough minds, and the potential of a tough mind is limitless.

Chapter 13

Finger-Licking Fun

"Make a powerful friend if you can. If you walk with an elephant, the dew will not bother you."
—Cameroon proverb

"Never ask, 'Who is my real friend?' Ask 'Am I a sincere friend to somebody?' That is the right question. Always be concerned with yourself."
—Osho

Hunger set in. My stomach rumbled for injera and wat. I searched the streets of Lalibela for a shack selling *messer* wat and vegetables. The sun burned the sky orange. Clouds hovered so low you could reach out and touch them. Watching the sunset made me salivate: the heavens were the color of the spiced lentils I ate for every meal.

Down the road, a group of people had gathered a few steps below a mountain terrace. A faint murmur of laughter undercut the evening silence. As I peeked at the group, a man with a commanding tone called out, "Hey! Come! Come sit. We have party. Many food here! Eat with us!" His deep voice shouted orders. "You comfortable here, okay? Me Eshetu. Me soldier."

Flustered by that afternoon's events, my hands turned clammy at the thought of dealing with more youngsters. I was especially wary of kids under 12. Psychologists would invent a new term, maybe even name it after me: Balarezojuvenilephobia. What an honorable way to impact the world. My eyes darted around, scanning the area for children. High-pitched voices shouting, "You! You! You! Money! China!" raided my internal dialogue. Songs of rocks plopping on gravel rang through my head, clouding my mind with chaotic fog.

I ached for human connection and longed to be with adults. Eshetu's assertiveness made me inclined to trust him. Besides, the spicy aroma of garlic peppered with a trace of ginger had my nose leading the way. My hunger was too strong to ignore.

I crept down a set of carved-stone stairs as my gut growled. Green lights hanging from the wall lit up an open area 20 steps below. A circular formation of chairs outlined the outdoor space. Only deep voices and the sound of adult women bantering in Amharic rang through the air. As I came closer, the fragrance of spiced vegetables had my stomach gurgling. Women in thin white dresses dashed back and forth with knee-high pots wedged between their arms. Lumpy stew steamed from metal plates, as turban-wearing men and wrinkled elders picked at their food with gooed-up fingers. Their homes of mud and tin made it appear the group was feasting beyond their means. Perhaps they'd pooled their resources to celebrate a major life event. It was great to see so many bright-eyed folks enjoying themselves.

"Come!" Eshetu shouted in a tone that could've made the stubbornest mule obey.

As I crept closer to the gathering, I saw that he was a superhero of a fellow. His arms and pecs rippled through a blue, form-fitting T-shirt. He yanked me in for a chest bump with so much force I lost my footing. I gasped as my scrawny torso slammed into his wall of brawn. He had a square jaw, shaved head, and a sharp stare that wielded authority. (*Idea!* Bring him along as my bodyguard?) One glimpse at his chiseled body would've had children racing for the hills. He was the soldier a *faranji* needed on their side during combat with local youngsters.

"Sitting! Enjoy! Be free!" Eshetu commanded, as if I were a junior military officer. The baritone voice complemented his intimidating physique.

I plunked down in a squeaky metal chair, and my relieved legs celebrated. I sat up straight, eyes wide with curiosity, and was ready to soak in this cultural experience. A woman rushed over and handed me a tin plate while bowing. My last wind kicked in.

"What kind of soldier are you, Eshetu?" I hungered to learn the life lessons of an Ethiopian soldier. I wanted to peel back the layers and listen to the adventure tales hidden behind his brawny exterior and commanding speech.

"For government."

"What do you fight for?"

"My sister cook food. Her name Selam. She good cooking. This wedding party. You eating. Injera!" Eshetu said, changing the subject.

Don't make him angry by refusing offers or broaching sensitive subjects. If he had piled my plate with fermented cockroaches and filled my cup with hyena blood, I would've scarfed it all down with an enthusiastic grin.

Selam wore a silver lace dress and a matching scarf. Thick hair draped her shoulders and whisked and whirled as she scooped clumps of wat onto plates. Her shiny red lipstick glowed in the green and white lights. It seemed like she'd put on half a bottle of perfume, filling the room with honey and lavender. She smiled with curiosity every time she came my way.

Selam passed me a dish and loaded it with soupy yellow lentils, toothpick-thin slivers of beets, and thumb-sized chunks of flesh from a slaughtered animal. I felt guilty accepting the boned beast. Someone else could've enjoyed it instead of their plant-eating companion. The gobbets of brown muscle and lard sat on my plate as I withered in revulsion.

"The meat very good. Goat special for wedding. Take it." Eshetu raised his eyebrows in anticipation of my reaction.

"Wow! The beets and messer are delicious. Thank you so much for this food. "*Amma sekee naroo!*" I said between bites while lowering my forehead in respect and appreciation. What an honor it was to attend such a special celebration.

I scooped the injera and vegetables into my mouth while poking around at the boned meat with my pinky finger. Grease outlined the wedge of flesh and cartilage on my plate.

"Try goat. This very tasty." Eshetu tore a wad of muscle off bone with his incisors.

"Thanks. But I don't eat meat. I'm fasting."

I thought of Haile Selassie's state meeting in Asmara, Eritrea, where a Chinese delegate spotted the Lion of Judah's vegetarian meal and declared, "If the Ethiopians are fasting, then the Chinese will too." The state ball in Asmara went ahead with everyone eating a vegetarian meal.

In similar fashion, I hoped Eshetu would stand up and proclaim, "If the *faranji* is fasting, then we will too."

No such luck.

"Just little bit eating. Today not fasting day. No problem." He lowered his voice a few decibels in sympathy.

I glanced up and noticed several other attendees staring in my direction, nodding and grinning. A bearded North American man with fingers wet with injera and vegetables was quite a spectacle.

"Eating goat!" Eshetu insisted. Louder, more assertive, and with a dose of frustration.

The situation flustered me. Do I keep my moral code or create a positive impression on the crowd by sucking on a corpse? If I didn't chew on flesh, how would the party hosts feel? I wanted to show them I accepted their culture and appreciated the hospitality. Which was worse—ripping apart another sentient being or offending a friendly host?

I peered at the steaming, dead goat on my plate. Damage done. I shut my eyes, grabbed the piece of meat, and nudged it into my mouth while mustering a phony grin.

My teeth shredded tough tissue into semi-digestible chunks as my stomach bubbled with nausea. I chomped and gnawed, convincing myself that the smaller the bits of meat were, the less inflamed my internal organs would be. As I chewed away, Selam pulled up a chair and plopped herself next to me.

"*Messer, injera, wat, gonjo!*" I pointed my slimy thumb toward the sky in approval.

After a few minutes of body language–infused conversation, Eshetu pointed at his sister's plate with a shrewd grin.

"She feeding you... my sister. Take it!" he said in a spirited tone while nodding toward Selam.

My lavender-scented hostess grasped a golf-ball-sized clump of vegetables wrapped in injera. Selam's cheeks rolled into dark-red dimples, and her squinty-eyed smile warmed my chest with compassion. It was as if she were getting ready to feed a baby. Only, after being pelted with stones, this infant had the appetite of a famished lion.

In Ethiopia feeding another person with one's hands is a gesture of endearment. After a stressful day that brought me to the brink of lunacy, I needed tenderness. Here it was in the form of a hand-fed meal. I was about to receive a gigantic piece of Selam's heart with a side of injera. It flattered me that Eshetu had created an intimate moment for his sister and me. *Give it to me, baby*.

I have no apprehensions about receiving food from someone else's hands since I've sucked on a plethora of fingers during mealtime in India and Bangladesh. The other person's germs give the cuisine a unique flavor and provide our gut with the bacteria it requires to flourish. Also, hand-based dining is an in-depth sensory experience that creates a closer connection between the feeder and finger-sucker. Before my vegetarian days, I had finger-fed plenty of South Korean women lettuce wraps filled with greasy pork flesh and fermented green onions doused with red pepper paste on barbecue dates. *Son-mat* is my favorite condiment and was a successful subliminal tactic to send warm fuzzy energy into mouths and hearts.

Hands slimy. Hearts open. Utensils overrated.

Selam stuck her fingers into my mouth and drew them out gently, allowing her fingertips to linger between my lips. Eshetu pounded his knees with laughter and let out a bear-like roar.

"Now you food to her. Give food your hand." Eshetu giggled and pointed at his sister.

I snatched a chunk of fermented bread and loaded it with beets and yellow lentils, thinking, *Let's see what she can handle*. Selam opened wide as I slid my fingers into her mouth. I withdrew until her tongue swirled around three of my fingertips. She let out a half-slurp, half-kiss that lasted a few seconds longer than expected. Fingers wet with Selam's saliva, I scooped up a clump of injera and thrusted it into my mouth. My glance went from her eyes, to her lips, and to her eyes again. Eshetu was rolling on the floor, laughing like a child whose mother was tickling its belly fat. My new friends didn't know they were dealing with a veteran hand-feeder.

"You go Addis Ababa. My sister cooking you food. She living Addis Ababa. My sister very beautiful. You Addis Ababa dancing together. She not married."

We hung out for an hour more, and Eshetu and his sister insisted on walking me back to my hotel.

Constellations of dippers and chopstick-shaped clusters twinkled above. There were plenty of utensils in the sky (optional when sharing food with friends). I scanned the overhead canvas for pinkies, thumbs, and palms but found none. Eshetu, Selam, and I had a total of 30 fingers, of which 15 could show affection during mealtime.

"Take." Selam handed me her thin, lavender-scented scarf, while her eyes traveled up and down my body and landed back at my eyes. She licked her lips as her gaze veered to the ground.

I had grown accustomed to her aroma over the past few hours, and now it tickled my nose and intoxicated my heart with longing. My imagination ran wild with possibilities. The temptation ripped me apart. My girlfriend was waiting in South Korea for my return. There was no way she'd know. A lust-filled night to finish the day would provide another stark contrast to the past 24 hours.

I couldn't do it. Loyalty was a virtue. I didn't want to be an animal without control of his sexual desire. One of my goals was to minimize the pain I imposed on others. While I could have had a few hours of passion with Selam, my girlfriend could've been frolicking with another man. Cheating would cause massive suffering. Deception and breaking one's moral code run counter to self-actualization. I had come this far, and any steps backward would've gnawed at my soul. I had to channel my masculine energy into other endeavors. Steep mountain passes and confrontations with Ethiopia and its elements lay ahead.

A few minutes later, I hugged Eshetu and Selam goodbye while whispering *amma sekee naroo—thank you*—one more time and returned to my room alone.

While lying on my bed that evening, I reflected on my moral dilemma. Maybe I took myself too seriously. Vegetarianism had become a more dominant part of my identity than I'd realized. How much did I contribute to animal suffering by consuming a piece of meat? My body would recover from the inflammation spike resulting from the consumption of animal protein. Did the psychological damage from my inner conflict cause more pain than consuming a chunk of flesh? I didn't slam shots of vodka or shoot heroin. Eshetu, Selam, and I gained the gift of friendship. I hoped the partygoers saw visitors to Ethiopia as humble, compassionate people with a genuine interest in their culture. All it takes is a single interaction to leave an enormous impression.

Perhaps I should've stuck to my guns and refused to eat the goat. Maybe abiding by my morals would lessen the inner conflict. I had to live with myself every day and would never see the wedding guests again. Could I have communicated my values more gracefully while declining the piece of meat?

Whatever the case, my openness had healed the wounds from a morning of dodging rocks. My hellish reality had transformed itself in only a few hours. It was self-inflicted. I would've sulked in my room in solitude without any drastic change in my emotional state. Yet all it took was a few minutes of interaction with friendly Ethiopians to return to heaven. Even during the worst of times, good people lifted me to extraordinary heights. Selam's tangy finger flavor still lingers in my mouth as I type these words. Kindness is the best medicine.

Eshetu and Selam inspired me to be a better friend, colleague, and family member while expecting nothing in return. I wanted to be more generous with my time, energy, knowledge, skills, and social connections. Generosity creates a ripple effect, enhancing others' success. It's easier to win with friends rooting for you. Having been on the receiving end of kindness so many times during my travels, I longed to do more for those around me. Thanks to the finger-licking fun that evening, I was ready to continue giving without expectations.

Chapter 14

Ignorance

"Real knowledge is to know the extent of one's ignorance."
—Confucius

The next morning, I stumbled out of my room at 5:30 to witness Ethiopian Orthodox Church ceremonies. I yearned to discover a magical place that Ethiopians bragged about with gleaming eyes, guidebooks listed as the country's top tourist attraction, and UNESCO had declared a World Heritage Site. After a 15-minute walk, I trotted down a set of stairs and dined on a sensory feast.

Lalibela's magic starts with its history and construction. In the 12th century, King Lalibela of the Zagwe Dynasty made a pilgrimage to Jerusalem and returned after the Holy Land fell to Muslim armies. The Ethiopian king wanted to create a new center of Christianity in his hometown and oversaw the development of eleven churches. The ruler excavated cube-shaped trenches while leaving enough soil and rock in the center to carve the monasteries from iron-rich red stone and dried lava. No one knows why King Lalibela chose the difficult construction techniques, but legend says angels helped him.

The Ethiopian Orthodox Church is one of the most ancient centers of Christianity. It began when the Queen of Sheba, who's mentioned in the Hebrew Bible, left Ethiopia (part of Sheba, founded in 1000 BC) for Jerusalem and met King

Solomon. They had a son who returned to Ethiopia as an adult and brought the Ark of the Covenant, a gold-plated chest containing two stone tablets inscribed with the Ten Commandments, to East Africa.

It was here that Haile Selassie spent three days in retreat after his army was defeated by the Italians in 1936, praying with monks right before leaving for England in exile.

Today hundreds of pilgrims walk for days, from their homes to Lalibela, and fast during the journey to show their devotion to the Lord. They hope God will recognize their loyalty and reward them with a place in heaven.

Overcome by divine energy, I inched toward a group of 20 orthodox monks standing in a semicircle in front of the church's main courtyard. Their pearly white cloaks shone as the sunlight reflected off red and white carpets. The contrast of dark-brown skin and creamy cloth had them resembling royalty from African history books. Their outfits were fit for modern-day Ethiopian kings. The sages lived at the UNESCO World Heritage Site, where the multitudes prayed for truth and happiness. They'd won the spirituality lottery.

The monks hummed to the beat of cow-skin *kebero*[1] drums and sistrums[2] as goosebumps formed on my arms. Tongues snapped and high-pitched voices cracked, adding a funky beat to the low-energy humming.

"Ayayaya ..." They skipped through octaves with zealous abandon.

I came to a halt and basked in pure musical wonderment. I was still drowsy this morning, my eyes half-shut, until the men sped up the pace and whipped my brain into an awakened state.

---

1. A double-headed, conical drum used in Eritrea, Ethiopia, and Sudan.

2. A sacred Egyptian rattle consisting of a wood, metal, or clay frame set loosely with crossbars.

My shoulders and head bobbed to the rhythm, which brought my spirit to life.

I sat and listened for two hours, which seemed like 20 minutes. Finally, I pried myself from my auditory trance to explore another section of the church grounds. After walking down several more flights of stairs, I found myself in the middle of a baseball-field-sized trench of crumbling stones. I was staring up at the Saint Giyorgis Monastery, one of the architectural marvels of the modern world. A gust of wind struck a blow of erosion against its walls. The four-story structure was carved out of a single stone, comprising a towering monolith. As I admired the monastery's brown and red walls, a wisp of air whispered in a raspy voice.

"Step forward and show your devotion."

It was King Lalibela, the leader who'd created an alternative to the holy cities of Bethlehem and Jerusalem in the Horn of Africa. Or maybe it was the ghost of Christ or Adam, whose replica graves lay less than a kilometer from the monastery. The two men had teleported themselves from Israel to Ethiopia to watch over their followers with compassionate eyes.

I marveled at the architectural wonder in front of me. The grainy red rocks were rugged with wear and tear. Hints of yellow permeated the stone walls, perhaps from centuries of exposure to rain. Diagonal, charcoal cracks split the wall into thirds, hinting at something of immense historical significance. Like the wrinkles on a legendary World War II hero, they oozed with wisdom and tales of struggle. Chiseled doors provided access to the desert air. Layered square window outlines, with four protruding knob corners and cross-shaped dark shadows, resembled the wooden structure where Jesus was tortured to death.

I went up a rocky staircase and entered the church from its main gate. As I tiptoed around people chanting prayers, a shaven-headed man caught my attention. Sweat glistened on his body as puddles formed on the floor. Globs of sweaty gray dotted his pants, and a cloth belt hugged his thin midsection. Lines of devotion engraved his torso; his spiritual practices must've blessed him with lats and abs that would have made a bodybuilder fume in envy. The man collapsed to a kneeling bow as he grazed his forehead against the carpeted floor. After crouching on his hands and knees for a microsecond, he shot up, exploding into an erect posture. Hands folded in prayer, he dropped to the ground. It was as if God had fired a revolver inside his blasphemous mind, propelling him to his feet to show allegiance to the image of a garish Jesus painted on the wall in front of him. The worshiper repeated this routine for over one hour. Burpees for redemption. This was religion in a country that produces the world's best marathon runners.

I circled the interior and stared in awe as devotees puckered up for wooden crosses and smooched images of saints on the church grounds. This was a type of Christianity that piqued my curiosity.

As I sat and observed, I reflected on my ignorance of Ethiopian customs and beliefs. My ignorance of how thousands of years ago people built artistic masterpieces, such as Lalibela's rock-hewn churches. There was so much knowledge out there, but I knew nothing.

After observing the Ethiopians in prayer and marveling at the colorful wall and ceiling mosaics for several hours, I made my way up the stairs and exited the church grounds. Not even a stone's throw from the monastery exit, I slipped into conversation with Kalib and Kofi, a couple of local kids named who'd recently graduated from high school.

They were much more mature than the handlebar-high troublemakers I'd encountered on the road and seemed to be harmless. So far, the adults I'd met were good people. It was elementary school kids on desolate roads with rocks in their hands that had my heart racing in fear.

After exchanging a few casual words about their lives in Lalibela and my cycling trip, Kalib and Kofi made me an interesting proposition: "Come our home. We have tea and injera, and you see how we live."

Offer accepted. My eyebrows shot up in excitement, and my body felt lighter as we strolled through Lalibela's inclined streets. The kids led me to a grassy path that spilled into a mud house where their mother was boiling a tin pot of tea next to a stack of injera. Their dwelling comprised a communal room, with three clay benches and a fire pit, and another space for cooking. The boy's grandmother sprawled out on a seat in dreamland.

The house was more modest than I'd expected. Whereas I sported dusty, black pants, a scruffy beard, and an eight-year-old used camera, the boys carried smartphones, wore chic hipster T-shirts, and kept their hair stylishly braided. If Kalib and Kofi only needed their simple home and family, then what, I wondered, had motivated them to spend money on flashy accessories.

After we'd shared tea and injera for an hour, my new pals had an idea.

"Let's go dance club and listen traditional Ethiopian music. Local celebrity dancer coming there. You liking very much. Don't worry. We calling taxi driver friend. You don't pay the money."

"Before leaving, you giving donation for food, please," said Kofi. "Anything okay."

I was glad to help although I found it odd that they'd asked for a monetary donation before emphasizing I didn't need to pay the driver. Going to the club sounded like a great chance to delve into Ethiopian culture. I couldn't pass up this opportunity and handed their mother a few birr before we piled into the taxi.

We traversed a bumpy road until we arrived at a guest house with neon lights and a staircase leading to a dark basement. The place put the "f" in *funky* and the "e" in *empty*.

"We so early," Kofi explained. "One hour more many people coming. We getting best seats."

I did a lap around the classroom-sized interior and gawked at the cultural museum the club seemed to be: traditional murals, musical instruments, and carved, wooden tables and chairs beautified the space. Red, green, and yellow woven cloth hung an arm's length above me from the room's internal support beams and spiraled around the entire ceiling. Furry white-and-brown animal hide, from cows or buffalo, adorned the walls next to pencil sketches of tribal art.

Women in colorful turbans served glass test tubes of *tej*, a bright-orange honey liquor. Experiments in drunken behavior and musical vigor were moments away. I was going to have a lab report's worth of tales about this eccentric place.

"You trying tej? Something special from Lalibela." Kalib smiled proudly.

"Thanks, but I don't drink."

"You sure? This not much alcohol. No strong. One or two percent."

I thought of my Ecuadorian aunt and uncle's warnings to never accept a drink from anyone in a bar in Quito. They recounted stories of drugged cocktails and criminals escorting naive gringos to ATMs to wipe their bank accounts clean. Then again, an ocean and thousands of kilometers separated Ethiopia from Ecuador. My intuition told me the kids were safe. This could've been my only chance to taste the infamous regional brew. Why not taste a drop or two?

"All right," I said. "I'll try it."

Smiles of excitement amplified; they called the server. Several minutes later, I was slurping the liquor out of a test tube. It tasted like the honey water I consume when losing my voice at the end of a semester of teaching. Tej was too sweet for me, but I nursed the tube throughout the night.

People continued to file in. Collared-shirt-wearing twentysomethings stuck their chests into the air. Silk-skinned women with thick hair tied behind their heads locked hands with waist-tall children. Gray-haired men with saggy cheeks and leathery hands chuckled with arms around one another.

The entertainment started when a drum-draped, middle-aged man with gray hair trotted around the room while pounding away at his instrument. His eyes were wide with intent as he gazed at audience members for several seconds at a time. Passionate Amharic beats filled the place with vibrant energy.

A fellow with braided hair shooting into a Don King skyscraper sprinted into the room. The tall, wiry man's shoulders bounced at speeds I'd never seen. The gigolo made the women howl and whistle at his showmanship. He picked out a lady with flawless skin, eyes traced with black eyeliner, and a yellow-and-purple dress that hung below her knees. Her cheeks reddened as the man pulled her, as beautiful as she was reluctant, onto the dance floor.

I sat in my chair and watched for 30 minutes. This man must've been perfecting his craft since birth. I was envious of the effort he'd put into his art. If only I had done something more productive as a child than play video games and watch basketball on television.

"This famous guy, I telling you. He have dancing skill. You go and dancing with him. You copy him and he teaching you," said Kofi.

My mind screeched to a halt. The wallflower of my teenage years wanted to curl up into a ball. My stomach bubbled with nervousness. In a moment of clarity, logic took over my internal dialogue. No one knew me here. When else would I get the chance to shake it alongside an Ethiopian celebrity? Time to make a fool of myself. My heart raced as I hopped up and walked toward the artist.

He stopped, slapped my hand, and bumped my shoulder. "Welcome!" he shouted and offered a white-toothed smile.

His gregariousness pierced my bashful inner adolescent with a dagger. The tension in my neck dissipated as I let out a lengthy exhalation. Seconds later, the dancer continued wiggling his shoulders, and I did my best to match his movements. My shoulders shimmied back and forth. My *faranji* hips twitched like a drunken grandpa finding his way home. Bobbing my head to the beat, my neck burned as sweat stains spread over my gray shirt.

The onlookers erupted in bellows of excitement and satisfaction. I lasted a solid 10 minutes before the fire in my trapezius muscles forced me back to my chair. I must've looked like a picture-perfect image of God knows what. It was a two-man show, starring the bumbling *faranji* and the Ethiopian Michael Jackson.

Soon the Lalibela locals got up and showed off their swagger. Adolescents. Wrinkled grandfathers. Makeup-caked women. Toddlers awake past their bedtime would've dominated me in a shoulder battle. Gyrating dance machines filled the place with funk.

Out of the corner of my eye, I spotted a shaven-headed guy whose arms and chest were popping out of his tight-fitting T-shirt. Eshetu, Selam, and the entire wedding crew stampeded to a table a few meters away.

I dashed over to greet him, and we embraced in a warm hug. It elated me to see my friends again, and soon Eshetu's powerful hands shoved me into his sister.

"You dancing with her. She happy dancing with you," his voice commanded above the thundering drumbeats and baritone vocals.

Selam and I shook our shoulders as she guided me through the movements. Her brother didn't waste any time in his chair and quickly humbled me with his dancing ability. His personality shifted from a tough soldier into a modern-day John Travolta with eight-pack abs. Ladies yelled roars of approval at Eshetu's rhythmic prowess. After a few songs, everyone retreated to their seats while grabbing their sore bodies. Only he could handle the vigorous workout. My soldier friend waggled his chiseled shoulders and neck at a lightning-fast pace as women wailed and applauded. His physical training enabled him to go at it longer than anyone else. Eshetu was a lieutenant commander on the dance floor.

Selam and I kept at it for as long as we could. Sweat poured down her cheeks and forehead, smearing her lipstick and eyeliner. We stumbled to our seats in fatigue, fanning each other with our hands.

At the peak of the frenzy, Kofi and Kalib signaled it was time to leave. I didn't object since my shoulders and neck throbbed. The day's events were catching up with me.

It thrilled me to see Eshetu and Selam again, and I ran over to greet them before I left.

"You okay going home?" Eshetu asked.

"Yes. The kids have a driver and it'll be fine."

"Okay. You contacting me next time you coming Lalibela," Eshetu barked in a serious tone as he escorted me up the stairs and into the parking lot.

Eshetu and Selam's sincerity and playfulness were so refreshing. I'd miss them while pedaling for long hours by myself. We pulled out of the driveway as Eshetu and his sister stood there waving. Tears formed in the corners of my eyes as my head and neck jerked from the bumpy ride. Sometimes the simplest displays of humanity and kindness etched themselves deep in my heart.

On the way back to the hotel, a familiar story ensued.

"I hate talking this George, but ..." Kofi paused mid-sentence. "We are tough situation. My grandmother no enough money to pay for house. We no payment three times and landlord say we go out if no pay again. I so worried. You helping pay? I bad feeling asking you but I don't know what doing. You from United States and have many money. Please help."

"I am sorry to hear that, but I can't help everyone in Ethiopia. If I had a magic wand, the first thing I'd do is give everyone in the world health-care access, shelter, food, water, and safety. I'm just one man who can't do that on his own. I hope you understand," I said in a sympathetic tone.

"Okay. I understand. You need pay taxi driver 300 birr," Kofi said flatly.

"Three hundred birr? Three hundred birr will pay for 10 nights in a village hotel or ten meals in a local restaurant. That's a lot. You said the taxi driver was your friend and wouldn't charge us. I tell you what, I'll give the driver 100 birr. That's more than enough."

"I scared driver will get angry. One hundred birr not enough," said Kofi.

"You said he was your friend and didn't want any money. I don't understand."

Seconds later, we pulled up to my hotel entrance. They took my 100 birr as I stepped out of the vehicle. Before I could even shut the car door, the high-pitched squeal of tires broke the evening silence. No goodbyes. Good luck wishes missing in action. Smiles absent. Only brows furrowed with scorn. Fake friends and game playing. That's where their cell phones came from. My head spun and my heart dropped to my stomach. Situations like this sink their claws into my spirit.

As I retreated to my hotel room, I chided myself for my ignorance. Their request for money didn't surprise me, but after spending an entire day together, they couldn't even say goodbye? How desperate were they? What drives someone to dehumanize others after not getting their way? I wanted to dissect their brains, peer into their hippocampus of memories and wet my eyes with understanding. Glance into their limbic system of emotions and soak my soul with empathy. I ached to accept their behavior for what it was but couldn't.

Ignorance was supposed to be liberating. Not knowing something should open infinite doors of possibility. My brain knew the kids would ask for money. It was obvious. However, my heart groaned from the beatings. Over the course of the day, I had grown attached to Kalib and Kofi. The shared dishes of injera, the walks around town, shaking and shimmying on the dance floor. I felt betrayed—by them and myself.

My lack of self-awareness disappointed me. I'd overestimated my ability to control my mind. I hadn't been able to perceive the truth and read the situation correctly. One of the essential skills for becoming actualized is an accurate sense of reality perception. I'd been off in Lala Land for an entire day. My chest throbbed with heat as I threw myself on the bed in disgust and stared at the spider web–ridden ceiling.

I was sick of it. Sick of being asked for money. Tired of children chasing me at every corner, assuming I was ready to hand out $100 bills like a CEO who doesn't know what to do with his wealth. I longed to change my plan. I wanted to burn my possessions and walk across Ethiopia butt-naked, white glutes reflecting the rays of sun, leaving permanent scars on everyone's memory. No one would bother me if my material items withered to ashes. I'd rather have people laugh and point at my pale skin and hairy chest than be asked for money again. No pockets. No credit cards. No bike. Survival from the mango and avocado trees and injera donations would liberate me. I'd walk until the bottoms of my feet turned into callused masses of concrete. Caucasian-guy stereotypes shattered within seconds. I wanted to yell and scream at Ethiopia, shock her with my boldness.

"Take a good look!"

Maybe I was being too hard on them. I'm from a place where the media rattle about gay marriage and abortion, problems rendered absurd in East Africa.

I wouldn't let them irritate me anymore. We'd had a great time together, and Kalib and Kofi taught me something important. I reminded myself why I came to Ethiopia—to enjoy a hard-fought battle while maintaining a growth mindset. The keyword was "enjoy." I wasn't enjoying the struggle yet. At least I'd realized my ignorance. Unconscious incompetence leads to stagnation and conscious incompetence is the start of development. Self-awareness is everything, and the twentysomethings had helped me find another slice of it.

In a matter of minutes, my mood changed. I wanted to thank Kofi and Kalib and shake their hands and tell them my realization. Witnessing the sincere appreciation in my eyes would help us understand each other's intentions. If you are reading this, my young friends, thank you for giving me a priceless gift worth an infinite number of test tubes filled with tej.

At least I'd seen Eshetu and his sister one more time. They'd offered kindness and hospitality with no strings attached. The hurt and anger I'd experienced were miniscule compared to the joy of genuine friendship. I vowed to leave my heart out there for others to tear apart or invigorate. Closing myself was no way to go through life. I had gifts of joy and love to spread. If the moon loves you, why worry about the stars?

Chapter 15

No Rest

"The Nile has no resting place as it travels around while carrying a log."
—Ethiopian proverb

"Many discouraging hours will arise before the rainbow of accomplished goals will appear on the horizon."
—Haile Selassie

I tossed my bicycle on top of a small van to evade a posse of rock-heaving children. No painting the dusty terrain dark red with my blood! I needed transportation with a metal roof and doors. The rusty white vehicle became my savior. I had never been so excited for a bumpy ride. A day off served me well as my legs were fresh, my stomach full, and my mind clear. My calling was calling.

That morning, I surrendered. A few days ago, my big-headedness had me laughing at warnings from locals regarding the dangers en route to Lalibela. Instead of listening, I followed my oversized ego.

Back in 2014, European tour cyclists in Central Asia had gawked in disbelief during my first two-month long 2,500-kilometer journey.

"You're cycling with that enormous bag? Doesn't that hurt your back?"

I became known as "the crazy American guy carrying a huge backpack." No panniers. All brute force. I was proud of my stiff neck and aching shoulders every evening when my body hit the stone-ridden ground. Mongolia. Siberia. Oman. Bangladesh. Each trip injected helium into my balloon of a head. My ego soared to unimaginable heights, but the children of Lalibela had burst it. I swallowed my pride, and its sour flavor stung my throat.

No more cycling around Lalibela. This time I let the van's tires and engine absorb the same potholes that punished my glutes a few days ago. The same youngsters that flung stones in my direction waved and smiled. It took us three hours to move sixty kilometers. It was the most comfortable journey since I'd arrived in Ethiopia.

Once we got back to the paved road, I stepped out of my metal cocoon. No more protection. No more vacation from my vacation. I yearned to ride out the momentum I'd built over the past few weeks. The Nile River didn't rest, and neither would I. I couldn't lose my edge.

My next destination was Woldia, another large city. The driver untied my bicycle from the vehicle's roof, and I strapped the panniers to my luggage rack in front of a coffee shack's worth of staring locals. Self-talk under control, I convinced myself the worst part of my journey was in the past—it couldn't get much worse than the malicious stoning on that dirt road.

Cars whizzed by and villagers twisted their heads. While pedaling, I reflected on the power of adaptation. Human beings were marvelous creatures. Rocks were fluffy pillows. Yelling became flirtatious whispers. Requests for money turned into humorous banter. The sun's equatorial rays were vitamin D–loaded beams of cancer-fighting energy. My mind was calloused while confronting threats. Pandemonium became normal. Hope and clarity kept me going.

Ethiopia was a character-building training ground. Resilience, leadership, and self-awareness, all of which I coveted, were invaluable meta-skills. I needed Ethiopia like a Navy SEAL needs a training pool. By forcing me to dig deep, Ethiopia had shown me that human potential was limitless. I longed to be unshakable in the face of chaos. The only way to awaken the warrior within was to stand and stare at danger until she became part of my identity. I couldn't celebrate until fear and anxiety were comfortable. The ability to tolerate pain without suffering was true freedom. The stones had taught me to stick my chest out. No flinching.

Or maybe Ethiopia had changed me into a battered child. Verbal and physical beatings were normal. A day without a whipping was an unforeseen gift.

Stop the useless self-talk. Don't fall victim to the wrath of doubt. My soul was growing bigger, glowing brighter, maximizing its power.

The midday rays pounded off the pavement and whipped me back to reality. The sun's position had spoken.

"You've been at it for three hours. No mercy!"

I entered a zone as devoid of trees as it was of shade. The upward-sloping, zigzag path peered at me from above and knocked the first, second, and third winds out of me. I reduced my speed to that of a Galapagos tortoise waddling to the ocean after laying eggs. As I crept along, ugly black insects scooted across the tarmac to the rocky, yellow soil and scurried beneath it. If only I could join them underground. What ingenious little creatures, digging refuges to keep cool.

As I continued ascending, the change in altitude had me huffing and puffing. A block of concrete lodged itself in my chest and each pant made it heavier.

Lungs going to explode. Why so slow?

"Huh ... huh ... huh ..." The sound of my struggle-induced breathing had me ruminating on an uncertain future. *Come on, Ethiopia! Give me shade!*

I pulled myself together by focusing on my breath. High-altitude meditation began, as a monk in Seoul had taught me several months before, with counting in Korean. *Hana. Dool. Set. Net* ... Hot air filled my nasal cavity for a count of eight, then I exhaled. Dried mucus blocked my left nostril, and soon my ears rang to the soundtrack of labored breathing.

After a hard-fought battle with the switchback roads, I continued along an inclined but straight path. I sighed in relief, and my lungs took a much-needed break. My cheeks and nose stung from the sunlight, but at least my breathing returned to normal.

My mind entered a time warp while my legs pumped. It had been a chilly Michigan morning. I was up before the sun again and wiped the crust out of my eyes. Two sweatshirts and three coffee mugs of lukewarm water later, I was at it. My feet pounded the pothole-pocked Michigan pavement. Knees stiff. Ankles cracked. My exposed skin yearned for warmth while the frigid breeze sliced through my neck. The hum of birds flapping through the air kept me motivated.

Glide! Glide like the birds.

The cobwebs of pain had disappeared. Only drops of wisdom remained. Bits of higher-order awareness resulted from observing the throbbing sensations in my legs. Seconds later, my thighs were tireless masses of rigid flesh. My inner dialogue fell to a whisper, enabling my body to weave around patches of ice. One hour and 30 minutes—15 kilometers—of struggle and ecstasy. It was over for now.

My research on Ethiopia had haunted me into a hellish workout regimen. British writer Evelyn Waugh had written: "In Ethiopia, most of the time I thought about how awful the next day would be." My muscles had several hours to recover before I was at it again. Locked in position, I stood upright. Legs shoulder-width apart, my hamstrings begged for mercy. Pearl Jam blasted through the gym speakers.

"Ohhh I am ... I'm still alive ..."

In times of distress and chaos, I fell back to the level of my preparation. There was a tiger inside me, and I brought it to the surface.

The moment struck, and I was ready for the test. I had prepared myself for struggle, blasting through hardship, and recovered faster than I ever imagined I would. My discomfort had schooled me in the law of impermanence. The relentless pursuit of personal growth kept me going. The training empowered me to make bold decisions in the face of danger. It taught me that answers are in plain sight.

My soil has seeds ready to sprout in time for the big harvest. Am I watering or poisoning them? This is the question that dominates my life.

The stone-throwing teenagers of life can appear when I least expect them. I must always be prepared to pry their weapons loose.

Chapter 16

Fight, Flight, and Friendship

When elephants fight it is the grass that suffers.
—Kenyan proverb

I peered up at the sky: turquoise without a trace of white. If God was up there, I needed His help.

Two shovel-armed teens stood on either side of me, blocking the road. Shorter than I by a few centimeters, they had muscled forearms and veiny calves. I'd put a thousand kilometers behind me and finally acclimated to the routine of being on a bicycle in Ethiopia, but the young man to my right jammed the handle of his shovel into the spokes of my front wheel to make sure I could go no further. The other gripped his tool as a weapon. A sand-laden wind stung my cheeks.

"Money! Money! Money!" they shouted.

Stabilizing the bike frame between my legs, I lunged for the nearest shovel. Grasping the handle with my right hand, I twisted and snatched the tool upward in a single motion. The young villager, caught off guard, countered my move but didn't put enough weight behind the maneuver. He lost his balance and stumbled back on one leg. I took advantage of his slip-up and wrestled the tool from his hands without dismounting from the bike.

The boys' eyes widened. The weapon and mental edge were mine. Gawking at each other, the teens bellowed, eyebrows raised in panic-stricken disbelief. They sprinted down the embankment, no doubt afraid I might use the shovel against them.

Go! Rocks are next, I told myself. "Come on! Pedal!" I yelled aloud.

With the shovel still in one hand, I gripped the handlebars with the other. My entire body pulsated as I glided uphill. My bike traveled at speeds I had never imagined possible, my legs pushing with unrelenting force as numbness spread across my lower body. The adrenaline never ceased.

Crack! Crack! I flinched at the sound of rocks striking the ground behind me. *Crack! Crack!* One landed an arm's length to the right of my bicycle. The other flew above my head, kicking up a cloud of dust where it landed.

At last, the thumping faded. The teens must have grown tired of their target practice.

Don't stop! Let's get out of here!

I wheezed and panted for air until the kids became specks behind me. There was only one road and open desert all around me. If they had a motorbike, they could be on my tail in minutes. I hopped off my bicycle and javelin-tossed the shovel deep into the rocks and sand beside the road. The last thing I needed was for them to catch up to me and use the tool as a weapon again.

I pushed myself until my legs couldn't take it anymore, cruising up and down hills and along winding roads. My hamstrings throbbed. My calves were knots of fire, becoming tighter and more heated with each pump of the pedals. Suddenly, the aching dissolved into nothingness. A few moments later, the agony and burning returned. The oscillating pain and numbness twisted my mind into a pretzel. Each time the sensations mutated, my eyes drooped. I couldn't stand not knowing how long it would take to find a safe place to rest.

I thought about my two-workouts-per-day routine leading up to the trip. The sets and reps of cleaning and jerking barbells, the mountain trail runs in the snow, the ring muscle-up competitions. The training had given me the confidence to react quickly and outmaneuver two kids 20 years my junior. I had trained like my life depended on it because it did.

After over 20,000 kilometers on a bicycle in Asia and The Middle East, I'd never been mugged. Heck, I'd never even been in a schoolyard fistfight. Luckily, those kids weren't armed with a Kalashnikov or a knife, or things could have ended much differently. I surprised myself and realized that I'm capable of ferocious intensity.

No one should ever have to defend themselves when they are simply minding their own business. Gandhi, a man famed for nonviolence, said, "When there is only a choice between cowardice and violence, I would advise violence." I realized I was capable of behavior I had once deemed unnecessary and brutish and was glad the situation hadn't resulted in anything more serious than a couple of bruised egos and jangled nerves. Violence is rarely the answer, but when it is, it's the only answer.

After another hour of cycling, I reached a village. It was a windy, chilly outpost at the summit of a steep hill. At the first sign of human life, I began a gesture-infused attempt at communication. "Sleep? Hotel?" I panted.

Seconds later, three soccer teams' worth of villagers darted toward me. I became the focus of a town hall meeting with no agenda and no town hall. People shoved and elbowed their way to the front of the crowd. Those toward the back jumped to catch a glimpse. Some clicked their tongues in rapid-fire Amharic. Others stood silently, resting their chest-high wooden staffs on the pavement. Villagers elbowed and shoved their way to the front with their muscled forearms. I was a circus act without a gimmick, a clown without magic tricks, jokes, or juggling skills.

Seemingly out of nowhere, the pulsing shifted from my legs to my bladder. All the water I had chugged that morning and afternoon had me ready to explode. I tossed my bike aside and pushed through to the edge of the crowd. Pants unzipped and exposed, a warm yellow stream splattered in the dusty sand. Too exhausted to be embarrassed, too fatigued for social niceties, I returned to my bicycle and resumed my query.

Onlookers took up the entire width of the two-lane road. In a normal state of mind, I would have been rattled by the crowd's sheer size. I wanted to push through the mob and catch some shut-eye on the rocky sand. Anywhere would do. I needed a break from the chaos. Suddenly, a welcoming voice rang through the air.

"Yes. Yes. Do you want a hotel? This way. Follow me. My name is Teka," said a man in near-perfect English.

Gauging another's intentions is an invaluable survival mechanism, and tour cycling had honed my intuition. Trust the wrong person and you sail in seas of peril. Open yourself to others and reap the rewards of sincere friendship. I had always opted to leave my heart open. Friendship and love are the world's most valuable gifts. I still keep in contact with Chilo, an *amiga* from my first backpacking trip (in 2007 in Nicaragua). Chilo assisted with volunteer work in a local hospital in the mountain town of Estelí. In 2008, she had come to visit me in Michigan. I took her apple picking, and, after she'd filled a bag with Granny Smiths and Fujis, the fall colors and sweet taste of the fruit brought her to tears.

In 2014 I taught at an orphanage in Bodh Gaya, India, with Indra and Vicky. After spending days writing English phrases and drawing maps on an outdoor chalkboard, we'd cook *litti choka* over an open flame. All these years later, we still share pictures of our everyday lives.

The bonds of friendship forged in adventure transcend international boundaries, and danger's fangs have never pierced my skin because of an intuition blunder.

From the moment I saw him, I knew Teka would become a friend for many years. His eyes sparkled like a polished mirror. He stared straight into my eyes, his gigantic smile unwavering, and seemed more from genuine excitement than temporary joy. Wrinkles etched his face with sincerity. He howled in laughter when I mentioned I'd cycled from Addis Ababa, over a thousand kilometers away. His soft voice, which rose several notches in pitch at the end of each sentence, communicated kindness and a willingness to help others. Teka seemed void of all hostility, as if he were incapable of raising a fist in rage. I knew I could trust him.

As I pushed my bike along the village street with Teka, the people trailed away. They lost interest in me and returned to their farm animals, billiard games, and lively conversations.

Teka led me to a compound of old, concrete buildings covered in crumbling, blue paint. A three-meter-high metal wall surrounded the rectangular hotel perimeter. A red door spotted with rust stood ajar, opening onto a downward-sloping ramp of soil and rocks. Grimacing, I awkwardly carried my two water bottles, banana-and-mango-filled panniers, and bike—one item at a time—along the entrance.

I stumbled into a courtyard. Devoid of weeds, flowers, or any other colorful plant life, it was filled with rocky sand. A pitcher of water and a bar of soap lay next to a wooden shack with black plastic bags nailed to the outside for privacy. I couldn't wait to use that outhouse and hand-washing facility. By my standards, it was a five-star accommodation. I would've pitched my tent on the rocks next to the outhouse if I had to. Anything just to know I could spend the night in a place locked away from the outside world. Safety and rest were paramount.

Teka introduced me to the hotel owner, a man in his sixties with a round, shaved head and a dimpled smile. The manager pounded on his knees and screeched in laughter upon learning of my bicycle journey. "Coming from Addis Ababa bicycle? Yaya!"

We agreed to a price of 60 birr (US $2) for one night's stay. The man led me up a creaky outdoor staircase of cracked wood. Our bodies wobbled back and forth with each step, and my chest sank to my knees as I nearly lost my balance on the way up. The manager brute-forced the door open with his shoulder and wiped the dust off the bed in two swipes. Four solid walls. Door with lock. Stable floor and ceiling. Twin bed. Sold.

I stood on the hotel balcony for a few minutes as the chilly breeze pummeled my back. The sky caught fire with red and orange streaks. This was the highest-altitude village in the Wollo

Highlands and the chilliest place I had visited in Ethiopia. I threw on the extra layers of clothing in my bag. My wool hat shielded my sun-chafed ears from the crisp wind.

I staggered down the wobbly staircase, and Teka signaled that we'd go for a walk.

He led me around the village as pop singers yodeled in between chorus lines through coffee-shack speakers. People struck each other on the shoulder amid familiar company. I felt gratitude and relief to have met Teka and found a safe haven. I could let my guard down for a few hours.

My new friend escorted me to his home, a small house with three rooms, including a common area for dining. His sister greeted me with a shy smile as pop music blared in the background. She avoided eye contact and busied herself washing dishes and preparing our meal. When I tried to make casual conversation, she shied away. Her daughter, hardly a toddler, wiggled her hips to the bass line of traditional music accompanied by words sung in Amharic. The little girl shook her shoulders and hips to the beat like a dancing doll. Perhaps this was a child prodigy before me? Teka and I chuckled and slapped a wooden stool in time to the music as the toddler imitated the singer's voice. To shake one's hips when you can barely walk! Now that was the way to enjoy life!

Infancy, it seemed, was life in its essence. Scream, smile, or defecate in someone's arms. Puke in someone's purse-lipped face while cradled. Unconditional love and tenderness were the root of humanity. No societal rules or judgment. That baby had it good.

So did I. That home-cooked meal was the best medicine I could have received after a draining day. We sat on a pair of chairs with a round tin of injera on our laps. The aroma of *berbere* spice filled the room. Shiro, a yellow chickpea-powder stew, steamed on my plate—also on my lap—and scorched my hands. Seconds later, I wolfed it down with fervent pleasure. Berbere-coated, shiro-soaked injera burned the roof of my mouth and tongue. Mushy, spicy, and sour. Absolute heaven. Teka's sister beamed with pride at each bite. Her cheeks glowed every time I said, "*Ammasekeenaroo, injera, shiro gonjo!*" *Thank you! Injera, shiro good*!

After the meal Teka took me to his favorite coffee shop, a two-minute walk from his home. One by one, I shook hands with khat-chewing men who appeared to have been there for hours. Music blasted from the stereo, and the sound waves reverberated in the streets. A cup of tea warmed my hands as steam blew through the thin mountain air. Teka translated while I answered the standard questions about where I came from and my thoughts on Ethiopia.

The village's high school English teacher greeted us with a smile. He looked 15 years my senior and, upon learning about my journey, tilted his head back and chuckled. His friends had nicknamed him Hyena because of his lively spirit and how much he laughs. Hyena explained to me what coffee, refined sugar, and khat did to the human body.

"These things are no good," he said. "Khat have bad effects on nervous system. We lose motivation and do not work. People being lazy, big problem. Khat very bad. I no like khat."

I asked Hyena about Ethiopian children and why they threw so many stones.

"I am so sorry. This Ethiopian culture. We always fighting one another. Always having violence."

I was sure he wanted me to have positive experiences in his country so I could tell a tale with many bright spots. It had been the same during all my previous cycling adventures. People sincerely wanted me to enjoy my time in their country. As a traveler, I became part of each nation's public-relations campaign.

We strolled the village, stepping around muddy puddles until we reached a home where snacks were sold out of a refrigerator, and villagers sipping coffee sat around a television. A man offered me a mocha-flavored, carbonated beverage upon learning that I couldn't handle Ethiopia's famed hot drink after dark. I explained repeatedly that I'd be up all night with only one sip, and everyone roared with laughter at the stereotypical non-Ethiopian who couldn't handle his coffee. It was impressive how ubiquitous the sipping of the bitter brew was after sundown. Many drank coffee compulsively and then snored well into the night.

Teka and I glanced up in wonder as we returned to my hotel. The stars and moon lit up the entire village. White clouds maneuvered across the luminescent sky, which flooded the landscape with varying shades of gray and yellow. The Big Dipper's ladle, shimmering brightly, reminded me of the large spoon used to scoop piping-hot shiro onto my plate during dinner. Nature was the greatest artist of all, bequeathing an image of beauty that lasted for mere seconds before morphing into a different one. The same constellation twinkled brightly on other continents. It was the same light combination I'd gawked at as a child in Michigan, the same glimmer that had served as my compass in the deserts of Oman.

I was nothing, yet I was everything. The universe dwarfed my petty existence. There won't be so much as a flinch in the galaxy when I leave earth. I was an infinitesimal speck that would be around for an instant in the grand scope of things yet slices of that instant were so meaningful. The stars aligned and rewarded me with life. Danger nauseated me, and Teka's friendship became my hot porridge. At that moment Teka was everything to me, and I was everything to him. Our new friendship energized us into laughter and smiles.

The moon cast a spell over the entire village. Silhouetted mountains in the distance watched us as we strolled along the muddy path. The night turned the yellow, sandy slopes into jagged, coal-colored peaks that stood guard over the village, isolating it from those unwilling to punish their motor vehicles or put their bodies to the test.

Two hundred meters ahead, donkeys, goats, and camels glowed in the darkness, an array of white light from the moon and stars beaming off their bodies. Perhaps the phantom mammals had risen from the dead, and since being separated from their brothers and sisters was too much to endure, had come to visit their families. Their calm spirits ran wild in the night, soaking in the village's love through a temporary resurrection.

Teka and I said our goodbyes a few minutes later at the hotel. "I so happy to meet you. It is so funny how we met while you looking for hotel!" Teka exclaimed.

I couldn't express what I felt. The right combination of words wouldn't come out. High altitude and fatigue had made me ultra-sensitive, and tears formed in the corners of my eyes.

"You are a good friend, Teka, and I'm so glad we met tonight. You're the friend I've been looking for in Ethiopia," I said.

Teka had no email or phone number, and neither did the hotel, and only fate knows whether we'll meet again. He was the shooting star who showed me the beauty of kindness and compassion only to disappear into the night without a trace. He will always be with me.

I felt whole again within my incomplete self. I felt a newfound appreciation for everyone who had ever done anything for me out of pure kindness. How lucky I was to have a loving family and a solid group of friends! How lucky I was to have Teka by my side that evening! They say a small house can hold one hundred friends, but all I needed was Teka and his friends to completely transform my mood.

Back at the hotel, I contemplated the day's events with utter confusion. One minute shovel-wielding teens had attempted to rob me, the next Teka had showered me with friendship. Each day was a nightmare and a fairytale.

In South Korea, my biggest challenge had been prying books out of students' hands for a few minutes to motivate them to get some sunlight, to enjoy the mountain air and cherry blossoms. Parents discouraged their children from going outside, playing sports, and socializing until they'd gained admission to a top-ranked university. Mothers and fathers taught their children that test scores were the most important measures of success. In Ethiopia I had to wrestle a tool out of a teen's hands just to continue down the road. I wondered what kinds of families those shovel-toting kids had. Maybe, as Hyena mentioned, violence and fighting for survival was the norm. The lives and experiences of people differ immensely based on the lottery of life.

Chapter 17

Popping the Big Question

"Dine with a stranger, but save your love for your family."
—Ethiopian proverb

After battling with inclines for several hours, I zoomed downhill. The tension eased throughout my shoulders and neck, and my heart calmed. At midday I stopped at a village café. It was a typical hangout, with plastic tables and benches set up around a room with microwave oven–sized speakers resting on the floor. I pressed my head against the wall and savored the cool breeze for one loop of the in-house playlist.

Alone time. Refuge from the sun and solitude. Suddenly, a man interrupted my plans by waving and introducing himself.

"Excuse me, sir!" Hearing words I could understand left me craving companionship since finding people to connect with on a deeper level was a challenge in Ethiopian villages.

"I like to have culture exchange with you. Please come my home and my wife make food and coffee," he offered.

After the incident with Kofi and Kafi and friendship with Eshetu and Selam ... Ethiopia kept me guessing. The man's smile and exuberant enthusiasm disarmed me. Eshetu wanted to hang out, so maybe this guy had innocent intentions. Or did he? Was this a ploy to extract money? The scabs on my heart hadn't healed.

While traveling by bike, invitations to homes at first greeting had been common, so his offer didn't surprise me. People had wanted to know my impressions of their country. It was a great learning experience for me since I could ask questions and see another person's daily routine. Exchanges were one of the best parts of being on the road.

"Okay, let's go." I motioned to the door.

"Me name Gebaya." He grabbed my hand up into a firm handshake that signaled humility and confidence. He was dressed in a tight-fitting, short-sleeved shirt with a collar and pressed pants and had a fresh haircut.

"My wife pregnant. She have baby after one week. I be father soon," he said with a big gleam in his eyes.

Gebaya and I strolled past several hut-sized, wooden kiosks selling snacks and cellphone accessories. Music from the stores faded as we turned down a winding dirt road covered with husky mango and banana trees. We entered a luscious, green entranceway beyond which squatting women wearing pastel kerchiefs spread beans and teff over sheets of cloth to dry in the sun.

We made our way to a newly constructed, two-bedroom home that had over 10 times the floor space of my apartment in Seoul. The main entrance led to a furniture-less interior with sparkling wooden floors and shiny, dark-pink walls. I glanced up at the ceiling, at least eight meters above my head—Gebaya's home was a mini Taj Mahal compared to the wood-and-mud dwellings I'd grown accustomed to over the past few weeks.

"I really like your place."

"I make this house myself. This I working for a long time. I am so happy here," he said.

Gebaya owned five houses in the village and rented them to neighbors. His ingenuity and business savvy impressed me. He seemed sharper than anyone else I'd met on my trip, and I wondered whether he'd try any shrewd moves to extract money from me.

This was his home now, he explained, but he had a vision.

"Village people old thinking. Not good. Just gossiping and no education. I live in village because cheap price," he said.

Gebaya—a teacher by day and a real estate developer, agricultural trader, and graduate student on nights and weekends—yearned to move to the mid-sized town of Woldia, a 20-kilometer downhill ride from his village.

"Teacher making 3,000 birr ($100) one month. This little, little money. I like teacher work but no money. Teacher hard job in Ethiopia. My students working in agriculture making money for family. School attendance big problem. My students no come to class and manager no pay full salary," he said.

More disrespected teachers. It was an echo I'd heard in Bangladesh, Guatemala, and Russia. The world's great minds avoided teaching because of the high levels of stress, low pay, and lack of respect. How can anyone support a family on $100 per month?

Gebaya was also a man of action. He could've simply blamed the Ethiopian government for his financial difficulties. So many of the villagers I'd met wasted hours chewing chat. He provided for his family despite having been born in a challenging environment. This was becoming rarer in today's world of quick fixes and life hacks that promised immediate results.

I was ecstatic to see Gebaya doing well, and he mentioned his grand vision several times. I found his goals admirable and was impressed with his accomplishments. During our conversation, I realized I should go after the things I wanted with relentless vigor. Watching him speak with satisfaction and clarity sparked a new level of motivation inside me. My mind ticked over the idea of doing more writing, pulsated over the prospect of more quality time with family and friends, quivered in excitement over additional physical training, soothed itself over more hours allotted to meditation. Hanging out with Gebaya motivated me to push my limits even further. His was an inspirational story. I needed to do more.

By way of recompense, I advised Gebaya on matters of health and food—after all, he was going to be a father soon. He leaned in with keen interest when I told him I fast every day.

The Ethiopian version of fasting means abstaining from meat consumption.

"Eating a whole-foods, plant-based diet can extend your life by five to seven years, and it increased my energy level so I can do more."

"Oh, thank you. I want know more. Tell more," he demanded. "In Ethiopia we no learn about this." Gebaya leaned in while I spoke about food and personal health. I felt like I was in the classroom with a knowledge-hungry student.

"I want make muscle like you. How I do that? I thinking you 25. How old you?" he asked.

"Wow! Actually, I'm 38." I burst into laughter, flattered by his innocence.

"No! No! You joking! Thirty-eight man no look like you in Ethiopia. You looking very strong." Gebaya dropped his jaw in surprise.

"Here's my Korean ID card to prove it." I pointed to numbers that displayed my birth year.

"How you cycling in Ethiopia? So many mountains? You no tired? How you strong like this? I want know your secret."

"Well, there are many things I don't do. I'm obsessed with energy optimization. No alcohol, no drugs, no meat, no dairy products, no refined sugar or processed foods, no smartphone, no air conditioning, no heat in the winter, no television."

These were the conversations I relished. This wasn't a mere cultural exchange but an inspirational session. Two people from opposite sides of the world motivating each other. Gebaya had won me over.

Amid our talk, he popped a question that threw me off guard.

"How much you making in month?" he asked.

Tricky. Although my salary was modest by North American or South Korean standards, it was one that most Ethiopians have only heard of in fables. I wanted others to view me as an average guy with an anonymous amount of money. Unfortunately, my skin color, manner of speaking, and style of dress had invited the same question in many parts of the world.

"One mango," I told him, "is 150 birr ($5) in South Korea. One coffee is 150 birr ($5), and I pay less than 11,000 birr per month for my small apartment. Your house is 10 times bigger than my place. In Korea, we have no mangoes or coffee. The mangoes are from Thailand and coffee is from Ethiopia, so it's expensive. There is a high population density in Seoul, so small apartments cost a lot. You have fruit, vegetables, and teff, but in Korea, the land is not suitable for agriculture."

He raised his eyebrows. In Ethiopia, one mango or cup of coffee costs three to five birr.

After I reluctantly divulged my salary, he said, "You moving here. Much better for you. Your salary one month you can building house like this in village. Your two-month salary, you building house in middle-size city no problem. You must invest Ethiopia."

My wanderlust had me fantasizing about owning terrain in various places around the world. It'd be nice to enjoy the mountain-domed landscapes, frothy rivers, tropical fruits, and friendship of warm-hearted people. Also, I wanted to give back. I could set up shop in Ethiopia and do my part to make sure everyone had access to adequate nutrition, education, and clean water.

As we sat in his big, empty room, Gebaya told me how he and a few friends planned on opening an orphanage for kids who needed protection. On cue, a little girl zoomed into Gebaya's home and slapped the wall with playful palms.

"She no have mother and father. Village people taking care of her. I want open place to take care of children like her."

How was there so much ambition inside his heart? I admired his interest in helping the less fortunate. I hadn't heard of communities in North America or Europe pooling their resources to raise orphans. Watching out for each other was another strength of collectivism. Gebaya made it sound as if everyone took her in without thinking twice. Humanity was inspiring to witness.

Before I left Gebaya's home, he had a final request, one that would entail immense responsibility, action, and wisdom. A mammoth question I never fathomed confronting.

"George, we have big tradition in Ethiopia. I have baby soon and one person becoming second father. Second father and first father having close relationship and make even closer. Will you second father for my baby?" he asked.

I was stunnumbed—stunned and numb. There I was, a seasoned Toastmasters member who answered crazy questions on the fly, in front of large audiences, and in his third language. It flabbergasted me that Gebaya thought I'd be qualified to be the second father. I had no experience raising kids and had avoided the two big life changes of marriage and children the way a vampire flees the sun. I doubted my competency as a parent and had always shunned babies, fearful I'd drop them or touch them the wrong way. This was a role that would shatter my comfort zone. The charcoal bats in my stomach were ready to blast through their container. I felt the discomfort of someone trying to dismantle a bomb, wincing in anticipation of the imminent explosion.

"Are you sure I'm the right person? What's the second father supposed to do?"

"You and me having closer relationship like brothers. You and me talking so much. We coming closer."

"What else is expected of me?"

"We coming very close relationship."

"Gebaya, we met a few hours ago. What about your friends from Ethiopia who understand the culture better? I'm sure there are many people you've known your entire life, right?"

"I know you good person. We coming like brothers and more close soon."

My mind took a journey to the time an Indian toddler had urinated on my lap during the second hour of a sixteen-hour train ride to the Punjab province. As if the puss-white, volcanic sweat blister on my hand, itchy, magenta, chicken pox–like dots covering my stomach, and drenching, oppressive heat weren't enough. To me, kids were unpredictable creatures that warmed your thighs with piss while stuffed in trains filled with the stench of rotting humanity.

Freedom robbers. How was I supposed to cycle around the world with a kid? Other people's babies were innocent and cute, but the thought of raising children overwhelmed me. I'd become a money slave, worried about providing a better life for my children. My carbon footprint was deep enough, no need to make my imprint larger. The handcuffs were too tight to bear.

What were Gebaya's intentions? Was this a scheme to extract cash? His motives could've been financially driven, but I didn't want to keep my heart closed out of fear. The genuine issue was responsibility.

As we sat in silence, I pondered my dilemma. Becoming a father seemed so alien. I reminded myself why I came to Ethiopia: it was about spiritual growth. To develop further, I needed the unknown. I didn't want to be a slave to my experiences and succumb to negativity about children my entire life. The only way to overcome my child-phobia was through exposure. If life's meaning was to leave something behind, then this would be a great opportunity to make an impact. I never ruled out having kids. In 10 or 15 years, I'd be a different person with an evolved philosophy. This could be practice for when I raise my own. The answer was inside the whole time.

"Okay, Gebaya. I'll do it. But remember, I don't have any kids."

"Oh great! I so happy your decision. We becoming close friends. Like brothers." He beamed, his smile stretching from ear to ear.

I knew I should take this on. There were plenty of people to ask for advice, and it could be a way to share something with the world. I'd said yes to love. I needed to cherish that baby as if it were my own. Now I'd become part Ethiopian, and the newborn child would be part North American. I felt like a stronger global citizen after accepting my role as a father.

Gebaya and I spent the afternoon in deep conversation over his wife's homemade cuisine and freshly ground coffee. His partner's face turned red every time I attempted to engage her in small talk. She joined us for several minutes and then returned to household chores.

The village baby stumbled in and out of his house, interrupting us with her innocent smile. Indeed, it does take a village to raise a child. I became part of the village that day. The

Ethiopian village where Gebaya opened his home and heart to me. His compassion and kindness inspired me to give more to the world. I needed to reframe my outlook on children and view them as little human beings that need to soak up the world's love.

I imagined myself returning to Ethiopia to visit Gebaya and his family. I envisioned us hiking in the surrounding mountains while stumbling across snakes and large insects. Thoughts of bringing the child games and toys from South Korea and the United States filled me with joy. The kid would read me Ethiopian fables and help me learn the Amharic script. I'd teach the youth English, Korean, and Spanish, and we'd toss around balls next to teff fields. Having an Ethiopian family made me more complete.

"Good. You staying here with me or going to Woldia and Aksum?"

Time was running out. I'd have to keep going if I expected to make it to Aksum. The goal-oriented part of my brain took over, and I decided to leave. Gebaya and I could stay in contact along the way.

The village had given me a warm feeling. Love was bursting from my insides. I needed to share it with the world. The unborn child would become my treasure. I couldn't wipe the smile off my face as I moved onward and pedaled toward Woldia that evening. My heart, mind, and outward gestures aligned along the skyward road of love.

Gebaya and I stayed in close contact via email and social media for several weeks after I returned to South Korea. We continued to send each other good wishes in the days leading up to his son's birth. I wanted to be his confidant.

One day he threw a wrench into the mix by popping another big question—a request for $2,200. I should have known. What a waste of effort, time, and emotional investment. If he'd requested $20 per month, I'd have agreed to help, but the enormous sum floored me. Part of me knew it was coming. Logically, it made little sense to have me as a second father unless I provided financial support.

After turning down his request, he persisted a few times while lowering the number until I grew tired of his nagging. My father had taught me that when you lend money to a friend, you lose your money and your friend. That was my answer. He wanted the cash more than the friendship. I couldn't blame him. He had his village to help raise the child. Why would he need a North American villager unless he thought they had deep pockets?

Our communication slowed because I left his emails unanswered. When we chatted, our conversations became one-sentence greetings of polite formality. I was sure he'd found someone else to be the second father in Ethiopia; neither of us mentioned our agreement after his brash request.

As I type these words, over two years have passed since my trip, and I have a different outlook. Perhaps Gebaya had looked at money through a lens of relative need. I told him my salary during our conversation, and maybe he figured I had several thousand dollars socked away. Ethiopia was the land of collectivism, and it could be common to give financial support to acquaintances and relatives. Even in South Korea, many friends had given sizable funds to community members.

I saw Gebaya's appeal as an offer to bring me into his inner circle. He felt close enough to ask for financial help since he'd appointed me as his baby's second father. It was impossible to know his true intentions, but this was the story I told myself. Ironically, this morning he contacted me and sent pictures of his wife and baby. He seemed content and invited me to his home after the coronavirus pandemic. I viewed him as a well-intentioned guy who wanted a better life for his family. That's one of the universals of being human.

This was the challenge of traveling in Ethiopia. Nearly everyone had looked at me with dollar signs in their eyes, and I was used to it by the time I met Gebaya. I had never seen the intensity of money requests as I did in Ethiopia. My friends in Bangladesh, Uzbekistan, and Xinjiang never asked for a thing. Instead, they showered me with gifts of generosity and compassion. Bitterness and resentfulness can immerse my memories of Gebaya, or I can view the situation with curiosity and be intrigued. The choice was mine, and it freed me from negativity. The world showed up the way it was. The wise accepted it and flowed with its waves, storms, and sunny days.

Chapter 18

Crumbs of Intuition

"The mouth is stupid after eating because it forgets where the food came from."
—African proverb

"The one who plants grapes by the roadside, and the one who marries a pretty woman share the same problem."
—Ethiopian proverb

Finally! A break from the switchback roads and steep, winding paths. My legs celebrated as I pedaled effortlessly and glided along the sparkling asphalt. Yellow pavement markings—freshly painted—signaled I was one of the first cyclists to test out this portion of the highway. Brown terrain dotted with rows of green crops surrounded me. Knee-high plants neatly distributed in rows swayed as a slight breeze cooled my skin. Mountain outlines covered by a haze and thick, gray clouds lingered in the distance.

Suddenly, a familiar sound rang through the air. "Ahhhh ... llahhh-hu akbar!" The village of Waja's muezzin's call amplified by loudspeakers. His muffled a cappella voice of devotion reminded followers it was time to pray, but for me it was time to take a break.

I stopped at an outdoor café and a man gestured to a plastic chair next to him. It was a seat on the perimeter of a semicircle of eight men who spanned at least three generations. The elders sported gray beards and white turbans. Several middle-aged men and teenage boys wore long-sleeved, collared shirts, jeans, and sandals.

As I grabbed the seat, a new sound surprised my ears. The speech changed from tongue snapping and air gasping between words to husky voices rolling syllables through scratchy tracheas. It was my first encounter with Tigrinya, a Semitic language related to Arabic, Hebrew, Amharic, and Maltese. I shook hands with the villagers one at a time as they greeted me with the Arabic "Wassalamualaikum" salute used throughout the Islamic world, followed by a friendly "Welcome to Tigray."

The Tigray province had been home to the kingdom of Aksum, founded in the first century AD. Also called the Aksumite Empire, it spanned at its peak a large swath of northeastern Africa and the Middle East, from Yemen to Eritrea and eastern Sudan. The city of Aksum, in northern Tigray, was its capital. The kingdom of Aksum had played a central role in trading between the Roman Empire and India, exporting ivory, tortoise shells, rhinoceros horns, gold, and emeralds while importing spices and silk. Because of its proximity to the Red Sea and Nile River, the people of Aksum traded with Nubians, Persians, and Egyptians.

Aksum has immense religious significance. According to the *Kebra Nagast*, a 700-year-old Ethiopian text, the Queen of Sheba—Sheba once comprised what is now Ethiopia and Yemen—traveled to Jerusalem, where she bore King Solomon a child. As mentioned several chapters earlier, their son, Menelik I, is said to have brought the Ark of the Covenant to Ethiopia after a visit to his father in Jerusalem. Many Ethiopians believe it resides in Our Lady Mary of Zion Church in the city of Aksum. Locals claim that only one man, the so-called "guardian," may lay eyes on the Ark, and he can never leave the chapel grounds.

He will stay at his post until his death, when a successor, to be named by him, will assume the responsibility.

Tigrayans traditionally wear white clothes with little adornment. Women wear long-sleeved white dresses that reach their ankles and are made of fine material. Men dress in pants that fit tightly from the ankle to the knee but are baggy from the knee to the waist. Tigrayans are known for their immense pride. They view themselves as mighty warriors who fended off Italian imperialists in 1896 during the battle of Adwa. This was the first crushing defeat of a European army during the colonial era. They are also credited with spearheading the 1991 overthrow of the Derg military junta, ending the 14-year dictatorship of Mengistu Haile Mariam.

For over two decades, the Tigrayans occupied most government seats based on their affiliation with the Tigray People's Liberation Front (TPLF) even though as an ethnic minority they comprise only six percent of the Ethiopian population. Many citizens loathe the TPLF for usurping power and using it against the majority Oromo and Amhara, who represent over 60 percent of the country's population.

Originally, Tigray was forest-clad mountain terrain, with a climate that provided adequate rain for farming. However, during the civil war (1974-1991), opposing forces cut down most of Tigray's trees to starve the population.

In 1991, after the civil war, the government undertook a project to end drought in the region. Workers terraced mountain slopes at elevations as high as 2,500 meters above sea level. This conserved rainwater for use during the agricultural season. Villagers also terraced vast stretches of fields. This was done by collecting stones from eroded mountain sediments and stacking them into walls. Locals planted eucalyptus trees on the highest terrace, creating a new microclimate. Several years later, Tigrayans boasted that their territory had a terraced area larger than Italy's entire landmass.

Only a few moments earlier, as I'd pedaled to the village of Waja, admiring the shelf-like mountain slopes, I thought of the negative stories I'd heard from the Amhara and Oromo about the Tigray. "They are selfish" and "Don't trust them" were frequent admonitions. Despite the rumors, I was excited to explore this region of Ethiopia, the ancestral home of the Tigray, and become acquainted with their customs and quirks.

Tribalism and rivalries exist everywhere—Pakistan and India, South Korea and Japan, Turkey and Kurdistan. Border regions often have bloody histories that, in the minds of locals, are still very much alive. When family members fall victim to an atrocity, life becomes a trauma-induced nightmare that repeats generation after generation. My adventures have taught me that people are just people. The tales they believe separate them into tribes differentiated by the gods they pray to, the animals they eat, the perceived corruption and greed of one group toward another, or oft-disputed borders. My prior experiences made me confident that the Tigrayans weren't bad, merely different.

So, here I was in the Tigray Province, sitting among three generations of men who just greeted me as though I were a fellow Muslim. Hearing "wassalamualaikum" opened a torrent of memories. I flashed back to sword-carrying Omanis gifting me cotton *dishdashas* to shield me from the Middle Eastern sun and locals from the Arabian Peninsula who had filled my water bottles with camel milk, professing its nutrient-dense properties by flexing their biceps. The thick, sour drink had kept me going during 80-kilometer cycling spurts in the desert when no towns or shops were available. I recalled Bangladeshi friends I referred to as *bhai* (brother) teaching me to navigate the chaotic streets of Dhaka and relieving me of the fear of becoming capital-city roadkill. The noise and sheer quantity of vehicles had rattled me. Having no confidence in my ability to cycle through one of the most densely populated countries in the world, my brothers organized group rides to serve as warm-up training. Thinking of the Turkish man who lent me the keys to his apartment while he worked the night shift imbued my mind with warmth and peace. All it had taken was a 10-minute, gesture-infused conversation for his offer of generosity. My crumbs of intuition told me this village was hospitable and safe.

I sat with the men for a few moments and chatted up a thin, bald guy who wore a collared shirt of dark maroon and had a firm grasp of English. After a few minutes of chatter about family and work, he offered me a tour of his farm.

"Leave your bike here. It will be fine."

"Uhh ... are you sure?"

After enduring so many Ethiopians hassling me for money and ravaging their way through the contents of my panniers, skepticism was almost a given.

"No problem." He shouted something to one of the older men. "My father will watch over your bicycle."

I reminded myself that I was in another ethnic region and the people were likely to have different values, morals, and stories. The countless gifts of hospitality and genuine kindness I'd received from Muslims on my earlier journeys had built up credibility points. The opportunity to visit an Ethiopian farm would most likely not present itself again, and in my experience villages and rural areas had been safer. Most of the village dwellers I'd met on my travels focused more on relationships than on greed or con artistry. In cities in the developing world, rampant unemployment had citizens stinging each other for pollen to fertilize their tribe, but not so much in the rural areas. My gut told me they were honest, and I made a decision. *The crumbs of intuition.*

"Sure. Let's go. I can't wait to see your farm." I hopped on the back of my new acquaintance's motorcycle.

As we sped along the paved roadway, my mind traveled to dark places. *What if he takes me into the bush and chops me into cutlets of hyena feed? This could be the grave error that ends my tale. What a stupid decision!'* I was thousands of kilometers from Oman, Turkey, or Bangladesh, and entirely dependent on the goodwill of my new acquaintance.

We turned onto a grassy path and left the village streets. My intuition warred with itself. *Why were we so far from the main road?* My eyes rolled into my head. Tendrils of terror started to wrestle my heart. I grasped the seat for dear life as we bumped along the meandering pathway. Why did I consent to a ride on a motorcycle? Were there not a million other ways to die! I was sure the risks would catch up with me as I stared in fear at the oncoming stones and muddy potholes.

I was caught helplessly in a web my mind was spinning at a breathtaking pace: *What was the best way to contort myself during a crash? Plunge shoulders-first to maintain the ability to walk? Perhaps it was better to land on my back while attempting a gymnastics roll while tucking my chin into my chest?*

Suddenly, my host spoke up.

"See that place. Tigers live there and eat the sheep. Big problems[1]."

"What? Tigers? Oh, you mean lions? Do they attack people?"

"Sometimes. Not all the time, though."

This just keeps on getting better. If I survived the motorcycle ride and could fend off this guy and his cronies, then hungry predators were waiting for me. Visions of drooling, saber-toothed cats pouncing on me from treetops had me quivering in my hiking boots. One swipe of a claw would thrust me into the underworld. I was 78 kilograms of lean, mean meat. Any ravenous beast would devour me first since the villager was a few "injeras" leaner than I was. As we sped along, I scanned the woods for glowing eyes, tawny fur, and salivating mouths of hunger.

A few minutes later, we zoomed out of the forest and into a lion-free zone. Rocky fields of unkempt weeds became organized rows of green leaves and stalks of hardened plants. Tanned faces topped by turbans shot up and down amidst the pastures as farmers gripped soiled roots with gloved hands. As I scanned the surrounding landscape, a set of white-domed, concrete structures caught my attention.

"This is my farm. Those are carrots. We export to China and the United States." He motioned toward green plants sprouting from brown soil.

---

1. There have never been feral tigers in Africa, so I have to assume that as a non-native speaker of English, he was confusing "tiger" with "lion."

A sigh of relief rushed through my body as the nervous energy dissipated, leaving me almost limp with relief. My friend really did own a plantation, and he really did want to give me a tour.

"These workers make 1,500 birr (US $50) in one month and help me so much," he said calmly.

"How is their work schedule?"

"They work 10 to 12 hours per day and we offer lunch and dinner."

Fifty dollars. I couldn't fathom how anyone survived on that. Their low wages and long hours reeked of exploitation. What profits did my companion make? Was he underpaying them or trying to conduct business in his version of the best way? It must have been a genuine struggle for the workers to provide meals for their families and pay for their homes. The confident yet humble tone in which this guy answered signaled he didn't have any malicious intent. Maybe he paid them the standard wage.

I thought of my 17-year-old self. I'd spent my weekdays heaving wooden scraps and unused concrete blocks into giant trash bins on Michigan construction sites. I lifted, squatted, and carried sheets of metal, asbestos, and pressboard until my youthful body ached. My boss told me I needed to be a leader by moving faster and disposing of the garbage more efficiently. He said I wasn't working to my potential. "You call yourself strong. Go! Go!" he'd shouted.

The work exhausted me. Seven dollars per hour wasn't cutting it. After a few weeks, I built up the courage to demand a raise. I convinced myself I ought to make at least $10 per hour. The sweat, sore muscles, and sunburn weren't worth $280 per week.

I gave my manager an ultimatum, but he refused. I stomped away, tossing pieces of broken wood into the air. In reality, I was replaceable. Any kid my age with a decent work ethic would've taken the job. Of course, my naïve teenage self hadn't known that.

In 1997 I'd earned over five times as much per week as Ethiopian farm employees in a month in 2019. Twenty-two years later and several thousand kilometers away from that construction site, I was ashamed of that teenager. I was a spoiled kid who thought he was a hard worker. I wanted to fly those workers to Michigan, search for my old boss, and work alongside the Ethiopians to redeem myself from the past embarrassments. We'd sweat together while sharing Granny Smith and Fuji apples.

Could anyone survive on their salary? The engineer in me resurfaced, and I did the quick mental calculations. If the average worker consumed only teff and 100 grams of teff has 250 calories and the average male workers requires at least 3,000 calories[2] to sustain themselves, they must consume 36 kilograms of teff each month. If the cost of teff is $1.33 per kilogram, they need at least 48 dollars per person every month for their minimum nutritional requirements. They'd need a lot more if they had families. I hoped the villagers had their own land to grow food. Luckily, the boss provided meals.

My inner deliberations came to a halt as we arrived at the concrete domes and my friend jumped off his bike. Green meadows and crops of varying sizes surrounded me. Jumbles of plants shot into the air, giving the brown soil a clean aroma. A group of pink and yellow flowers aligned in an intricate circular design separated the domed structures.

"This is where the workers stay. Everyone eats lunch here together. Let's get some food. It's fresh."

Empty floor space with a wide column in the middle comprised the dome's interior. Small metal benches lined the perimeter as sweaty employees picked at the day's meal with their bare hands. A woman behind a counter used both arms to handle a wooden ladle that must have been half her size as she struggled to mix the fresh grub. A mist of steam doused the area with an aroma of vegetables and spices. I stepped closer to inspect her work, and my eyes feasted on a colorful array of green, white, yellow, and orange. It was simple, yet promised to be delicious.

---

2. Dietary Guidelines for Americans 2020-2025, Office of Disease Prevention and Health Promotion.

A pile of raw, unpeeled onions lay on the floor next to the woman. The tennis-ball-sized veggies gleamed with red, cancer-cell-destroying energy. They appeared to be the same vegetables I'd purchased several weeks ago at a grocery store in Michigan. Maybe they were from Ethiopia. Flashbacks of my dad hoisting mesh bags of onions into our cart entertained my brain.

"We have steamed vegetables with bread. Take a plate."

I nearly ripped off the chef's arm as she scooped a pile of broccoli, onions, cauliflower, and carrots onto a plate and handed it to me. My mouth foamed at the prospect of taking a break from injera and shiro. My taste buds craved a rest from the tangy, fiery mixture of crushed beans and injera, which I had consumed for several weeks straight. I longed for change. Now I had a fresh, healthy one.

The meal was for the workers. They deserved it. Their bodies must've ached from hours of bending over in the sun. They struggled for a meager salary while I had the resources to order three meals at any street shack.

I felt embarrassed by my ravenous cravings and reminded myself that I'm not my thoughts, which were out of control. Let them flow. Bubbly waves crashing on the shore.

I said grace in Arabic: "Allah *hamdulillah*." I was thankful for the sweat and pain that had produced the meal on my plate. I was humbled, reduced to a micro-version of a man. As the steaming vegetables burned my fingers, I thought of thrown-out leftovers. I remembered how my university friends had poked fun at me for eating their pizza crust. To them I was a "cheapskate," a "bum." After an 18-year-old's explanation of global food scarcity, they continued their juvenile rants. Fuming, I chomped on leftovers even though I knew I had broken North American social norms. The laughter and pointing didn't surprise me. They were ignorant. It wasn't their fault.

I promised myself that day that I'd never stand back and watch someone toss a piece of food in the trash again. My crumbs of stubbornness were still alive 20 years later. Avoiding external conflict leads to inner strife. In South Korea, it was common to see others ordering large amounts of food, taking pictures and uploading them to social media, and letting half of it go to waste. Their vegetables could have been imported from this farm. Sticking up for humanity and the Ethiopians was imperative. I needed to speak up and not let their sweat go to waste.

After lunch, my friend took me around his farm. He gained my confidence by pushing the mute button on my growling stomach. After the meal, my breath and heartbeat slowed, and the tension in my wrists dissipated. Maybe if he'd given me a spicy plate of injera and wat I'd have been on edge. The mild, salted cuisine relaxed me into a state of trust.

What about my bike and panniers? They'd been out in the open for several hours. Did the village children take every banana and string of cotton? What about the elderly man who was supposed to watch it? Had he grown weary and retreated for an afternoon nap? Someone could lift my quick-release tire levers in a few seconds. They were worth at least $100 a pop—two months of a farm worker's salary.

We sped past the lion-infested bush and cruised in and out of potato and cabbage fields. Moments later, the village elders were lounging in the same plastic seats I'd seen them in, chewing the same khat leaves, and sipping the same cups of coffee. My bike was leaning against the same wooden pole, and my bags and belongings were intact. It was like time had frozen.

My worries faded. I felt lucky to have had a special experience with my new buddy. He dropped me off and zoomed away to take care of personal business, but I was thankful for his hospitality.

I should have trusted the crumbs of intuition at my disposal. My brain had created threats that didn't exist. Survival instincts, however, often trumped higher-order critical thinking, and I became hyper aroused. I clouded my mind by doubting my intuition. When faced with a grand error, mind control is paramount. Hesitation can lead to more mistakes under pressure.

My values were strengthened by the farm tour. Observing the worker's glistening faces invigorated my enthusiasm for food conservation. Even though it was a gift courtesy of the farm owner, I felt guilty eating the cooked vegetables the plantation workers had spent days cultivating. The memories of all the wasted food had me feeling guilty and I decided I'd never let a single drop of sweat go to waste. From then on, every crumb on my plate was a cherished grain of nutrients. My mouth received a valuable education and will never forget where my meals come from.

Chapter 19

The Elephant Within

"The slimming of an elephant and the losses of a wealthy man are not noticeable."
—Ethiopian proverb

I'd been at it since hearing the roosters crow that morning, weaving up and down hills in the blazing sun. I was spinning on my metal machine, my waist hoisted above the seat, pumping my legs as my bike and I battled a headwind. Villagers along the road swatted at their animals with long wooden canes. Children stood still as thousand-year-old trees with roots embedded deep in the earth's crust. Their glassy eyes followed me up the path, and their heads turned in my direction. The breeze became cooler by the minute as the sun dropped behind mountains. I was on my way to Mekele, the next large city along the highway and the jumping-off point to the Afar region. I couldn't wait to sweat in the world's hottest location.

I realized that if I didn't move swiftly the Ethiopian night could drop its curtain on me, but I enjoyed the tension. Quick decisions about sleeping had my stomach buzzing with life. I'd been at it for three weeks and 1,200 kilometers. By now I was used to the routine.

A day on the road had three stages. Stage one: the slumber, first wind, and midday break. In the morning, my back was sore from uneven mattresses in $1-per-night shacks or from lying on concrete. My neck cracked and my spine jolted itself into place. Breakfasts of nuts and fruit dragged on while I savored the downtime. I chugged water until my bladder fought back. I somehow believed that the more liquid I consumed at the day's start, the more obedient my body would be when my brain attempted to silence rebellions of soreness. After loading up the bike, my aching thighs and calves needed a pep talk. "Come on! Get ready for work!" The first hour was the toughest. Sharp pulses of oncoming arthritis attacked my wrists because gripping my handlebars, once so trivial, drained my mental fortitude. Ankles cracked in protest as my tendons and ligaments became loosened by the sudden motion. After a few uphill climbs, the pain withered away. I was warm.

Two to three hours later, it was time for a breather. I scoured the landscape for a café, tree, bridge, or culvert where I could protect myself from the sun, refuel my body, chat with locals, or take a nap. The duel with midday laziness began as my body stiffened from the contrast between action and rest. My mind searched for excuses: heat too intense. Wind too punishing. Distance too far. Villagers too friendly and talkative.

When I got lucky, I was in a mud shack with a pile of food and an endless supply of water. My brain rehydrated. Comfort glued me to my chair. On unlucky days, I shared slabs of concrete or rock beds with scorpions, ants, and other insects. Even then it wasn't too bad. My "don't bother them and they won't bother me" logic never failed. I have never stomped, swatted, or swung unless provoked. The tiny creatures had the right to live, and I considered myself a guest in their territory. They have always treated me with hospitality, allowing me to rest next to their holes, hills, and webs. Even insects sensed my fatigue.

I grew attached to my "spot," whichever one I picked out for the night, and its unique characteristics. Insects became wordless companions, a tree my refuge, and rocks a familiar mattress. I was often awakened by rapturous moments in my vivid dreams, surrounded by bugs and critters. Snapped back to the reality of sweat pools, I stretched my aching muscles while admiring the moist, dark outline of a human body on the ground (punctuated by the deep-brown shade left by my glutes). A few seconds later, the abstract sweat art had evaporated.

Once I motivated myself to continue, stage two began. The sun's reflection off the pavement abused me until tears soaked my eyes. It had lasted 10 to 30 minutes but felt like an entire afternoon. My vision became foggy, tears streamed down my cheeks, and I continued at a slow pace or pulled over into the shade to let it pass. Once the crying spell was over, the self-talk started. "It's only a sun overdose. This is part of the journey."

After a few more hours of pedaling, I stopped for a late-afternoon meal. Once I'd replenished my energy, I had a newfound zest to tackle the road and finish the day strong. Surges of glucose to my muscles and brain uplifted my spirit. The sun's rays weakened and transformed the sky into a burning mosaic of pink and dark red. Cool air was my savior. The accumulated momentum had me ready to push on throughout the night. Thinking had ceased, and I reached speeds unattainable during other times of the day. I was alert and had to convince myself to stop before daylight disappeared. My body was a high-performance machine.

Long days had resulted in nights of nine to 10 hours of sleep. Not a tossing-and-turning, semi-conscience rest. A blacked-out state only a major earthquake could disrupt.

I was accustomed to my daily routine and had become comfortable with pressure. Swift action and spontaneity were normal. Impending darkness didn't rattle me as it had a few weeks ago. Maybe I had learned to trust myself and play from excellence instead of panic.

I reflected on Tetsuya's calmness. At last, I related to his unwavering stillness in the face of unpredictability. He'd developed the equanimity necessary to master the world's chaos. I was learning to become a bigger rock so the pebbles tossed at me ricocheted to the ground. My shield of positivity triumphed over malicious behavior.

As I continued up an incline, watching the sun hide behind yellow mountain peaks, a sound as loud as a gunshot murdered the late-afternoon stillness. My bicycle stopped dead. Was my tire frame busted? I could never find parts out here. The Internet information had warned me that self-sufficiency was a must in Ethiopia. I turned around to see my luggage rack held up by my rear tire. The rack's left joint had snapped, and a screw was missing (too many bumps and rattles). There was no way I could continue while carrying my bags. What now? With the tire caught under the rack, I couldn't even push my bike to the next village.

One choice was to ditch my bags, use my tools to pry the rack off the tire, and push the bike to the next village. Or I could choose the bags over the bike and abandon my hunk of metal and rubber. The other alternative was to hitchhike to Mekele and search for a mechanic.

I contemplated traveling with nothing. Leaving my possessions in the sand for a lucky villager. Complete freedom. One pair of clothes, passport, and money. The essentials with no extra weight. No fear of having my goods stolen. Non-attachment. Gautama Buddha walked through India and Nepal with nothing before his enlightenment. I could simplify things and complete my journey on foot. Rid myself of the metal-and-rubber contraption and push my flesh-and-blood machine to the limit. Toe blisters. Knee and ankle pain. I wanted to own the agony. Observe it at its source and conquer it. Limp to the finish line. Nothing worth achieving comes without a struggle.

I thought of the cash I'd spent on the bags. They'd run me half the monthly rent of my studio apartment. My panniers were more expensive than my worn-out shirts, Mongolian tent, and spare tubes. That hard-earned money would be gone. During my next trip, I could leave my luggage at home and take nothing. The taste of freedom accompanied by non-attachment from material items must be more succulent than an apple after a week-long hunger strike. That flavor had to wait.

Mechanical issues were commonplace on bike tours, and the locals' ingenuity always had saved me. In rural Mongolia, for example, a man had rummaged through a scrapyard and tied together two metal rods that functioned as a makeshift spoke and lasted a thousand kilometers. It took three days of tracking down mechanics and welders, with whom I communicated via body language, to get the job done. In Tajikistan, I went through a new Russian tire every day. The rocky paths and potholes were too much for my thin tires and hybrid bike. Something told me Ethiopia would be no different. Everything would be fine.

I waved down a van headed toward Mekele and watched the workers tie my bike to the luggage rack. A man half my size rested the bottom frame on his shoulders, grabbed the ladder with one hand, and pulled himself up each step while maintaining a shiny-toothed grin.

I didn't have to speak. The guy read my facial expression like a fortune-teller.

"Don't worry," he said. "You no problem."

I came from the land of lawsuits. Slip on the ice if a neighbor doesn't shovel their driveway? Lawsuit. Burn yourself with McDonald's hot coffee? Call a lawyer. It was refreshing to spend time in a country with fewer rules. No more worries about my prized possession. If my bike tumbled down a mountain, I could buy another and bring home an Ethiopian souvenir. It was only metal and rubber.

After three weeks of moving at the pace of an overweight turtle, being in a motorized machine was surreal. A universe of adventures zoomed by. Trees. Children. Thatched houses. Steeply inclined roads. Nobody paid any attention to the world outside our safe compartment.

While I sat in the van, my mind ran through the stark differences in travel speed and how they had affected me. When moving fast, borders and towns had become more separate, underscoring the imaginary lines drawn on the map. Planes and vehicles catapulted me into the chaos of the underdeveloped world. One minute I was watching a movie or taking a nap or chomping on snacks, the next moment horns, music, beggars, and the stench of fermenting trash took over. Rides, hotels, drugs, prostitutes were on offer. It forced me to sink or swim.

While riding the bike, everything changed gradually. Quiet, rural paths became louder and wider until roaring engines, sirens, and horns replaced chirping birds and my squeaky chain. Barren terrain of sand, rock, and sparse patches of grass changed to concrete and asphalt. Dry, sandy air turned into a smoky, exhaust-filled atmosphere that left the corners of my eyes with chunks of black mucus. Tall buildings loomed in the distance, inspiring me to daydream for hours about the modern services and conveniences that lay ahead. The transition was less startling while pedaling.

I had changed. The inflated inner narrator would've been irate over taking a vehicle. *Don't be weak and get off your bike. Push your big hunk of metal and rubber*!

I realized I had nothing to prove. During unpredictable situations, the only choice was to ride the wave until it passed.

While sitting in that van, shimmers of calm moved over me. I had more equanimity and was learning to stay cool while the world threw its stones and threatened me with its shovels.

After an hour, we arrived in the big city. The vehicle dropped me and my bicycle off at a hotel, and I crashed hard that night.

The next morning, I woke up early to explore Mekele. Economic prosperity was everywhere. Shopping malls, posh cafes, and upscale hotels filled downtown with a buzz I hadn't experienced in other parts of Ethiopia. People strutted with an air of confidence. Men wore designer aviator sunglasses and sparkling sneakers. Women painted themselves with imported cosmetics and clicked their high heels on paved sidewalks. For a split second, I thought I was in a fancy neighborhood in New York City.

Mekele has a deep history. In the 1880s it was known as The Emperor's city because Yohannes IV, the Emperor of Ethiopia and ruler of Tigray, chose Mekele for its proximity to rich agricultural centers and the Afar salt region. The city's growth can be attributed to the establishment of residential quarters for the nobility and court servants. Yohannes leveraged his political capital by establishing a trade market in Mekele, drawing on northern trade routes and salt caravans running through the town. The Italians, who occupied the city in the

1930s, also contributed to its modernization by reorganizing roads, installing water pipelines, electricity, and postal services.

Peering into a coffee shop, I saw a pencil drawing of an elephant and reflected on the giant beast's symbolic significance. According to Hindu texts, the god Ganesha, represented by an elephant, is a symbol of success, wealth, and prosperity. Ganesha-like beings disguised as humans pranced around me in their material abundance. I felt out of place in Mekele. Its chic cafés and upscale restaurants were alien after weeks of meals served in wooden shacks and open, hilly terrain. My eyes stung with pain as multistory buildings masked the area's natural beauty. The concrete edifices, blaring horns, and overpowering colognes left my senses shocked and my mind appalled.

I was a different elephant. One who went too long without spraying himself clean with his trunk. I was a beast whose dusty shirt, soiled socks, and oil-drenched skin emitted the pungent stink of ruggedness and raw, wild energy. I'd sunk my tusks into the same two foods almost every day. Hunger, thirst, and fatigue were familiar. My baby fat had disappeared. I was the elephant that had stomped away from the herd, an animal striving to tame itself while becoming less civilized.

I felt the change in myself as I sat in that café, surrounded by modernity, and stared at the pencil sketch. Amid comfort, I itched for discomfort. Amid safety, I yearned for danger. While taking a dip in Mekele's deep pool of amenities, I thirsted for the stinging winter wind. Struggle had hardened me. I blasted through my limiting beliefs. My momentum had me ready for more unpredictability. Mekele made my blood gurgle.

I took advantage of the city's comforts by finding a bicycle mechanic the following morning. He wasn't just any repairman. This guy had traveled abroad with Ethiopia's top cyclists and helped them deal with mechanical issues mid-race. With that experience, he might've been the best bike technician in the country. Thankfully, my bike had broken down near Mekele. He knew what to do, and it was ready a few hours later. No price gouging. No haggling. Only a big smile and a fixed machine. My broken piece of metal and rubber had become a bicycle once again.

While in Mekele, I purchased a flight from Aksum back to Addis Ababa. I still had about ten days left on the bike and figured a flight would help maximize my time to enjoy Ethiopia instead of taking a two-day long bus ride back to the capital right before my flight to Seoul.

While pedaling back to my hotel that evening, I ran into a group of cyclists coming back from a ride in the mountains. Decked out in helmets, sports sunglasses, and form-fitting shorts and shirts, they shot past me in a single file.

"Hello! Where are you from?" A man smiled and pulled up next to me.

"I'm from the United States. I cycled here from Addis."

The man whistled and yelled to his friends. They u-turned and before I knew it, I was shaking hands with 7 guys on bikes.

"Wow! Addis? Let's go eat together. I'll buy your meal. You must be hungry after all that work," the man said.

Over dinner, I learned that my new friend was from Eritrea, a northern border country a mere 170 kilometers away. The two nations had a long, bloody history. In 1974 the Marxist Derg staged a coup on Haile Selassie, triggering a civil war that lasted until 1991. The Tigrayan People's Liberation Front (TPLF) and the Eritrean People's Liberation Front (EPLF) joined forces to overthrow the Derg and install a transitional government in Addis Ababa.

After fighting side by side to end Marxist military leadership, the two groups became enemies. During the next few years, the TPLF governed Ethiopia, while the EPLF led the newly independent nation of Eritrea. The groups came into conflict over a series of border disputes, a conflict heightened by philosophical differences in ruling. The EPLF was determined to have Eritrea liberated from Ethiopian rule as a single state despite its nine linguistic groups and two major religions (Islam and Christianity). Conversely, the TPLF's primary goal was forming a Tigrayan state. In 1998 Ethiopian forces attacked an Eritrean platoon, killing five officers and triggering a three-year war that resulted in a death toll that some claim exceeded 100,000. Tensions continued in the following years, until Abiy

Ahmed ended the conflict in 2018 by implementing a peace treaty, which won him the Nobel Peace Prize.

It was great to see Ethiopians cycling with a guy from Eritrea. What a grand symbol of harmony after such a long, bloody dispute. Bicycles were a tool for friendship-building, even between rival countries. In the end, people are people despite differences of opinion. World peace inspired me to pedal forward.

Chapter 20

To Hell with Comfort

"Counsel and advise him, but if he refuses to listen, then let adversity teach him."
—Ethiopian proverb

"Ears that do not listen to advice accompany the head when it is chopped off."
—African proverb

Hell.

Every Ethiopian I'd encountered characterized Afar using the same word. The value in experiencing hell must have been related to appreciating heaven. If heaven was so splendid, then I needed hell. I itched for self-imposed combat, so hell called me with its raspy voice.

My mind descended into fantasy. Children hurled rocks of fire. My tires popped from the volcanic heat. Armed youngsters surrounded me, ready to forage through my panniers until I surrendered my sleeping bag and bananas. The gates were wide open. The youths challenged anyone who entered to come out alive. Only the strong survived. If I could laugh at a hellish reality, then nothing could stop me. This is the story of life.

"Afar is hell. You going and sweating in Afar. I no going there," said the Ethiopians in their highland villages.

I'd heard plenty of warnings. "Don't do it" became the motivation to "just do it." Don't move to South Korea. The peninsula is still at war." "Don't camp on that mountain. Wild boars will attack you." "Don't cycle across Western China. The people are terrorists." "Don't visit Pakistan. The Taliban will slit your throat." "Don't cycle across Ethiopia. Children will stone you." "Don't go to Afar. It's hot as hell."

Over the years, I had learned whose advice to follow. Did this person stay in their comfort zone? Where did they get their information? Even though warnings had frightened me, I went for it. Every bold decision pushed my limits and bliss waited for me at the end of the road.

Addis Ababa was a three-week bike ride behind me. After huffing and puffing up mountain passes, dodging flying stones, and exposing myself to the blistering sun, there was no way I'd pass on a journey to hell. It was February, one of the milder months in Afar, so it couldn't have been that bad. Militant attacks on tourists several years ago resulted in rigid safety requirements. My only choice was a guided tour. I stowed my bike at the tour office in Mekele and looked forward to a break from the saddle. Food, water, and safety. Worries about the big three had dominated my thoughts until then. Not anymore.

Off we went. This time in an SUV overloaded with water bottles. A thin guy in a white, cut-off T-shirt was my guide. Khat leaves dangled from his lips as he gripped the steering wheel. Our vehicle hugged and traversed mountain curves at speeds that had my stomach churning. Within one hour, the mountains vanished, and we found ourselves in a different world. We descended from an altitude of 2,200 meters to 125 meters below sea level in minutes. As we traveled farther from the ridges, goosebumps formed on my arms. I'd miss those goosebumps in a few hours.

We entered the Afar Triangle, an expansive desert landscape that divided Ethiopia, Eritrea, and Djibouti. Lava lakes. Steaming fissures. Eighteen species of scorpions. Villagers who hadn't changed their way of living for over 2,000 years. Even the microorganisms were unique; scientists came to Afar to study extremophiles, tiny microbes that live in "extreme" conditions, to investigate the possibilities of extraterrestrial life. Afar had everything needed to tickle an intrepid traveler's palate. This was the cradle of humanity. It began with the discovery of a 3.2-million-year-old humanoid fossil. No matter how strongly we believe in the story of nationalism, we are a single family of Ethiopians.

As our vehicle made its descent, the landscape flattened and crumb-sized black specs appeared in the distance. They looked to be shadowy camel caravans or ancient villages. Green plants vanished. Brown soil and baseball-sized rocks replaced turban-wearing locals. Paved roads became tire tracks in the barren ground. The air grew heavier, and the sunlight turned into a misty haze. A chalky gray sky added an extra dose of gloom as a faint melancholy descended on me. Even though I had many reasons to smile, the depression had me depressed.

Our vehicle skidded from side to side and left a smoky trail of dust. I gripped the bottom of my seat with one hand and tugged on my seatbelt with the other. If our SUV crashed, we'd spend eternity in hell. The driver chomped on chat leaves and sang along to the pop music blaring from the radio, unfazed by excessive speeds. My eyes widened as I glared at him. *Drive safely!* I wanted to yell. While on the bicycle, I had control. Now it belonged to someone else. I hadn't gone this fast since backpacking in India six years ago. This was why I'd transitioned to bicycle touring. My life was in the hands of a guy high off the local drug. Death should be on my terms, not his.

I simmered silently in my thoughts. Uptight tourists who didn't trust people who made the trip to Afar multiple times per week weren't cool. Several deep breaths later, I chilled out.

The hair-raising ride ended at one of the poorest villages I'd ever seen. Shelters were constructed of sticks and palm fronds bound with sandy pieces of cloth. Villagers had nailed plywood of varying sizes into walls and roofs. Stone foundations circled the dwellings' perimeter. Women were responsible for constructing the nomadic homes. They spent hours weaving palm fronds into mats.

As I strolled around, smiling people waved from inside their houses. They stood huddled together, cups of coffee in hand. Locals were a head shorter than inhabitants of the highlands and much thinner. I wondered whether their shelters kept them cool and how much protection they provided from sandstorms. Life here must've been tough.

"You will sleep here." The guide pointed to a thatched cot, a frame covered by a lattice made of a tree-derived material. I'd lay my head right beside a series of local homes in the middle of the desert.

"Perfect," I said with a smile. What a delight it'd be to crash under the stars alongside the villagers.

After spending a few minutes testing out the cot, we continued our tour. We drove through fields of brown interspersed with white patches. A few radio songs later, snowy powder surrounded us and we stopped the SUV. The cool air ceased blowing from the air conditioning vents, and the fiery climate took its toll. This was what locals referred to as the *gara*, or *fire wind*. My eyes teared and twitched. The hot earth breathed at point-blank range. Nose hairs fused together, and each inhalation brought me to the point of dizziness. A mad scientist had laced the atmosphere with the vapors of her superglue invention in a perverse attempt at biological warfare. The surreal environment literally took my breath away.

I got out of the car and stood in the middle of the world's second-largest salt flat, one of the lowest locations on earth. It hadn't always been this way. Tens of thousands of years ago, oceans covered Afar. Salt remained from the dried sea. But the primary reason for the white, crunchy grains lay beneath my feet: a huge, volcanic engine drew salt water from the nearby Red Sea, pushing it through the earth's crust. Sedimentary rocks deposited in marine settings were horizontal, but these stones tilted along massive cracks in the earth's surface, acting as fault zones.

Rail-thin men used pickaxes to split, lift, and shape the salt into slabs. Miners hoisted pearly blocks of salt above their waists and loaded them onto camels and donkeys. Their strength would've baffled a powerlifter. I turned away as glistening faces grimaced in pain. Bloodshot eyes stared through me. Their gazes communicated everything: *Don't stand there and watch, you spoiled wimp.*

Donkeys pinned to the ground by weighted blocks surrounded the men. Their hooves shifted in meek attempts to return to their feet. Disappointment. Hopelessness. Despair. Each animal had a different expression, but they had one thing in common: eyes wet with pain. The animals knew they'd never escape their hellish existence. Whips cracked across torsos, painful demands to get up and move. The animals whimpered on the ground while groaning in pain. They'd trot to camp to rest for a few hours and do it again the following day.

Even though they were a picture of suffering, the donkeys and camels displayed an unrivaled toughness. As their owners placed more weight on their backs, they tumbled to the sand. I imagined they'd throw in the towel. A few moments later, they crawled to their feet. The same pattern repeated for several minutes. Life must've tired them out, yet they never quit.

I turned my attention to a guy with a gray, hooded sweatshirt, blue shorts, and neon-green sandals. He was half my size, yet heaved blocks of dead weight onto his camel's back as sweat glistened on his shaved head. The man's choice of clothing had me intrigued. How could he wear a hoodie in this unforgiving heat? His ancestors had lived this way for over 2,000 years, and his body was biologically primed for superhuman feats of endurance. It was February in Afar and maybe the heat didn't faze him. Historical records from 1911 state that villagers worked naked during the summer months. Perhaps he felt chilly during Afar's version of winter.

His blood-red eyes locked with mine for a few seconds. His stare sent an electric chill through my torso. My arms shivered amid a blazing inferno. I clenched my fists and my shoulders tensed. This was his turf. What was I doing there? Was this ethical tourism? Maybe he didn't appreciate others gawking at him.

His eyes darted to the bottle of water in my hands. He cupped his palms together and tilted his head back, asking if he could have a drink.

A swimming pool of thoughts flooded my imagination. I wanted to teleport him to an oasis. Send him to Michigan with me in the summer and give him a vacation while exchanging our life stories over fresh cherries and strawberries. He deserved it after a grueling work schedule of 365 days a year.

This guy needed water, and our vehicle's trunk was full of it. I was on an all-the-water-you-can-drink tour. None of the villagers stopped to rehydrate. How did they keep going? I could switch places with the man before me. He'd cool off in the air-conditioned SUV while I loaded up the animals. Why did we have so much liquid? We weren't doing manual labor in the earth's hottest region. Women typically made water runs at 2 a.m., leaving their homes with donkeys and returning at 11 a.m. My water run was only a few steps, and in two days we'd never go through all the bottles in the back of our truck.

I handed the miner my drink. A few giant gulps later, he tossed the empty bottle to the side. Then he continued strapping blocks of salt to his animals. This for $2.75 US at the end of a 12-hour day.

The history of salt as money runs deep. The word "salary" comes from the Latin for salt, "sal" because it was a valuable commodity during the Roman Empire. Until 1930 salt blocks were used as currency in Afar. An Egyptian traveler first recorded its monetary use in the sixth century although many historians agree it existed long before then. The price of the salt bar, or *amole*, was a function of supply and demand, so it's no surprise that in ancient times salt was very cheap near the mines but worth its weight in gold in faraway locations where it was scarce. As a valuable export, it was subject to taxation at customs posts throughout the country.

Animals were frequently overloaded, and if they collapsed from fatigue on the road, merchants threw away amoles so their livestock could continue the arduous journey. During the rainy season, wastage risks were high, and villagers attempted to preserve their amoles by packing them in wood ashes under their hearth or suspending them above the fire from the roof. Animals robbed their owners at night by licking the salt, a temptation too great to control. Caravans included up to

15,000 animals. Amoles changed hands many times before winding up in cooking pots.

How many kilometers, I wondered, would this miner walk? Villagers made long treks to the highlands to sell salt blocks for 10 birr ($.33) each (the days of taxation and currency use were gone). As in ancient times, the price increased in proportion to distance from the mines, so merchants were incentivized to travel far. What an amazing feat of human endurance.

I stood there in shame—ashamed of every piece of meat I'd ever consumed. Ashamed of the new car I'd bought with my first paychecks after graduating from university. Embarrassed by my closet of unused outfits. My greed had tugged me toward a life of wastefulness. I was a pawn in a system that gave minor consideration to the destruction it had created. I'd been brainwashed by a culture that worships consumption. My energy-intensive actions caused the temperature to increase[1] in Afar. I had blame to bear.

The stinging reality of my softness awakened me. I'd forced myself to lift heavy objects to prevent a premature death related to overconsumption. My workplace was a cool classroom with fluorescent lighting. A utopia. Standing for six hours a day drained me—what a joke.

---

1. In pastoral communities in Ethiopia, climate-induced shocks and stresses, such as droughts and temperature increases, impacted water availability and led to animal deaths (Conway, 2008). There has been an increasing frequency of extreme water scarcity in Ethiopia because of global warming (Institute of Development Studies, 2008). The country has confronted severe droughts at least twice per decade for the last five to seven decades, with the most serious ones occurring in 1972–1973, 1984, and 2002–2003 (Mideksa, 2010; Tadege, 2007). The inhabitants of Afar believe droughts have divine origins and often pray for rain.

What about this trip? Flying to Ethiopia in search of truth and global knowledge? Couldn't I do that in my backyard without taking a plane? I questioned everything, but the damage was done. The best I could do to offset my wasteful behavior was to share these words and motivate others to live a more environmentally friendly lifestyle.

Observing the Afar miner ignited an inner blaze: Don't complain. Ever.

The SUV sped along white-encrusted flatlands, a highway in its saltiest form. The haze became disorienting and eerie. If zombies had arisen from the bleached, crumbling ground, I wouldn't have been surprised.

A few moments later, we arrived at another salt plain. This one had a whirlpool-sized hole of murky, blue water. Near the pool's edge I sampled the ground and coughed at the pungent flavor. It felt as if I'd inhaled a shot of wasabi with no sushi or soy sauce. Salt, in its natural state, is more potent than the condiment served in restaurants and sold in supermarkets.

Time to cool off. My insides vibrated at the thought of relief. An oasis of blue liquid in a Martian desert. I hurled myself into the water and felt a burn along my back. The jagged pool wall pierced my skin, but I didn't flinch. Excitement overpowered everything. The murky liquid was more viscous than anything that had ever touched my skin. Slimy blue molasses. It felt as if I'd waded through a hot tub whose contents had been mixed with salt from a dried ocean on Mars. The liquid was too thick to give a cooling effect. No matter how hard I tried to submerge myself, it pushed harder upward, making me super-buoyant. I was in a mysterious state of weightlessness, floating effortlessly across the pool. I stuck my face under and grimaced at the burning. The sodium and chloride ions seasoned me with an extra tablespoon of pain. Even bodies of liquid in Afar showed no mercy.

As I waded through the viscous salt water, I stared in awe at my surroundings. The dull, cracking landscape resembled an elderly woman's face. I was a microbe, floating on her wrinkles. Miners dug into her pores, creating creviced age spots. Bits of her salty skin were exchanged for flakes of paper, which, in turn, were swapped for goods and services. No one seemed to realize our entire world would become a wrinkled Afari fire pit in a few years if we continued on our path of economic growth while ignoring environmental externalities. "See what you've done!" she bellowed. "This is a preview!"

After squinting off the sting, I stepped out of the pool and my body felt crustier than it usually did after a good sweat. The white material solidified within minutes. I turned into a salt ghost.

We drove back to camp and prepared for nightfall. That evening, while I lay on an open-air bed, the sky gifted Afar with sporadic sprinkles of rain. *Give me rain! Give me relief!* The heavens must've sent angel tears. They wept for the villagers' harsh life.

As a pitter-patter of raindrops graced my skin, I stared at the misty sky. Afar had rendered my clothes crusty, sweat-soaked towels. My face tingled and twitched in discomfort. Mother Earth had nailed the doors shut. Christmas songs went off in my head as I reminisced. *Let it snow! Let it snow! Let it snow!* I stripped to my underwear. That was the best I could do. The hair on my legs and arms clung to me like a thermal blanket. Much too soon, the rain stopped. There was no escape.

My mind ran wild. The Afari mystified me. February was one of the coolest months in the region. I couldn't hack hell in its mildest form. How on earth did the Afari carry out their daily routines during the blazing summer months? Didn't they want to move to an easier place? Weren't they tired of life? Perhaps they had no choice but to sweat it out to make a living. Forget growing mangoes, coffee, or teff. Nothing but camels and the toughest humans on the planet could pull off survival here. People's ability to adapt to their surroundings, no matter how harsh, was awe-inspiring.

The next morning we went to Dallol, a geothermal desert 130 meters below sea level. I crept along an uphill walkway of red and gray stones that had once been magma. The ground crackled beneath my feet. The odor of spoiled eggs intensified as I inched closer to the hill's summit. A hydrogen sulfide breakfast. I covered my nose. The stink seeped through my fingers and continued its wrath. If I couldn't get rid of it, I'd have to enjoy it. I forced my brain to visualize Saturday mornings when my mother had cooked omelets and French toast. The smell of eggs frying in oil had my nose leading me out of bed during childhood. I grew nostalgic until the stink knocked me off memory lane. Afar eggs were a few months past their expiration date.

Once we crossed the hill, a science fiction movie began. I stood at the edge of the world's largest subaerial volcano. The sour odor reached its zenith. Towers and ridges of crystal. Hissing gas vents. Gurgling pools of bright-yellow sulfuric acid. Gray steam spouting into the air. The contrast between red sand, white salt, and yellow sulfuric acid riveted my gaze. African egg-drop soup.

As I walked deeper into the abyss, the colors became brighter and more varied. Yellows, whites, and oranges dominated the desert-scape. Terraced pools of sky-blue liquid were nature's watercolor masterpiece.

For a second, I pondered jumping into one of the boiling ponds. Wait. This was sulfuric acid, a tissue-destroying substance. A stroll around the abyss was the better choice.

I tiptoed along the terraced edges as a guide scolded me. The man pulled his pant leg up to his knees, revealing a series of blotchy scars. "Look here! The ground collapsed beneath me one time."

Don't play here. Be vigilant.

With its beauty and geological significance, how was this area not a UNESCO World Heritage site? Did the heat keep experts away? I was lucky to walk freely in such an extraordinary place. No fences, signs, or "Danger" signs. Only gurgling mounds of colorful terrain to explore as one's heart desired. Even more impressive, scientists predicted the entire Horn of Africa would break from the continent, giving birth to a new ocean. Layers of the earth's crust were pulling themselves apart along the Great Rift Barrier, exposing a layer of magma. While experiencing the odor, sights, and sounds of Dallol, I was also standing atop a volcanic engine.

After a stroll through the multi-colored abyss, the SUV sped us up the mountains, and we completed our journey to hell. We stopped at a restaurant on the way to Mekele, where tourists sprawled out on benches. People in drenched shirts complained of stomach cramps and lightheadedness. I hoped they'd recover after returning to the highlands. How terrible to develop heat stroke after traveling so far. I sent them wishes of health and strength.

The experience in Afar spurred me to reflect. I had trained myself to endure South Korea's climate without air-conditioners or fans. I bundled myself up on frigid nights with no heat to stimulate hormesis[2]. Whenever I second guessed myself, a voice screamed—often in the tone of a high school football coach—*Toughen up! No machine-made air for you!*

The air-conditioning culture in the economically privileged world outraged me. Michigan hospitals, shopping malls, and theaters were much colder than New Delhi or Guatemala City winter evenings. Locals carried jackets to protect them from cold air spouting out of every crevice in buildings constructed within the past hundred years.

How ironic our desire to control indoor temperatures as we babble on about climate change. It cools off inside, but outdoors it becomes hotter. Shouldn't we end the vicious cycle before we destroy ourselves? The Afari proved humans were capable of more.

---

2. Hormesis – mild oxidative stress associated with exercise, fasting, heat or cold exposure that can cause favorable adaptations in order to protect the body against more severe stresses and disorders.

What if we adopted new educational programs to motivate people to dismantle their temperature-control devices? A live-in coach would help residents of the developed world adopt a nature-aligned way of life. The program would start with one hour per day without air-conditioning in the summer and one hour without heat in the winter. We could increase the time by one hour every second day until everyone lived in homes ventilated by outdoor air. Wouldn't this result in a tougher, healthier, and agreeable human condition?

I'd love to be part of the movement. Despite being a guy who's slept on the ground for the past 10 years, I am sometimes tempted to crank up my floor heating in South Korea, especially when my body craves relief after hard exercise. I have no right to preach about something I don't practice all the time. The role would motivate me not to slip.

My first targets? The CEOs of Shell, Chevron, and ExxonMobil. Don't those responsible for polluting our world and spreading doubt about climate change deserve a proper education? The scene played out in my mind. Cushy leather chairs, each large enough to seat three middle-aged men from any village in South Asia. State-of-the-art computers discarded— "updated" a year after being acquired—and shipped as electronic waste to Ghana, where children burn them for the rare minerals they contain. Lunch meetings, where beet-red cheeks waggle while teeth chomp Kobe steak. Plump fingers clutch sterling silver forks while poking at French caviar. Cherry-sized Adam's apples shift while sipping German ice wine.

We could teleport them to a place they deny even exists. A personalized tour through hell—pin-striped suits, jet-black ties, and designer dress shoes intact. A stroll through Afar would awaken them to the havoc they've wreaked on the world. At the time of this writing, global warming doesn't affect oil executives and their families as it does the lives of millions in Bangladesh, Indonesia, or the Philippines, but in Afar they'd feel the heat of their decisions. People over profit instead of profit over people.

Schools worldwide could require every global citizen to complete a yearly "two weeks in Afar" educational program during summer vacation. We could teleport students to the Danakil Depression. They'd spend their days digging up salt, loading camels, and walking 20 kilometers back home. They'd exchange their Nike cross-trainers and smartphones for open-toe sandals and turbans. Youngsters would create lifelong memories by spending a few days in one another's footwear. Pupils would earn $3 a day. Some might call it child abuse, but aren't resilience, emotional intelligence, gratitude, adaptability, cross-cultural and environmental awareness qualities everyone should strive to develop? The ability to find my third or fourth wind has been one of the most important skills I've ever gained. Tour cycling helped me learn it. I'd sweat right next to them and let Mother Earth share her wisdom.

One mild summer day in South Korea, my students requested I turn on the air-conditioning. A visit to Afar every year could help with those requests. One by one, participants would sweat themselves into environmentalists. They'd dread the slightest increase in temperature the following year. After the first visit, beans would replace chicken on dinner plates. Closets would have only three outfits. They'd ask for bicycles instead of gasoline-sucking cars.

Lifelong friendships would form. The camaraderie of completing an arduous training program would rear its flushed face. Hindus sweating alongside Muslims. Han Chinese hoisting blocks next to Uyghurs. Trump supporters grunting next to Trump haters. Imagine participants talking out their disagreements. Flashes of anger would cause losses of precious energy, energy needed to load salt blocks onto camels. In hell, energy efficiency takes priority over personal differences. Egos deflate to the size of a fire ant.

The only way to mitigate climate change is for individuals to change their beliefs. What if we make training in Afar a required educational program before anyone earns a dollar, euro, or Chinese yuan? With great money comes great power and, as Voltaire said, "With great power comes great responsibility." Come to hell and strengthen yourself into a humbler, more tolerant, more resilient, and more culturally intelligent global citizen. Become a part of the solution to the greatest challenge of our time. Let adversity teach and lead the way.

Chapter 21

The Holy Commute

"No matter how many times you wash a goat, it will still smell like a goat."
—Ethiopian proverb

The highlands cast their spell on me. Goosebumps formed on my inner forearms. Mountain air whisked and whooshed. The brisk wind pelted my skin, providing relief from yesterday's onslaught of heat. I snaked along roads that cut into spectacular cliffs. The sight of unfamiliar, jagged slopes had my dimples aching with delight. Stone buttresses rose out of the ground like the torsos of malevolent ancient spirits. Absorbed by my environment, I lost myself in the euphoria of another uphill climb.

My goal was to tackle a new giant. In Afar, I'd heard about the rock-climbing monks of Abuna Yemata Guh. The legend of the church hewn out of rock for Father Yemata, founder and builder of the world's most perilous holy site, reeled me in with the promise of a knee-shaking experience.

Since the fifth century, priests have climbed to their holy sanctuary every day, and no one has perished along the treacherous climb. Legend has it that the patron saint protected those who fell with wind, returning them to the ledge. Father Yemata chose the spot for increased proximity to heaven, enabling pilgrims to meditate and pray with greater clarity. Others argue it's a strategic location to avoid enemies since Ethiopian Christians were being persecuted at the time of its construction. Whatever the case, followers made the spiritual quest, risking their lives while climbing jagged walls. Parents even took their babies on the hazardous trek to get baptized. There had to be mystical energy up there, and I yearned to let it run through me.

The table-shaped rocks on the distant horizon were mesmerizing. As I pedaled on, small hills changed to yellow-and-red behemoths. Cliffs shot straight up into the clouds. The absence of terraced inclines resulted in clammy hands and an eager heart. How is a guy with no climbing experience supposed to scale the vertical slopes and reach the church?

Finally, I arrived at the edge of the mountain, stared at the giant rock, and found an uphill trail. The sand-covered path weaved around a set of chest-high boulders leading up to a three-dimensional tower of phantasmal proportions. Awe-struck by my surroundings, I cocked my head back and glanced up while my boots crackled along the sandy trail. Horizontal crevices shaped by wind gusts had my mind screaming with delight amidst the silence. The spiritual energy had me in deep focus.

After an hour of creeping up the trail, a giant halted me in my tracks. "Come on, you wimp!" It taunted. "Look at you trembling!" The stone cliff shot straight up and had me by at least four body lengths. Flimsy branches and rocky wedges too small for my hands to grip dotted the wall. The ledge I stood on was a bicycle-length wide. No net, no rope, no soft surface to land on. If the unthinkable occurred, I'd become a falling mound of helplessness. This wall was a death sentence.

So what's it gonna be? After six hours on the bike and one hour of hiking, you're going to turn back?

How many tourists had injured themselves here? I was an intrepid guy, but heaving myself up a vertical slope was a whole other animal.

Several minutes later, a group of Thai women and three Ethiopian priests confronted the same challenge. Without hesitation, the first lady slid her fingers into the wall's grooves. At the halfway mark, she stopped, and her legs shuddered. Nowhere to go. Two monks scaled the rock and guided her feet. Another effortlessly glided up and seized her hand, pulling her to the next step. Amazing agility and strength. The holy men must've been in their early seventies, but had the balance and coordination of twentysomethings.

"Right foot. Right hand. Left foot. Left hand," they said in English while guiding her moves. Moments later, the traveler stood on a ledge, panting in exhaustion. The woman gasped for air with her eyes closed. How lucky she was to be alive.

Faces red with terror and adrenaline, the other women climbed to safety one at a time. Observing the small Thai ladies overcome their fears made me want to prove I could do it.

The priests motioned to me. "You! Up!"

These guys had been making the trek their entire lives. Their presence gave me confidence. God had to be on my side. I glared at the heavens and asked the saints to catch me.

"You! Go up!" They repeated.

I pried off my shoes and socks so my feet could better grip the rock and started. The desert heat rose off the sandstone. I jammed my toes and fingers into the rocky grooves and pulled myself up. After a few steps, I glanced down and realized I was three body lengths high. The sweat on my hands welded to granules of stone until my fingers slipped free from the small holds. I jerked my body closer to the wall's face and hung on for dear life. The helpers formed a group around me and guided my every move.

"Right hand here. Left hand. Left leg. Right leg."

Are you stupid? If you fall backward, you're done. Shut up, George! Thrust yourself up there. Focus! I clung to the wall and tried to halt the useless self-talk.

"Left wood." They pointed to a frail tree branch embedded in a crack.

Wrist shaking, I grabbed it. Unstable. Whoa! Hand slipped. Left arm flailed. My heartbeat stopped. I pictured myself gliding through the air, my fall broken by a pile of rocks.

"No wood! Wood not good!" I said, panting frantically.

Desperate to move upward, my arms continued to vibrate as I regained balance.

"Here!" The man at the bottom pointed at a groove in the stone. I grabbed the wedge and uprooted myself, my back and forearms burning from fatigue.

A priest catapulted himself to the top ledge and stood above me, arm extended.

The end grew nearer. I gazed down as the two other guys directed me. My eyes focused on my toes to plan the next step. The horror! Damned peripheral vision! No other way of getting it done. A minuscule part of my three largest toes supported my entire weight. The steep drop shot an electric chill through me. My torso and legs trembled. *Come on! A little more*. I took a few deep breaths through my nose to calm myself and stop the shaking.

Out of nowhere my mind became clear. Coordination razor sharp. God sent me His energy and vigor, or maybe my adrenaline response shifted to overdrive. The ghastly structure turned into a simple flight of stairs with railings. I yanked myself up and gasped for air on the ledge.

"*Ammasekeenaroo! Ammasekeenaroo!*" I folded my hands and bowed to the priests.

I stared at my accomplishment with pride. It looked every bit as treacherous from above, but the euphoria of completing an arduous task cleared my head of cobwebs and trivial worries. Three seasoned men had helped me do it. It wasn't a victory over the wall; it was a triumph over myself. I shattered my limiting beliefs that day, showing myself I was capable of more than I'd ever imagined.

Being close to death changed everything. I didn't have time to let anyone bend me out of shape. My capacity for inner peace increased tenfold. I was ready to give love to those with the worst intentions. How lucky to breathe and be free of suffering. Life was a gift to cherish. I needed to embrace the highs and lows, the struggles and pleasures, enjoy the moments when children threw rocks, and smile at the countless locals who pestered me on the street.

I caught my breath and continued up the winding path. Two dusty skulls housed in a microwave-oven-sized niche startled me. Teeth straight, no signs of rotting. A giant white bone with dark grooves of decay sat in between them, creating a divide where the spirits shared the same enclosed space. Soul roommates. Having one's remains outside the holy site was more honorable than a ground burial or cremation. Their ghosts lingered, protecting the monastery from evil. They had watched over me as I'd clung to the wall moments ago. I folded my hands in appreciation of their help.

The last section was stunning and horrifying. Sharp sandstone rocks shot out of the desert foundation, fists protruding through the ground, elbows embedded in the sand. I crept along one final ledge as the cool, smooth rock tickled the bottoms of my feet, barely providing enough room to stand with my legs shoulder-width apart. I glanced downward. Deadly drop to the left. No room for error. The piney scent of incense infiltrated the air and helped my mind relax and focus on my steps. I was close to heaven. God's helpers must have visited Tigray to create the pilgrimage site.

The narrow ledge led into a cave monastery, with an entrance hole about the same diameter as my height. The cave's entrance was only several feet away from the steep drop. One wrong step from a spiritual trance would result in a premature trip to the afterlife. I tiptoed inside in order not to disrupt a monk's deep humming. The turban-wearing, wizened man stared at a Bible of sheepskin written in the ancient language of Ge'ez in ink from minerals, fruits, and flowers. The cave was split into three areas as was typical of Ethiopian Orthodox Churches—an area for music, a place for Holy Communion, and another section that held a Covenant. Colorful murals of the Bible's protagonists illuminated the walls. Portraits of the pure exposed the entire face. Sinners, however, were depicted in profile, with only one eye visible. This made it easy to separate good from evil. The paintings were as mysterious as the monastery's construction, drawn by unknown artists 1,000 years after the church's founding. The dry climate, remote location, and the cave's absence of sunlight must've helped preserve the artwork.

The ancient portraits, hair-raising climb, and devout chanting gave the place an intense vibe. Perhaps the priest felt the vitality of nature pouring through his spirit, giving his words robust meaning.

I sat, crossed my legs, and focused on my breath as the rhythm of his chanting became more familiar and warmer. His voice soothed my nerves and relieved the tension in my shoulders and neck. As oxygen infiltrated my brain, electrical impulses radiated from the tip of my head to my navel. My feet tingled with cool energy. I focused on my wrists and observed the throbbing that had plagued my grip for days. The pain trickled away, rendering my palms and fingers limp, their youthfulness replenished. My heartbeat still banged from scaling the vertical wall and creeping alongside steep drops. A few moments later, it slowed to a light patter. The soft pressure against my chest reminded me of my girlfriend's smooth hands as they kneaded my body into relaxation after a taxing session of physical training. Adrenaline lingered, and the God within me woke from its slumber. The mind, nature, and the divine worked in mysterious ways.

The monk's chanting trailed off into humming at a baritone pitch. I stood up and felt rejuvenated. An hour must've gone by, but I was nimbler than after a day at the spa. Cracking elbow joints turned silent as I pushed myself upright.

After collecting myself, I started the trek back. The descent looked more hair-raising than the upward climb. My shoes were a distant speck of brown in the yellow sand. How was I supposed to survive this one? The tension returned to my body. My shoulders and forearms ached from the thought of hanging on for dear life. I stood there in panic-stricken defeat. Amid a fantasy about how my family would ever go on without me, voices from below became louder. The rustling of sandals on stones broke my defeatist thoughts.

The priests! I waved my arms in desperation and screamed "Salam!"

Within seconds, they shot up the wall and stood next to me. One man held a beige rope.

I bowed to the monks in respectful panic, eyes focused on the rope.

"Use rope. One hundred fifty birr" ($5 US). Eyebrows furrowed and wide-eyed with seriousness, they pointed to the rope and strap.

I would've cleaned out my entire bank account and handed them the clothes off my back to use that rope. Luckily, I had 150 birr on me. I hoped they'd buy extra vegetables or a new pair of sandals with the money.

As I inched downward, the rope's security made it easy. In a worst-case scenario, I'd lose my balance and slam into the wall. Much better than tumbling to my death and becoming a midnight snack for hyenas.

The priests released the rope, and I crawled along the same wall that had my limbs trembling hours ago. I felt helpless, no longer in control. One blunder by these men could end everything. The training I'd done to prepare for my trip meant nothing. The running in the cold and sweaty afternoons in the gym would be rendered worthless. I'd never expected to dangle off the edge of an Ethiopian mountain. The monks had the power, and my safety was in their hands.

I made it to the bottom unscathed and collected myself. The day's events had me surging with life.

I had new respect for these holy men, who commuted to work by scaling mountain walls. Barefoot and empty-handed commutes accomplished by sheer skill, strength, and experience had to make them feel alive. Or were they so accustomed to rock-climbing that it became as painstaking, mundane, and aggravating as sitting in gridlocked traffic on a North American freeway? Somehow, the latter case seemed impossible.

I thought back to my days as a commuter in Detroit, Michigan. My daily one-hour trek to the office was duller than George Orwell's pencil tip. Riding in a motorized vehicle with temperature control, adjusting the light with a sunroof, and listening to a high-quality stereo that blasted the latest rap beats had turned me into a spoiled brat. At the push of a button, my car sealed itself off, airtight, from the outside world. Comfort and luxury resulted in complacency, dissatisfaction, and boredom. Everyone around me drove a car to work and complained. There had to be another way.

Everything changed with a decision to pedal to the office. Mundane roads became thrilling, unexplored territory. Trees rustled in the breeze. Gray clouds signaled a storm's attack. Wind gusts pushed from behind and assaulted from the front. Sunlight glanced off the Detroit River and splashed my face with tingling heat. After cycling to work, it was impossible to not have a grin on my face. Back then, my adventurer's spirit gleamed through the darkness of my cubicle. The journey nourished my soul. I'm sure the monks of Tigray could relate.

Even though the priests of Abuna Yemata and I couldn't communicate on a deep level, I felt a camaraderie with them. Barefoot walks and rock-scaling, a centuries-old tradition, must have replenished their life energy. Perhaps their holy commute was a big part of their secret. Whatever the case, I'm forever grateful they saved me twice.

Chapter 22

Swimming in a
Sea of Sin

"Do not blame God for having created the tiger. Thank him for not giving the tiger wings."
—Indian proverb

My final destination, Aksum, was one day of cycling away and I was looking forward to taking a plane back to Addis Ababa as my reward for completing the journey.

I'd been climbing uphill for three hours and at least 15 kilometers. My legs shook as I grasped my handlebars and pedaled unceasingly. My thighs felt blown during the uphill struggle, yet I was enjoying the work, knowing my body was becoming stronger with each grimace and movement. Everything slowed down. I crept past rocks and twisted and turned around curves while focusing on the tiny houses that were a distant drop away.

After an hour of pain, my mind became quiet, and my legs pumped themselves into numbness. Throbbing hamstrings were a fair price for the euphoric silence in my head. I accessed a stronger version of myself, a guy who could continue on the bike deep into the night while staring down hyenas and yelling "Salam!" at ghosts. Three village homes and 20 minutes later, the endorphins and endocannabinoids took full charge. The feel-good chemicals had me humming, beatboxing, and rapping.

"Biking in Ethiopia, not hardcore.
First wind, second wind, third wind, four!
Pedal all day, not saddle sore.
Wat, injera—can't wait for more.
Fuel to keep me goin' till Ecuador.
Throw stones, I wave, build rapport.
Not rocks, hit me with Tigray folklore."

Once at the summit, I celebrated with large gulps from my water bottle. The natural beauty beckoned me. Goosebumps formed on my arms at a single glance of the undulating, yellow hills and rocky canyons scorched red. A parched river created a white, curvy stripe that faded into the distance, a snake thriving on drought and sun—desert art created by the arid climate and the imagination. Craggy mountain ridges created a strand of white film where they met the clear, blue sky. Trees—patches of green—gave the rocky slopes relief from the unrelenting sun. Birds of prey glided below me, about halfway down the canyon. I grinned and took another swig of water while congratulating myself on having made it higher than Ethiopia's flying desert creatures. Now it was my time to fly downhill and collect my reward for the morning's work.

I sped past waving villagers and screamed, "Whoo! whoo!" while pumping my fist in the air. The bike accelerated and my stomach and chest churned. Cool air walloped my entire body, blow-drying the glistening sweat on my arms into grainy chalk. The brisk wind made my eyes tear and pounded against my helmet, creating a stereo of fuzzy feedback, like an FM radio station in a distant city. My ears popped as the abrupt altitude change muffled the whooshes into murmurs and then back to whooshes. An entire morning of uphill pedaling for a priceless view and 20 minutes of downhill fun. Sixty kilometers of pedaling in the Ethiopian mountains was the best way to start the day.

As I wound around curves and looped around jagged, towering mountains, the air became hotter and hotter. Before I knew it, I was gliding along the bottom of the canyon and the sauna door was wide open. Heat reflected off the pavement and beamed at my exposed skin—the ground was a furnace. My face reddened as ultraviolet rays penetrated my exposed skin. The burning sensations stung, and the tip of my nose tingled.

The small of my back received the most punishment. I thought I was clever, bringing my quick-dry T-shirt along for the trip, a gift tossed to me by a seductive Korean cheerleader at a volleyball game in Seoul a week before my journey.

At the game she'd tucked the shirt into the rear side of her white miniskirt. Her thighs were perfect. Etched outlines of muscle above the knee with enough thickness at the waist to fit perfectly in my lap. My imagination ran wild with lewd ideas. She picked me out of the crowd of yelling fans and tossed it in my direction. Destiny! The threads emitted her vanilla perfume for days, and I had to bring it on my cycling adventure before her scent wore off. A prize bequeathed by an angel; it was sure to keep me safe during my trip.

Aside from attached superstitions and its pleasant aroma, the shirt was a practical item. In theory, its white fabric would reflect the sun's rays, keeping me cool in the sun. In practice, it was the worst idea ever. I didn't realize that by leaning forward to grab my handlebars, a baseball bat-sized portion of skin above my tailbone lay exposed to the elements. I felt blisters forming along a thick horizontal line. Bubbling hot oils of burned flesh. The tattoo lasted for eight months, a piece of Ethiopia branded into my body as the perfect souvenir. I wore the dark brown line as a badge of honor. Every time I showered, I gleamed with pride at my accomplishment, starting the day with vigor and enthusiasm, knowing I'd made it across Africa's most mountainous country on a bike.

Along the bottom of that Ethiopian canyon, nature and man worked against me. The night-black tarmac reminded me of the volcanic lava that had melted my rubber shoes into an unrecognizable lump of trash several years ago in Guatemala. I had to get the hell off the volcano to retreat. Now I had nowhere to go. The road had sucked me dry.

What a blessing to have dark skin. SPF 100 wasn't doing it for me. I zoomed by locals on the street, strutting barefoot with their livestock, slapping each other playfully on the back. I was the only one suffering, and I loathed them for their built-in protection.

I winced from the pain of fatigue, shielding my body from the sun's wrath via my helmet and sunglasses. My watch battery had died several days before, and the sun became my timepiece. By my estimate, I'd been exposed to the heat for five hours and needed a rest. I was green with envy and red with sunburn.

Then came the sandstorm. Pebbles sprayed my burned cheeks. Sand hurtled against my helmet, creating a chorus of grain on plastic. It found its way into my body's exposed orifices. I sniffed crusty grains, tasted crunchy granules, and my eyes turned into useless, watery gobs. Adrenaline withdrawal combined with the sand assault left me depleted.

Luckily, the storm only lasted a few minutes, and I blinked my eyes back to normal. I scoured the periphery for a shaded place, and, as I sped around another curve, two surreal boulders grabbed my attention. The red-and-yellow rocks seemed to protect something, perhaps housing a tribe of indigenous residents. The landforms gave the area a spooky vibe, and their mysterious energy brought me to an abrupt halt. I gawked in awe, forgetting the hot weather, wondering how Mother Nature had created the mammoth structures.

The heat caught up with me, and I continued riding.

A few hundred meters down the road, houses dotted the terrain, and a signpost informed me I had entered the town of Siero. I spotted a store with a large tarp set up near the entrance. Food and shade. Please!

Four people sat together in the tarp's shadow, one of them a monk dressed in a red cloak, a large wooden cross around his neck. The bottom of the cross rested below his waistline, and the top poked the lower portion of his chest. A nice ornament to go with the yellow turban on his head. I threw my bike aside, took a seat, and asked, "Injera? Injera?"

The monk opened a pillowcase-sized burlap sack and handed me a piece of bread that must have weighed more than a full-grown toy poodle. Round like a pizza though without cheese or toppings, the bread had my mouth watering before the first bite. I devoured it within several minutes as the gathered Ethiopians chuckled at my appetite.

A thin man sitting beside the monk spoke impeccable English. He wore a faint-blue button-down with sleeves rolled up to his elbows. An orange undershirt stuck out below his collar, providing a sky-on-sunset contrast. Clean gray slacks hugged his lean thighs. This guy dressed more formally than the Ethiopians I generally encountered in rural desert areas. He sported a scraggly mustache and goatee, not more than a centimeter thick, which added a few years to his face. Concave eyelashes lined the entrance to a pair of wide, dark eyes with faint crow's feet in the corners.

He launched into his tale, touched the bottom of his chin as he spoke, and maintained strong yet compassionate eye contact. He talked slowly, in a gentle tone that radiated peace and tranquility. His smile was calm, Dalai Lama-esque. I felt as if he was completely with me, with nothing else on his mind. His movements were deliberate and graceful, absent of the slightest nervousness. Deep-red capillaries filled in the white of his left eye. Despite the discoloration, his eyes soothed me into the comforts of his story. I knew I had much to learn from him.

"Wow, you rode your bike from Addis! Amazing! I hope you are enjoying Ethiopia. Welcome! My name is Henok." He gave me a shoulder bump as we grasped hands.

"And you? Where are you from and what are you doing here? You're not from this village, are you?"

"Oh, funny you ask that. It's a long story, but I think you have time. I'm from Addis Ababa and come from a rich family. My father sent me to India to learn the family business and study Hindi. I lived alone in India but messed up my chance there. I drank alcohol, smoked cigarettes every day, did cocaine sometimes, and became addicted to sex and other bad things. I did nothing my father intended me to do in India and ended up getting deported. I failed, so I came here."

A phone call interrupted Henok's story, and he excused himself.

An addict? Why did he come out here? Was Henok high right now?

He wasn't spacey or aloof, switching between English and Amharic with ease. Maybe a philanthropy junkie pulling all-nighters, helping the destitute at the local hospital. That would've explained his red eye.

I turned to the monk. I folded my fingers into the prayer position, pointed off into the distance with my index finger, raised my eyebrows, and threw up my hands. The monk smiled as he put the cross to his lips and puckered up.

A woman sitting off to the side interrupted our attempt at conversation and translated. Someone else in rural Ethiopia with amazing language skills, her English was flawless: "He lives in an Orthodox church nearby and says he wants you to bring him to the United States to talk about God."

I figured since I was in Ethiopia, a country with a sacred history where most locals ate vegetarian food two days per week to seek redemption for their sins, I'd stay open-minded about their version of Christianity. After all, legendary emperor Haile Selassie used to wake up at 3 a.m. to attend church, then drive to the outskirts of Addis Ababa and visit the poorest neighborhoods where he handed out banknotes. The giving of alms was mandatory in the early Christian church, and he took this duty seriously.

After pondering on Selassie, the Elect of God, I smiled and nodded, keeping my views to myself. *Listen and ask questions. Don't judge others, especially in here.* I had to be a blank slate.

A few moments later, Henok returned and continued his story. "So I came here to cleanse myself. There is a church over those hills that's very powerful. I've been here for two months and don't have cravings for cigarettes, sex, drugs, or alcohol anymore. I'm pure again. The devil was inside me in India, but it left." The wrinkles under his eyes deepened.

"Tell me more." I nodded to encourage him.

"The monastery does amazing things. It has cured over a thousand people with HIV. Visitors are relieved of cancer and mental illness. Murderers come to the church and are kept in chains until the devil leaves them forever. I had the devil in me as they did. Now I am clean. My friends in Addis Ababa can't believe the changes I've made in my life. The priests have special power. They knew I had sex with many girls. I couldn't even remember how many girls I had until I counted. The priest was correct in his guess of 61. He made me bow to the image of Jesus 3,000 times per day for punishment. I've been bowing so much and feel great. It's incredible."

"That sounds amazing, Henok. I'm glad you're clean." I took a swig from my two-liter water bottle.

"Come with me to the church," he offered. "It will be a very special experience for you. This place is underground. Several thousand people are staying in tents, waiting to become healed."

"I don't know ... I'm tired."

"You can stay with me in my tent. No problem. You'll never forget it. Amazing things happen there that you won't see anywhere else."

"I don't know Henok ... I'm not a religious guy."

"You must come. We have over a hundred million people in Ethiopia, and only several thousand are staying at the church. People know the monastery by word of mouth. They don't advertise. Ethiopians hear about the amazing power of the church and come to get healed. You'll never forget it there no matter what your religious beliefs are." He held up his hands and exposed his palms.

"I've been riding for a month and am exhausted," I countered.

"You can rest in my tent there. It will be a great Ethiopian cultural experience. No one will try to convert you. Just come and enjoy."

I deliberated over his offer. On one hand, his passion and sincerity were convincing. His persistent advertising had piqued my curiosity, and I craved a spiritual awakening. Enticing indeed. I wanted to investigate the place and witness the Ethiopian magic.

Was it a hoax, or was there special energy?

But the heat had depleted me. A glance at the hills in the distance made sweat trickle down my forehead. Trotting along the path while the midday rays pounded on my skin sounded painful. How was I supposed to walk in the desert when my body was a lump of dead weight? Nutty idea.

My final destination was 70 kilometers and eight hours of cycling away. My opportunity to ride in Ethiopia was slipping away with each passing second. If I stayed at the monastery, I'd have to put my bike in a taxi van to arrive at the airport on time for the flight the next day.

Then again, I was on the bike every day and had dealt with enough hardships along the journey. Opportunities like this were rare. No matter how exhausted, I could dig deep to muster enough energy to trek through the sun for one more hour. If this place was as special as Henok claimed, I'd be energized soon. I needed an oasis.

"Let's do it," I said.

"Great!" Henok extended his hand to pull me in for a second shoulder bump.

I said goodbye to the monk and others at the shop and began the walk. We strutted along the winding path as my new friend recounted tales in remarkable detail. I was at full attention. Fatigue decimated by distraction, it was a morning stroll in a crisp forest.

"There was a cave monastery in those rocks. That's a holy place too. People still go there to pray sometimes." He pointed at the two creepy boulders I'd marveled at earlier.

"There used to be a big snake guarding the church from intruders. The serpent knew who to let in and who to turn away. It was eight meters long. Ten years ago, they started using people instead of the reptile," he continued as our feet pounded the sand. "You have to bathe in holy water before setting foot on the church grounds. I'll show you how. You'll be clean of all evil."

I didn't want to criticize his stories and become the outsider preaching about science and the West's superiority. I was there to observe, ask questions, and gain a deeper understanding of Ethiopian spirituality.

We stripped off our shoes and socks while on the approach to the church grounds. I winced at the stones pressing against my heels. While I stumbled, the local churchgoers strolled gracefully as though they were stepping on soft, ankle-high grass that tickled the bottoms of their feet.

"Ha-ha! My toes were hurting too," Henok said. "Now that the evil is gone, walking here is no problem."

We approached a stream cordoned off by red and pink blankets, which provided users of the holy bath privacy. The water sparkled and shimmered in the sun. My heart leapt with excitement at the prospect of ridding my body of filth. It had been several days since my last shower.

"Let's go. You will get baptized here. This is a special day."

I staggered down the rocky slope to the water, and we stripped off the rest of our clothes. Water spewed out of a large pipe, which guided the water into a stream that unloaded along a small ledge—perfect for sitting and bathing. Washing myself in public bathhouses in South Korea was one of my favorite pastimes, so it wasn't awkward taking a bath next to another naked man.

Henok squatted and let the water pour over his head and flow down his body. He looked so serene as the liquid glistened on his forehead and cheeks.

"You must let the holy liquid touch your forehead first. This will cleanse your mind of evil thoughts."

I followed suit and took a seat next to Henok under the cascading stream. Vigor surged through my body. Tingling currents of energy started from my head, passed through my chest, ran through my legs, and reached a reverse zenith at my toes. My torso went into a brief state of paralysis from the drastic change in temperature. A welcome shock. Fatigue had burned me to the core, and now, as the icy water hit my skin, intense power replaced the soreness. The surge had me ready to fight the Ethiopian mountains. This water was special.

"Wow! You didn't make any noise. Usually, people yell when they feel the water. You must be very pure already."

I was far from pure. I'd used the Lord's name in vain countless times while cursing out the rock-heaving kids and envied the locals' comfort while strolling around in the unrelenting sun. I swam in a sea of sin. My sea might not have been as deep and turbulent as Henok's once was, but if one uses the Ten Commandments as a baseline of morality, I was a good distance from God's example of an ideal human being.

My lack of reaction to the bath could have been because of my daily habit of bathing in cold water. Several years ago, I had shrieked and cringed when confronted with cold liquid. I was a soft kitten. After reading about the health benefits of brown fat production through cold exposure,[1] I slowly learned to relish it. At first, I'd tiptoe my way into the shower, bracing myself for the shock. I'd stare at my shoes, clean my room, or surf the web in order to put off an exercise session in the winter. Now I jump for joy when the temperature falls below freezing, strip down to as few layers as I can tolerate and enjoy a deep feeling of accomplishment as steam issues from my mouth during winter sessions of high-intensity interval training. It clears the mental clutter, forces me to focus, and slows down my sense of time. Wolves don't shriek at the idea of jumping in cold water or running around in the winter. I long to become stronger and ignore the social programming trying to brainwash me into being a kitten crawling back into my mother's womb. I'm still a wolf in progress.

People in the economically developed world have become weak. Industry thrives when we spend money to medicate ourselves with alcohol, food, and external stimuli, which leads to diseases of despair, such as addiction, depression, and anxiety. People in North America are now more likely than ever to kill themselves. Evidence shows that suicide didn't occur during nearly all of human history. My goal is to stab diseases of despair in the heart by awakening the beast within, choosing uncomfortable tasks and making them routine. It's time to jump into the ice water, struggle for air during snowstorms and

---

1. For more on this topic, read David Sinclair's book "Lifespan: Why We Age and Why We Don't Have To."

embrace the essence of what it means to be alive. If suicide is one of humanity's biggest sins, then comfort is its best friend.

We have developed into victims of our successes. Concept change[2] says that as our lives grow more comfortable, we lower our thresholds as to what we consider a problem. In the end we have the same number of problems, and they become increasingly shallow. Bathing without a water heater could be a big problem for some, but before they were invented, no one would have complained about cleaning oneself while cold or chopping firewood for hot water. Likewise, a student had complained about traveling without GPS and the awkwardness of asking people for directions, but to old guys like me, who prefer flip phones, the issue sounded trivial.

Nonetheless, I'm also a victim of this mindset. I'm sure I'd complain if I had to write this book on a typewriter or go through engineering school without a spreadsheet and sophisticated software programs after using a computer. We are always moving the goalposts no matter how good we have it. When new comforts are introduced, we adapt, and old comforts become unacceptable. Comfort creep is real. We need to control our use of technology and not let it control us.

Every generation and culture has its own strengths and weaknesses. Its own beauty and ugliness. Suffering occurs when two eras collide or overlap. I was caught in a transitional era between excessive comforts and the natural human tendency to use the mind and body for survival. Machines and technology offer so much free time. When I visited villages in Bangladesh, Ethiopia, and Uzbekistan, frowning faces were rare. There were no choices about fetching water, eating, or farming. People used their bodies and had strong community ties. Their lives were aligned with nature: They slept as soon as the sun went down and woke when it rose the next day. No diseases of despair. Just movement, smiles, perseverance, and the great outdoors. Now

---

2. Psychologists often refer to this as prevalence-induced concept change.

is the best time to be alive, but we can't forget where we came from and the value of hard physical work.

The people at the church had a set of problems different from the array I'd grown up with. Ailments, diseases, and horrifying, life-changing decisions left Ethiopians with no choice but to seek the monastery's healing power. I was ready to listen, observe, learn, and trust Henok's guidance.

Chapter 23

Sleeping With Angels

"When angels appear, the devil runs away."
—Egyptian proverb

After the bath Henok escorted me to the church. It was a single concrete story the size of a middle-class home in suburban North America. A tilted, silver cross atop the highest point of its double-tiered, dome-shaped roof glimmered in the sun. It shone like the star I'd attached to my family's Christmas tree as a child. Green, yellow, and red stripes painted on the roof provided a pleasant contrast to the sandy desert hills and blue sky. The colors of the Ethiopian flag reminded me of the country's vast history: green was hope, or the land and its fertility; yellow symbolized peace and harmony between Ethiopia's ethnic and religious groups; red represented blood spilled defending the nation. While glancing at the colors, I silently wished Ethiopia and its people peace and a prosperous harvest season.

I followed Henok as he completed a lap around the holy complex. The opposite end of the monastery's aqua-colored walls was adorned with paintings of Ethiopian saints. The red, yellow, and green murals stared at me. The saints' glowing eyes spoke thousands of words, echoing a charitable spirit to help society's destitute. After listening to my friend's magical accounts of healing, I expected them to leap out of the wall waving magic wands. Perhaps their mystical energy helped him overcome his addictions.

Henok appeared giddy. The creases below his eyelids and baritone laugh signaled he was happy to be with me. His changes were incredible. I admired him for facing his problems. His spiritual beliefs, it seemed, had led him in the right direction.

My friend guided me around the premises. A labyrinth of makeshift tents surrounded the church. There must have been at least a hundred of the chin-high shelters. Plastic bags bonded together, supported by wooden scraps, became the churchgoers' home away from home. Small creases in the plastic walls revealed groups of three or four locals boiling coffee and tea as the melody of tongue-snapping Amharic textured the air. The place resembled a refugee camp where the displaced waited to gain asylum.

Henok brought me to another housing complex, this one with a floor area the size of a tennis court. Here, followers set up blankets and pillows in single-file lines. Bodies were pressed together, each person given less than an arm's length of personal space. Legs were chained to metal columns with only a few feet of slack. The leashed men sat cross-legged on the ground and chatted, appearing content with their absence of freedom.

"Those men are violent criminals," Henok said, gesturing at the chained men. "They came to be cleansed of evil spirits. Satan possessed them to murder, rape, and terrorize the innocent."

Rather than gassing them to death, they were given a shot at redemption. This is nobler than labeling the convicts beasts and denying them any possibility of rehabilitation, which virtually guarantees they will return to crime when released from prison.

While on our stroll, Henok grabbed hands with, and shoulder--bumped a middle-aged man who held a Bible and wore a white turban.

"See that guy I greeted?" Henok asked. "He killed three people. He was in chains for many weeks. The priests made him bow in front of Jesus several thousand times per day, and now he is much better. The evil has left him. This church is powerful, right?"

What did I get myself into? I was walking amongst murderers. My jaw dropped and my neck shuddered as an icy chill of fright shot through it. I glanced around at hundreds of people in the room. How many others were homicidal?

How incredible someone could be transformed into a peaceful human after taking a life. I could never comprehend the level of rage and hatred necessary to kill. Perhaps he'd acted in self-defense. The man appeared content with spending time at the monastery and worshiping his god and saints.

After contemplating the man's transformation, the day's events threw me into turmoil. Mind in overdrive, the stimulation had overwhelmed me. I had crept along treacherous mountain passes, received pizza-shaped bread from a monk, stomped through the desert sand at midday, bathed in icy holy water, and observed Henok shooting the breeze with a murderer. Experiential overload.

I gathered my senses once again, and Henok led me through the maze of tents outside where his friends had set up shop. I slipped off my shoes and ducked into a corner as a lady passed me a crumpled-up newspaper to sit on. A woman with a black cross tattooed on her forehead boiled tea and heated a frying pan; the aroma of spices had my nose's utmost attention. The tradition of facial tattoos had started in the Middle Ages when Muslims kidnapped Christians for slaves. In the eyes of their captors, the marks of faith symbolized Christ's death and resurrection, reducing slave value and motivating the Muslims to select another victim. Slavery is no longer so common, but people still carry on the tradition of tattooing their faces.

Seconds later, a petite woman in a yellow-and-purple dress and shiny green eyes stuck her head in the tent. A purple bandana held back curly hair and exposed flawless, beige skin. She was a stunner, and I took my time while admiring her beauty.

The chaos began when she shoved her way into the tent without removing her shoes. Her speech was slurred in between tongue pops and deep breaths. Maybe she was an alcoholic trying to become sober.

At first sight of me, her attention changed. "*Faranji*." She wrapped her arms around me and pulled me in for a soft hug. Her green eyes scanned the rims of my glasses as her head bobbed. Her face was a thumb's length away from my temple as she inspected the hinge joint of my frames. Coffee-scented breath pressed against my cheeks. The moisture of her breath temporarily relieved my sunburned skin. Fingerprints clouded my vision as she grabbed at my spectacles while her tongue cracked out rapid-fire Amharic. I removed her hands from my glasses as a woman jabbed her shoulder in disapproval.

"This woman is an electrical engineering student," Henok explained. "She was normal a few weeks ago. She promised to stay here for several weeks but secretly left during the night. Then, a few days later, she started acting crazy. The devil found her and punished her for leaving early. Her family took her to Addis Ababa to see psychologists, but that didn't help. They brought her back here, and she is doing much better now. The evil is disappearing. See? The church is powerful."

The girl's story floored me. Studying engineering at university requires intense concentration over long periods of time. This girl couldn't string sentences together without slurring her words and was acting like a five-year-old. She was a toddler stuck in an adult princess' body.

The woman with the tattooed forehead pulled her off me as the engineering student kept reaching for my glasses. Strip me of everything I own, and I'll flash a white-toothed grin. Take my glasses away and I'll shudder in fear. Panic pounded through the core of my stomach. Blurry vision and one wrong step into a canyon meant death. Don't toy with my specs!

My glasses still intact, I tiptoed out of the tent with Henok, while the girl nibbled on snacks and sipped tea.

"It's time to meet the head monk. It is a great honor to talk with him. He's a special man," Henok said, as we climbed up a hill toward a concrete cube.

We entered a small room with a double-bed mattress. It was lined with cream wallpaper, and there was a life-size mural of

Jesus Christ surrounded by a group of Ethiopian Saints. Several folded-up, white cloaks lay in a corner and a wooden staff rested against a wall. A middle-aged man with a curly black mustache and a sparkling cloak greeted us. Carrying a wooden staff in his left hand and smiling serenely, he greeted us: "Salam."

"This guy is so pure. They say he is still a virgin." Henok motioned toward the head monk.

Celibacy elicits mixed feelings in me. Deeming sex immoral goes against human nature, as the future of the race depends on the craving for sex. The goal of all creatures is to replicate and pass on their genes, yet Christianity makes us feel guilty for wanting sex. Denying this vital urge could be detrimental and lead to sexual misconduct. There are enough examples of celibacy gone wrong in religious institutions around the world.

On the other hand, overcoming cravings is a key to spiritual awakening. I had given up consuming food and drinks that weakened me. If I could choose salad over pizza, monks could opt for celibacy over sex. However, intimacy and the touch of another person help optimize the hormones responsible for our mental and emotional health. I'll never mask my desires for women—sex is one of life's greatest gifts—so perhaps I'll never achieve full enlightenment.

Henok translated the monk's words while I contemplated sexlessness.

"This church makes Ethiopia special," Henok said. "In North America, you have science and money. Here, we have spirituality. The white man tries to take away our culture and told us Lucy was the first human. Many Ethiopians believe Lucy is a lie. Adam was first and we don't believe the white scientists."

Lucy is the name given to several hundred bone fossils discovered in 1974 in the Afar region of Ethiopia by a group of anthropologists from Cleveland, Ohio. The specimen dates back 3.2 million years. This ancient ancestor, who was bipedal and walked upright, acquired the name "Lucy" because the scientists were listening to the Beatles' song "Lucy in the Sky with Diamonds" at the time of her discovery.

Several churchgoers brought Henok and me a piece of injera covered with multicolored wat; it was big enough to feed an entire football team. We dug our hands in and stuffed ourselves until we couldn't move. Next, the monk passed us glasses of fermented barley. I took one swig and my head spun. After battling with the scorching sun and mountain passes, listening to mystical stories, and interacting with the sick, I needed a solid rest. I never drank alcohol, so finishing a cup would've knocked me into a state of blackness, accompanied by frequent interruptions in my sleep cycle. Subpar sleep would weaken me, so I declined when they insisted I finish my cup.

I didn't understand why religious leaders would drink alcohol. *Spirituality is supposed to strengthen us*, I thought, *but alcohol weakens the body and mind and is a barrier blocking our hopes and dreams*. Isn't it hypocritical to consume a toxin during religious gatherings? *Isn't the body the soul's monastery?* I was sure the priests and monks didn't want to deteriorate their temples and churches. *Why'd they put a poisonous substance into the flesh and blood that shelter the soul?* Sure, hallucinogens have thousands of years of religious history, but the trip isn't permanent and once you come out of it, one is more likely to be depressed, or even have a bad trip that can traumatize the user. Instead, it's better to achieve a state of peace and bliss through many hours of praying and meditation. The answer is inside of us. No good things in life come easy and a quick fix isn't the answer.

Henok gulped several cups of fermented barley while explaining how natural and free of industrial chemicals the beverage was. The head monk downed a few glasses as we continued our conversation about my trip. *Stay humble*, I reminded myself. Perhaps they'd been guzzling the brew for ages as part of an ancient tradition. Or maybe alcohol consumption was too difficult to quit (habit often wins out over reason). Maybe they needed a drink after a day around criminals. I reminded myself that spirituality and culture triumph over science here, and I didn't want to push my "Lucy stories" on them. *Listen, ask questions, and stay curious. Be a blank slate.*

"The monk wants you to stay here, in his room, tonight. What great hospitality! It will bring us closer to the angels," Henok translated.

The monk's offer flattered me, but I didn't need special treatment. An open-air night with lions and hyenas prowling around sounded fine. With everything I'd been through that day, I'd send the beasts shaking in their shabby fur with my roaring snores. Besides, I felt unworthy of sleeping in the best room in the compound. I wanted to be treated as an average person. One reason I followed Henok to the monastery was to enhance my sense of humility. I wasn't anyone special. Just a guy on a bike curious about Ethiopian culture.

"Tell the monk *amasekeenaroo,* but I prefer to rest outside. I don't deserve to stay here, and I'm excited to spend the night in your tent."

Henok translated my message and pleaded his case again. His eyes had a new fire in them, wide with the hope of redemption.

"George, I need to tell you something. By bringing a foreigner here, God will forgive my sins. Sleeping in this room is a special opportunity. I'll be here with you. While staying here, we'll be with the angels, and good things can happen."

I pondered his words. My new friend had led me to a magical place, shared his stories, and loaded my mind with ideas. Peace filled my heart and nourishment permeated my soul. I wanted to help my companion thrive.

"Okay. Let's stay here," I said.

His eyes became wide, and his eyebrows rose. "This will be incredible." Henok rested his hand on my forearm as the dimples in his cheeks deepened.

This was the best thing I could do to repay Henok, and his elation made it worth it. Spending the night in the priest's room would give him the extra spiritual strength to go for his dreams while staying on a wholesome path.

The monk smiled and nodded when we accepted his offer and left his room to us a few minutes later. I hoped sleeping with the angels would bless me with good luck for the rest of my journey.

My eyes drooped shut, but Henok whispered to me before I could plop myself on the bed: "Can you stand well?"

"What do you mean, stand well?"

"Tomorrow morning, we should go to service at 3:30 a.m. We have to stand for three hours."

"Okay. Wake me up at 3:30 a.m."

It was past 11 and I needed at least eight hours of rest to function well the following day. However, my days in Ethiopia were ending, and I could sleep on the flight back to Seoul. This might be my only chance to attend an early-morning church service in the Horn of Africa.

Several hours later, I awoke to Henok tapping me on the shoulder. My companion handed me a large white cloak and staff in the head monk's room to wear for the service. Wrapped in their traditional church-going outfit, I was wearing the same garb as the locals on the street. It was a privilege, after all the taunting, to clothe myself in their wardrobe.

The Ethiopians had finally adopted me as one of their own. For a whole month I'd heard the words *faranji* and *money* everywhere. No matter how much I strived to be equanimous, the wish to be part of the tribe proved too strong to conquer. They used me, and it wore me out. I longed for warm smiles, extended arms, and listening ears. With those clothes on my back, I felt human again.

Tight social bonds were the secret to making it to a healthy old age, and isolation was toxic. It stung venomously every time kids tossed stones in my direction.

If Jesus existed, I had a newfound respect for him. He had a deep love in his heart for the ignorant people who'd hung him on the cross. I was a slave, elated when others clothed and fed me and distraught when they made me a sacrificial lamb in the name of amusement. My heart was too small. I didn't have enough love inside for those who had harmed me.

We made the five-minute walk in the dark to the church, as a smattering of stars glittered yellow in the sky.

The monastery interior, surrounded by several wooden benches, encompassed a large gathering space. Rods in hand, white cloaks covering their bodies, turbans tied to their heads, the congregation formed a semicircle around a Jesus painting in the center of the room. The painted savior hung from a cross in the middle of a grass field while white clouds hovered in the blue sky. A gold, moon-shaped circle surrounded Jesus' head. His head hung down, and his eyes were closed with sadness.

A haze of incense smoke floated through the building, adding a thin layer of gray to the air and masking the odor of dozens of worshippers standing shoulder to shoulder. Men chanted in unison, keeping the rhythm steady and clapping to an Ethiopian gospel beat. The church had the proper acoustics to amplify the sound and leave echoes during brief interludes of silence. The chanting filled the room with vibrant energy. High-pitched yodels gave my eardrums a familiar melody to relish. The power of belief instilled vocal cords with an unmatched strength that put me into a trance.

Clanking metal interrupted the slow drumbeats and ancient hymns. Middle-aged men with their hands and feet bound in rusty chains waddled and tripped over their bondage links. A Bible circulated from one person to the next. The book was the size of my hand, its brown cover and pages wrinkled with age. One by one, members of the congregation pecked the holy text the way a mother brushes her lips against a newborn baby's head.

One thought entered my mind: *Germs! How many of these people had brushed their teeth?* As anal as I am about taking care of my yellow-stained pearly whites, I didn't have time to brush before stumbling to the church hall. The congregation spread their bacteria on the book's cover.

Before I knew it, the bible had traversed the room. All eyes were on me—the guy who'd slept in the head monk's bed with the angels. I wanted to pass the book to the person next to me, but a great pressure weighed on me. Big decision. Smooch and share germs with the masses or refuse and offend a congregation of friendly hosts. I pride myself on being a rebel and going against the grain. Not this time. Peer pressure got the best of me. I'd have been a disrespectful outsider if I hadn't brushed my mouth against the age-old document. I longed to be accepted. This was my chance to become one of the in-crowd. I shut my eyes and puckered up to the thick leather binding, hoping the love of God and Jesus would help me return home free of sickness.

Next, a monk circulated a hand-carved wooden cross and waited for everyone to follow the same two-kiss procedure.

Whenever the cross and Bible came my way, I smooched and prayed, asking God to ward off the germs. The ritual repeated itself, and I must've puckered up more times in three hours than Casanova did in his whole life. Now I was living on the edge.

Sleep deprivation had me wanting to crawl back to the head monk's room for four more hours, but I knew I had to stick this one out. My legs ached, and I leaned my weight against the staff. Now I understood the role of the wooden staff in Ethiopian Christianity—to prevent one from being injured while falling asleep during lengthy church services in the middle of the night. This was spiritual torture. *God help the pulsating sensation in my knees and lower back!*

My eyelids twitched and drooped until my vision blurred to a field of blinking cobwebs. The eye spasms kept me from blacking out and plunging into the men in front of me, each sporadic movement serving as an alarm clock that shook me into consciousness. I watched the time like an office worker waiting for the weekend, ready to sprint out of the temple and find a place to sleep when we hit the three-hour mark.

As the minutes crept by, Henok insisted I sit on the bench behind us. *Oh Lord, relief.* Was I wrong for having thoughts of boredom and wanting to escape? Under ordinary conditions, I'd have been thrilled to stick out the session, but last night's injera smorgasbord didn't provide the strength I needed to stand without adequate sleep.

The service ended at 6:30 a.m. as chanting came to an abrupt stop. After a brief prayer, everyone filed out of the monastery. The experience was much longer than the church services of my childhood on Sunday mornings. If I have children, they won't endure such a grueling punishment.

After the religious ceremony, I needed to return to Siero village to catch a van taxi to the airport. We rushed out of the sanctuary, and Henok's uncle picked me up in his truck. Suddenly, a wailing sound broke the early morning calm.

"*Faranji*, don't go! Don't go!" It was the mentally ill student who'd grasped my glasses and hugged me earlier. She stomped toward me in despair as raindrop-sized tears rested in the corners of her glossy eyes.

She latched on to me like a child separated from her mother on the first day of school. This time she was much more forceful and dug her fingernails deep into my upper back. Her torso pressed against mine, and the aroma of coffee seeped through her pores. How endearing. A baby, not afraid to let her true emotions shine, stuck in an adult's body.

Several guys tugged her away after a brief struggle. The yelling, now a high-pitched siren, was heartbreakingly genuine. It was the way I'd felt whenever separating with a friend I'd likely never see again while traveling. My heart had always screamed and howled, but I remained calm and collected. Society said men weren't supposed to wail and let tears flow, and my emotions had stayed deep inside.

I stepped into the front seat of the vehicle and shut the door. She freed herself from the men and dashed toward me again at full speed, tripping over her green-and-red dress. Her arms flailed through the open window for a few seconds before the men overpowered her and pulled her away. "*Faranji! Faranji!*" she screeched while fighting to pry herself free of the men. Dust kicked up around her as her feet struck the ground in horror of separation. My vehicle zoomed off as a congregation of people accumulated to check out the commotion.

Henok and I said goodbye to each other once we reached the village. We'd spent less than 24 hours together, but I was in tears when we separated. My heart bellowed more loudly than the ill woman had, but, again, I kept my emotions at bay. Henok had gifted me unconditional friendship, which was the perfect way to end my journey in Ethiopia.

"You are my spiritual friend," Henok said. "We had wonderful talks. I hope you come back here."

I hugged him and my van pulled away as he waved in the distance. One thing is certain: I won't forget Henok, and I'll forever be thankful to him for helping me become a member of the tribe.

Chapter 24

Vomit and Drool

"Only the man who is not hungry says the coconut has a hard shell."
—Ethiopian proverb

"One never knows what the next day will bring."
—Ethiopian proverb

Concerts. Musicals. Fine dining. So many ways to celebrate an accomplishment. Five weeks and over 2,000 kilometers on a bike in the most mountainous country in Africa. I was proud, and I deserved a treat. My reward was a flight to Addis Ababa before returning to Korea two days later. Comfort awaited in the form of a window seat, unlimited drink refills, and a toilet with soap and running water.

At the end of my past trips, I had chosen the cheapest way back to the major cities, which was the most adventurous. In Xinjiang, China, nothing could compare to lying on the top bunk of a sleeper bus for 30 hours. It was fine at first, but they designed the space for someone one head-length shorter than me. I crouched in the fetal position and straightened my knees over the aisle to relieve muscle aches. Being up high meant I couldn't sit up without banging my skull on the roof. I never would've guessed I'd be sorer from lying down in a vehicle than from traveling 2,500 kilometers on my bike in the Tianshan Mountains.

The ride in Xinjiang was comfortable compared to my 500-kilometer taxi-van journey in Mongolia. Locals had told me I'd make it to Ulaanbaatar in 12 hours. The Mongolians didn't factor in extra time for flooded roads, mechanical issues, and sleep. Pushing our vehicle through the mud and inspecting popped tires were amusing ways to stretch my legs and develop a rapport with fellow passengers. I enjoyed the unpredictability.

Later that evening in Mongolia, the granddaddy of delays came at nine o'clock in a Gobi Desert town. The driver parked our van beside a gasoline pump until the attendant arrived the next morning to turn on the machine. With 20 of us crammed in the vehicle, it was an all-night war for personal space.

The guy beside me hunched over and used my lap as a pillow. His bowling ball of a bald head dug deep into my quadriceps. During his first 30-minute round of snoring, my thigh muscles thanked him as his skull probed my sore spots. The massage made me doze off into a lucid dream. I was on the steppe beneath a blue sky dotted with fluffy, silver clouds. Animal-skin yurts and brown goats were scattered over the green grass as I lay on my back. A cool breeze brushed against my arms. A sticky liquid tickled my leg. Drip by drip, it trickled along the side of my leg.

"ZZZZZ ..." A loud snore snapped me to reality. I was in the van. The man's chin glistened with saliva. He'd dribbled a trail of white, bubbly drool onto my lap. The horror! My eyes widened, and I let out a quick breath of frustration. I jerked my knee, snapping him out of his slumber. His head shot upright and looked around in a daze. I gave him a deadly glare as he shifted for a few seconds and fell asleep. During the next few hours, the pool of spit dried on my leg as visions of tissues and napkins clouded my hazy, unconscious world.

Although that gas station wasn't an ideal place to crash, I was thankful we'd stopped. It could've saved my life. We only had one chauffeur for the entire 40-hour fiasco. At hour nine, a passenger took over to relieve him. After a few minutes, the substitute operator slammed on the brakes, woke up the sleeping man, and jumped into the back seat. As the original driver settled in behind the wheel and wiped the drool off his chin, a police car zoomed towards us. Seconds later, an officer was checking the driver's ID. Our try at letting the chauffeur rest had failed. No matter how uncomfortable the night was, that guy had needed his rest. A sleep-deprived person at the wheel could've led to a flipped vehicle and a date with Genghis Khan's ghost. I prefer drool over death.

Before boarding the plane back to Addis Ababa, I had another ride in a vehicle coming up. Time was of the essence. Three hours and 100 kilometers to the airport in Aksum on newly paved roads—an immense contrast to Mongolia's dirt-tracked highways. I hoisted my bike onto the roof of a van taxi, paid the driver, and prayed we'd make it for my flight. No mechanical issues! No gasoline shortages! Please!

The van was simple and squared off, with three rows of seats. The vehicle and I must've been the same age, but it had more dents than I had wrinkles. Its faded, white paint was dotted with copper spots of rust. Thirsty doors screeched from an oil deficiency.

By North American standards, it should've had at most 14 passengers—four in each row and two up front. But this was Ethiopia, and our vehicle was packed to double capacity. I squeezed myself into the second row, torso pressed against a pair of men on both sides, scrunching my legs into a mesh of throbbing ligaments and muscles. My shoulder blades were compressed into positions that would've made the world's most flexible yoga practitioners wince in pain. A couple of children sat across from me, close enough to get a whiff of their breath, a mixture of coffee and spiced vegetables. The guy to my right reeked of cigarettes. Sweat dripped from the bottoms of our chins to our knees. The drops of brine gave my lap an illusion of cleanliness: my dusty pants needed a scrub. Now they were half jet-black and salty white.

We were like chickens on a factory farm. This was the closest I'd gotten to that horrid environment. As we maneuvered around curvy, uphill corridors, I thought of the animals who lived out torture sentences. For me, it would end in a few hours. For them, it was lifelong abuse.

My mind time-traveled to high school basketball in Michigan, where away games had meant pouring into a yellow bus. The seats were wide and comfortable, and an aisle ran the length of the vehicle, enabling us to stretch out our legs. My clothes soiled from playing basketball, I couldn't wait to douse myself with soap and water. Back then, I'd complained about being sweaty for several hours after the game. I hadn't appreciated the luxury of knowing when I'd be able to take my next shower.

As we maneuvered along the Ethiopian highway, I shifted in my seat while rubbing my hips against the passengers next to me. I clutched my camera with both hands and dug my heels into the floor. My stomach quivered with nervous energy. *Only two hours until my flight.*

Midway through the ride, several people behind me screeched in fear. Voices shouted in Amharic as the driver let out a piercing bellow. Squeezed by passengers on both sides, I couldn't contort my body to check out the terror.

The man next to me clenched his fist and, after a double-take, his eyes widened in disbelief.

Goosebumps dotted my forearms. My nostrils flared, and the skin ruffled on my forehead. My feet tangled themselves into a knot beneath my seat as nervous energy flowed throughout my body.

Seconds later, the driver slammed on the brakes. I thought of the delays I'd experienced while traveling by motor vehicle in Mongolia. Why were we stopping?

As the passengers exited the van, I caught sight of a purple-faced woman in the back. Her eyes had rolled into her head, and her sweat-stained forehead leaned against the window. Her neck, it seemed, was too weak to support her head. Strings of viscous and opaque saliva dribbled down her lips. A few minutes later, she stumbled her way out of the taxi and sat cross-legged on the sandy soil.

It must have been a nightmare riding in a crowded vehicle while sick. I hoped she'd get better after breathing some fresh air and taking a break beside the road.

The sour odor of fermented food infiltrated the air. It reeked of urine and spoiled injera, with a faint hue of coffee.

There it was. Gobs of green-and-yellow liquid laced with bright-red speckles of pepper paste covered the van floor. The viscous blob crept toward the rear luggage storage area. Chunks resembled my favorite Ethiopian lentil dish, messer, mixed with bile and acid. The black interior became an abstract oil painting with a putrid stench.

My toes curled in my boots, and I jerked myself away from the mess. A bitter taste flowed through my mouth and my throat burned. My stomach churned since the previous evening's meal had me bloated and heavy.

I wanted to grab my bicycle and flee. Ninety minutes until takeoff. How far was the airport? My heart sank as I glanced at the gigantic mountain slopes. I threw my hands into the air in frustration and sighed. I couldn't cycle there in time. It was out of my control.

I stumbled out of the vehicle, happy to stretch my legs for a few minutes and free myself from the pungent stench. My knees cracked and the fiery sensations along my lower back subsided. I extended my arms upward and glanced at the sky while my shoulders celebrated the open space. I was sure factory-farm cows didn't taste freedom every few hours. How lucky I was to have been born a human.

The sick woman was on her feet and talking to several other passengers with a smile on her face. I was glad to see her better after looking so ill only a few moments ago.

The driver grabbed a fistful of leaves and branches and shaped them into a makeshift brush. He pulled out the luggage bags one at a time and cleared off the waxy mixture as leaves dripped with the slimy goo.

A few seconds later, horror ensued. The chauffeur held my bag in his hands, only it was vomit-yellow and covered in bile, saliva, and phlegm. *How was I supposed to touch it?* I lifted it by the only black corner left and watched the vile liquid drip to the sand. The man grabbed another set of branches to help clean the exterior.

I stumbled back a full body-length. My jaw went slack as I expelled my breath. I felt disoriented as my cheeks flushed with heat. I muttered a few words ... "What ... bag ... why ...?

Chest puffed out and chin high, the driver wiped off my pannier. "I cleaning for you. You no worry," he said, lifting his gaze to mine.

The guy scrubbed until, at a glance, it looked clean. I held my breath while inspecting the damage. The vomit hadn't penetrated the bag's outer shell. My sleeping bag and underwear had been spared. Luckily, I had a large bottle of water and was able to use the last drops of what remained to restore my gear to its original color. At least a neat exterior would serve as a placebo, making my stuff appear germ-free. Mind over microbes!

Germs were crawling all over my pannier in search of a home. I dealt with the situation by handling the puke-free corner of the bag (until such time as large quantities of soap and water became available). Microscopic monsters filled me with terror.

Someone barfed on my stuff! I can't believe it! My upper body tensed up after I exhaled a sigh of frustration. I could outsmart hyenas, baboons, and lions, but germs had my mind racing. Weren't germs responsible for more deaths than wild animal attacks over Ethiopia's several-thousand-year history? To make matters worse, my immune system might've been weak from sleep deprivation. My day had started at 3:30 a.m. with cross- and Bible-smooching at the monastery. Germs, germs, and more germs!

I wanted to ditch the bag. Were the two months of gym-membership fees I'd spent on the pannier worth a few sick nights? I could wear my clothes instead of lugging around contaminated gear. Three T-shirts, three pairs of underwear, three pairs of socks, and an extra pair of shorts would make the sweat pour. But wasn't the perspiration better than contracting an unknown illness?

If I left the pannier behind, I'd be an ungrateful *faranji* who discards germ-ridden items. There had to be a solution. I constructed a makeshift glove for my right hand with a spare plastic bag. A temporary fix.

After a few moments, we boarded the vehicle for the ride (vomit-free). An hour later, I unloaded my panniers and bike on the windy airport driveway. Forty minutes! A sprint's worth of panting and heaving later, I arrived at the terminal, hoisted my bicycle onto a metal detector, and dashed to the Ethiopian Airlines check-in counter.

On other flights, I'd taken the wheels, handlebars, and pedals off my bicycle and packed it in a cardboard box for airplane storage. I had nothing this time—and the clock was ticking.

In 2014 I had rolled up to the airport in Tashkent, Uzbekistan, with my bike intact. A tall, buff woman with forearms the size of one of my thighs strolled out of the cargo office and scolded me in Russian. Eyes steaming, painted-on eyebrows slanted in a V, and fists clenched, she tore into me. "*Velesped samaliot niet*"—*bicycle, airplane*, and *no* were the only words I understood. I pleaded for at least 15 minutes, using body language and survival Russian. My heart nearly burst at the thought of losing my bicycle. It was my fault. Perhaps she'd have been reprimanded by her superiors if she allowed my unpackaged bike on the plane. The lady was doing her job.

Finally, she said the magic words, "*Da, maladez.*" *Yes, okay*. And I nearly hugged her giant, muscle-swelled body.

I braced myself for a similar conflict with the Ethiopian Airlines employees.

Twenty minutes left. I needed a backup plan. My eyes darted around the terminal, searching for someone my height who'd enjoy a mountain bike from the United States. My trusty machine had survived Ethiopia, Siberia, and Mongolia. What a run! On the way to Mekele, I'd been ready to ditch my hunk of metal and rubber. How was this different? The worst-case scenario wasn't all that bad: the new owner would appreciate the bike more than I ever could.

My nervous energy turned into a calm wave of satisfaction. Bike or no bike, I'd made it to Aksum. A month on a bicycle in Ethiopia: mission accomplished. I'd shown myself no challenge was too daunting if I tackled it one day at a time. My worries disappeared as I pushed the bike down the airport corridor.

I sprinted to the check-in counter and spotted an airline worker with a thin build who was a few centimeters shorter than I am, a perfect fit for the bike.

"Hello, sir. I cycled here from Addis Ababa and am returning by plane." I pointed to my machine with a proud grin.

"Oh! Bicycle only? You very strong!" He exclaimed in a squeaky voice while clapping his hands together in amusement.

"I'm not that strong. Thanks to the injera and shiro, I made it here." I held the man's smile with my gaze. His eyes put me at ease, and I knew he'd be a great bike owner.

"Okay. I happy you like Ethiopian food. Ha-ha! So ... your passport, please?" He stuck out his hand. His willingness to make small talk despite the time crunch shocked me.

"How should I load this onto the plane?" I asked the big question as a jolt of warmth shot up my chest.

"Oh ... your bicycle ..." He tilted his head to the side and placed his hand on his chin. Then he shouted in Amharic. A short guy with a shaved head and goatee strolled over, and the two slapped hands, shoulder-bumped, and exchanged words.

With 15 minutes until takeoff, there was still time for a friendly greeting and a chat. No matter the situation, finding time to put people first and smile is a beautiful way to live.

"Okay. My manager say put bicycle there." He pointed to the far end of the terminal.

"Oh great! Only 15 minutes left. Do I have enough time?"

"Of course. No problem my friend!" he said with the same expansive smile.

I leaped into the air and forgot about the puke incident. Pangs of relief ran through my chest, and I had to restrain myself from hugging the airport worker.

I boarded the plane and gazed out the window during takeoff. The struggle, bypassed in one giant swoop, went on below. Wild animals, canyons, and mountains left to their own devices. Coffee shacks, monasteries, and makeshift homes were specks in the beige landscape. Naughty children, cross-kissing priests, and staff-carrying villagers with trails of goats became invisible as we soared higher. The plane's shell protected me from sunlight, sandstorms, flies, and heat. Cute flight attendants refilled my water cup and handed me extra trays of food. What a difference one's mode of travel makes. Slow speeds sparked struggles for survival.

I couldn't wait to go home and rest. I longed for my apartment floor's cool wooden tiles on the small of my back. The firm surface always had lulled me into the unconscious world of recovery. I'd have a kitchen to cook pots of seaweed soup with fresh tofu, mushrooms, and fermented bean paste. I was ready to sit cross-legged on my pillow and focus on my breath while birds chirped outside of my window. A toilet with running water and a washing machine at my disposal. I had a shelf full of books to rummage through while my rice cooker steamed and a pot of Bengali black tea and ginger boiled on the stove. Reading, cooking, and shirt cleaning—done simultaneously.

I needed a break from cycling. Over the course of a month, I'd become a one-dimensional athlete. Every day I had used the same muscles, sat on the same seat, and wore the same helmet. I couldn't wait to do front squats, muscle ups, power cleans, pull-ups, and burpees until tears streamed down my cheeks. I was ready to trash-talk my workout partner. "Quit stalling, you chocolate milk–chugging, pasta and cheese-chomping, protein powder-mixing old man!" I could hear his reply ringing in the back of my head. "Alright then! You bean-eater!"

My heart longed for Seoul, but I needed to survive the last few days in Addis Ababa. The adventure was far from complete.

Chapter 25

An Ethiopian Ice Storm

"One who hides their illness cannot expect to be cured."
—Ethiopian proverb

"Anyone can start something, but the real art lies in carrying it through to the end."
—Haile Selassie

After the flight, my task was to ride my bike to the campgrounds. This time, the city was different. Goosebumps covered my forearms. I put on long pants and a long-sleeved T-shirt. *What was happening? The locals weren't bundled up in sweaters and scarves.* A man in a green shirt and purple shorts pushed a cart of sugarcane along the sidewalk. A woman with sandals and a flowery dress shouted at her cellphone over the sounds of blaring automobile horns. The chilly Addis Ababa breeze left me astonished.

"Where you go? *Faranji*!" yelled a guy in a tank top. A forehead full of wrinkles, he leaned on a wooden cart, which was surrounded by a yellow-and-red mosaic of mangoes.

I got off the bike and mustered a slight nod as the sun shot its beams into my eyes. Tears flowed down my cheeks from the bright light as my vision clouded and made a blurry mess of the cracked pavement. I stopped for a moment and squinted—the stinging had penetrated deeply.

"*Faranji*! You no looking good!" shouted the mango salesman, handing me two pieces of fruit.

"Thanks for the fruit. I'll be fine in a few minutes." I held my forearm over my eyes. The man's generosity touched me, but I couldn't find the energy to give him the attention he deserved.

"This mangoes making you better!" said the man gregariously.

"*Amma seh kee naroo,*" I muttered as the chilly breeze rushed through the microscopic gaps in my sleeves and my arm hairs rose in shock.

Eyes stinging and body shivering, I stood there dumbfounded, the bike resting between my legs, waiting for the stinging in my eyes to pass. A few minutes of tearing later, my eyes had cleansed themselves, but my limbs grew heavier and the quivering more pronounced.

I waved goodbye to the mango man, got back on my bike, and pedaled at a crawling speed to counter the chilly wind. My head ached more with each minuscule expenditure of energy. Ready to kiss the world good night, I fought off my cloudy vision with hard blinks that gifted me a few split seconds of clarity.

With each pump of the pedal, the temperature crept lower until I pushed through an Ethiopian ice storm. My body quivered and my thighs struggled to create enough force to move my bike through the sun-soaked streets. It was like someone had shot me with a dart that had rendered me a weak, dizzy mess. The more I pedaled, the more fragile I became. The guy with chiseled legs couldn't use his muscle mass for the slightest functional movement. I was an imposter.

I weaved in and out of crowds at the pace of a slow walk. Men in collared shirts jumped to the side as I swerved and zigzagged. A heavy woman wearing a purple-and-orange dress and sandals let out a high-pitched shriek as my front tire came within a thumbnail of her painted toes. The thought of backtracking a few bicycle lengths to apologize was daunting. Empty concrete spaces tempted me to plop down and surrender. My eyelids slid downward, cutting off my peripheral vision and reducing the colorful city to a grayish haze. If I didn't get off the road soon, I'd collapse into a world of darkness.

I broke the trip into small pieces by focusing on every upcoming pavement crack and coffee shack. Once I passed a landmark, I pressed on to the next. Each minor victory gave me the strength to keep going. Each tiny battle was another repetition in a bizarre workout.

In 45 minutes that seemed like several hours, I reached my campground. A month had gone by but nothing had changed. The same green grass, the same spotted dog with the same limp, the same wooden picnic table were waiting. There I was, a sickly version of the guy who, four weeks ago, had oozed with the energy to explore an unknown land. Returning to a place that hadn't changed triggered something. That campsite was so welcoming, like an apartment full of memories. It was the closest thing I had to home in Ethiopia. If resting there didn't nurse me back to health, I didn't know which place would.

I crawled on my flattened tent and snoozed as equatorial sunshine scorched my face a darker shade of red. I sprawled out on the plastic sheets as my crumpled-up poles lay beside me. When I regained consciousness, my arm shook as I reached for my bottle of water.

My head was stuck in a vise and every thought twisted it tighter. Pulling and crushing, followed by more pulling. Sweat trickled down my forehead while I shivered with feverish compulsion. I stared at the grass and listened to the dog stomp and bark as my mind ran wild. *It can't be malaria!* I was in denial.

What if this was it for me? My imagination went through a series of images. Teary-eyed family members stood around my casket. Lifelong friends in black suits embraced in hugs of grief while trying to keep it together in front of their wives and children. High school and university graduation, old sports photos, family vacations, travel adventures—a photo-collage of my greatest hits stood at the entrance to the church's worship hall as organs blasted religious hymns. I didn't tell anyone what kind of funeral I wanted to celebrate my life. Death was a faraway destination I'd never reach. It should be different. Not at a church. Not without one last goodbye.

I yearned for more time. Time to cultivate relationships with my loved ones by listening with open ears and gazing with eyes wide with concern. Time to stroll through snowy forests while inhaling crisp winter air. Time to feel the world's beauty through the compassion of its people. Time had escaped me, and I didn't know how much was left.

Determined to stay afloat, I forced my mind away from the pain and delved into problem-solving. A 24-hour water fast would do the trick. Water, water, and more water. I had to drown the illness before it drowned me.

Somehow, I mustered the energy to stumble to a nearby store and bought a few liters of water. On the walk, I thought of the great minds that had used hunger as a medicinal tool. "Fasting is the first principle in medicine," said Rumi. If Rumi was wrong, then I could count on Hippocrates, the father of medicine: "To eat when you are sick is to feed your sickness."

Water fasts had become part of my routine over the past year in South Korea and transformed me into a leaner, more energetic version of myself. I battled with food cravings every Monday and Wednesday and taught my students with renewed enthusiasm and vigor. It had made me tougher, and I became used to the hunger after a few weeks.

The plan was to chug water and allow my body to concentrate on its fight. Fasting and liquid were my bow and arrow. Starvation would focus my body on the battle. With each swig and every hour, my aim would become more precise. The illness could never handle my immune system in its optimized mode. Time, starvation, and water would pulverize the evil illness into oblivion. In the morning, only germ carcasses would remain, flat on their backs, dead from warring with my juiced-up white blood cells. Digestion would get in the way. No distractions.

Perhaps it wasn't malaria. Anything could've triggered my sickness. Maybe pathogens had infected the holy water stream. The cool, sacred water had cured me of fatigue for a few hours, but now I was paying for it. It could have been the early morning church service. Smooching the same cross and Bible that had touched the lips of hundreds of worshipers had exposed me to plenty of germs. If that didn't seal my fate, then the woman who puked on my bag must've tainted me with her illness. How I became ill wasn't important anymore. I had to man up.

My mind wandered back six years to backpacking and hitchhiking in Namibia, Botswana, Zimbabwe, South Africa, and Mozambique. The day I returned to my Seoul apartment after that trip, I'd dropped to my ice-cold floor and wrapped myself in blankets while my limbs vibrated. My eyes burned, and the energy had fled my body—even standing upright left me panting for breath. I had prayed to a God I doubted existed that it wasn't malaria. I pried myself off the ground and plopped down in a cab that took me to a hospital, where I learned it was an intense fever, the result of overnight travel, sleep deprivation, and exposure to a new set of germs. Nothing could have prepared me for that illness.

I had, however, at least been in South Korea and had had access to a hospital. Now, despite my sickness, I had to pack up my bike and go to the Addis Ababa airport the next morning. Somehow, some way.

I set up my tent, moving each limb with the utmost concentration. My legs heavy and unstable, I stomped on plastic lining to put poles through loops. I knelt on all fours while focusing on untangling strings, but the tremors in my hands resulted in one miss after another. "What the ...!" I muttered while throwing the cords to the side in frustration. *How did such a mundane task become so energy-sucking?*

Sleeping on the grass while feeling the cool ground against my limbs and absorbing the earth's electrical field seemed heavenly. More than anything, I wanted to avoid the tent setup. The task had me flustered and made me realize how weak I'd become. I was the same guy who'd pedaled across Ethiopia's mountainous terrain, threw weights in the air, and ran through snow and against frigid winds to prepare for the adventure of a lifetime. No matter how ready I'd thought I was, the power of nature dominated me whenever she asserted herself. She reminded me I was nothing but a speck in an infinite universe. She kept me grounded as I lay on the ground in a lethargic mess.

Sprawled out on the grass, I glanced up at the sky for several minutes as my skull continued to throb. My eyes shut, turning the day black. The sound of heavy breathing gradually became overpowered by images of the past month. Baboons scavenged for berries; dancing coffee-shop patrons shook their hips and arms; and turban-wearing men pushed overflowing mango carts. My unconscious filled to the brim with unique experiences in what I once considered a bizarre world. Now it was normal.

While lost in that dream, I realized that Ethiopia, once a mysterious land that had generated fear, curiosity, and excitement, had become my home. A place full of spontaneous conversations and impromptu friendships around every corner. A country whose topography carried a mystical energy and kept me pedaling despite a multitude of physical and psychological setbacks. Those setbacks had become routine. Instead of responding with aggression, I could smile at the children tearing through my bags while I enjoyed the blistering sun and quadriceps-sculpting, uphill climbs. No need to fantasize about sitting in a shaded coffee shop. I could greet the Kalashnikov-armed villagers instead of gawking at the deadly weapons strapped to their shoulders. In one month I had adapted to life in the Horn of Africa. If I could make it in Ethiopia, then I could make it anywhere.

As I basked in my dreams, chanting from a nearby Orthodox Church brought me back to reality. The headache and chills whipped me wide awake. *Come on! Set up that tent!* More than a resting place, the tent functioned as a mosquito net, protecting me from parasite-injecting insects. *This is just another workout! The second round starts now!*

The day faded into night as I struggled to untangle knots and balance poles. Finally, my job was done and I could rest. I collapsed in the plastic refuge area, and my eyes welded themselves shut while my hands and feet quivered.

But no. Ethiopia wouldn't let me relax. *Boom! Boom! Boom!* Pounding bass lines wreaked havoc as the sound of club music blared through a set of speakers at a nearby concert hall. The vibrations entered through my ears and infiltrated my cranium.

My teeth chattered and my head still pounded. This was no way to treat a sick man.

The full moon's white rays shone into my tent. My eyes itched, but I willed my fingers away and kept them folded in a prayer position below my navel. My only choice was to face the music and embrace the moonlight with ears and eyes wide open. I scanned the midnight sky for hope, strength, and life energy. When times got tough, I had to accept reality. *Turn up the volume and shine brighter! Give it to me! Come on Ethiopia!*

As I continued to stare at the glowing satellite above, tears slid down my cheeks. Calmness and stillness overwhelmed me. Ethiopia dealt the cards and I accepted them. Day by day, kilometer by kilometer. I stared reality in her deep-copper eyes and knew attempting to alter their color was a fool's game. I sobbed and shivered yet felt peaceful. Laughs and chuckles mixed into the bizarre set of emotions and reactions.

Minutes later, everything became clear. I was at one with Ethiopia and embraced her for who she was. I felt a love for her and her people; for the cloud blankets she gifted me as cool relief from the burning sun; for her jagged peaks, which scratched the sky; for her canyons, which dug deep into the earth's crust; for her teff crops and her coffee and mango trees, which nourished me and gave me the strength to continue. For so long, Ethiopia had been a dream, foreign to experience. The closed door had a key called *fantasy*. After so much anticipation and waiting, I stood on the porch of her home and stared in awe at her terraced balconies, where people shared stories and sang. Screams of dissent and horror echoed from her cellar. By sheer will and determination, I opened the door and shriveled in her basement of terror. I basked in the excitement her gifts of hospitality induced. Now I was at her exit, crying alone in my tent on my last evening.

I smiled and reflected on the people I'd met. Ethiopia had given me the gift of friendship, on cue, several hours after each mini-crisis. I thought of Eshetu and Selam, shoving endless plates of food at me after I'd dodged golf-ball-sized stones. I thought of Teka and his genuine sincerity, our stroll around his village and his baby niece's dance moves. His warm and gentle demeanor had calmed me into a state of ease after confronting shovel-brandishing teenagers. After saying goodbye to Teka, Gebaya took me into his home and impressed me with his ingenuity, curiosity, and charm. He adopted me as a family member and made me part Ethiopian. I sent his unborn child love and positivity. The memory of Henok and our spiritual talks, the holy-water bath, and his giddy reaction at sleeping with angels in the head monk's bed shone brightly.

I thought of the children. Their persistence and boldness enabled them to push and pull at my bicycle, tear open my bags, and toss stones in my direction to keep me alert and aware. They'd forced me to grow as a person by arousing anger, helplessness, and shame. Through them, I gained the power of forgiving and learned to regain control of my mind and create my reality. Instead of blaming them for hurling rocks, I blamed myself for the intense reactions of rage and aggression. I had learned to forgive out of love and compassion for others, and most of all, for myself.

The children of Ethiopia instilled lessons in humility. Stones can break my bones, which heal themselves, but humility lasts a lifetime. Before my trip, I thought I'd accomplished so much in the realm of adventure travel. The kids knocked me off my pedestal by making me their target-practice dummy. They showed me that the superhuman who'd cycled along the Pamir Highway and pedaled against balance-shaking headwinds in the Gobi Desert was a foolish guy with an inflated ego. I was a man who couldn't control his temper and fought stones with more stones. Troops of humans half my size bullied me on their playground. It was an enormous wake-up call. A reminder that I was nothing. An indication that any slip-up, any spout of fury, any rage-inflicted reaction was my fault. Between any stimulus and response was a space of time, and I needed to use that time more wisely.

My tears flushed away the unconscious pain and toxic energy that had accumulated in recent years. The blood of deep-seated depression and anger trickled down my cheeks. Resentment toward the uncontrollable. Fury at my inability to change things that are unchangeable. Frustration at others who view the world differently. Outrage at those who brush off climate change, poverty, and hunger. Rage at a society that bullies people into addiction, depression, and suicide. Anger at an education system that fails to teach self-confidence, freedom from fear and suffering, and financial literacy. Repressed sadness, excitement, and happiness surfaced. Finally, I was empty.

I felt clean and proud. Purged of the ego-driven cravings for attention. Cleansed of the inner turmoil from the events of the past four weeks. I was proud of the preparation for my Ethiopian trip and ecstatic to have another adventure under my belt. It'd been nine years since my grandmother passed away and I'd cried this much. Ethiopia gifted me nine years of life experience in one month. Every three days I aged a year. Now it was time for my once-every-nine-years cry.

Ethiopia had congratulated me in her unique style. After a soul-breaking obstacle course, which drenched me in sweat and tears, she uttered her message with bone-vibrating ferocity: "Take this soap and water. Congratulations! You did it!" she howled. I lathered up in the fetal position as her moonlight cast its spell.

Ethiopia groomed me into a more complete human being. I was a 38-year-old man who completed his rite of passage into middle age. She pushed me farther than I'd ever imagined I could go, and I battled to the edge of delirium. I proved to myself that my potential was limitless.

Being sick in my tent was one of my happiest moments. I observed my bodily sensations with perfect equanimity. One second, a hammer pounded into my forehead; the next, hot coals dug deep into my scalp, followed by another bout of chills. The seasons of life were wrapped into one evening and I lay there, my face wet with tears, smiling in the moonlight. I knew I could handle any challenge the heavens threw at me, even if it was self-inflicted.

They say when the student is ready, the teacher will appear. Like a superior educator, Ethiopia made me believe in myself. In the future, when the rocks of difficulty strike, the blood will dry up, turn into a scab, and the wound will heal itself. The scars a reminder of life lessons.

Ethiopia became the merciless college professor who piled on assignments right after midterm exams. She was the educator who made her student's head pound. She was the teacher whose pupils all thought: "How am I supposed to get through this semester alive?" The professor who means well but can't understand her learners are taking six other classes besides hers. The instructor who makes her students pull all-nighters, shortening their life span and increasing their risk of Alzheimer's disease. The universe was giving me what I deserved for piling on the work at my university in South Korea. It was my turn. Only my test was outside the classroom, a struggle with life and death.

The next morning, beams of sun poked through the gaps in my tent. I sat up and crossed my legs while my eyes were still glued shut. I took a few deep breaths and my brain replenished itself. Each drawn breath made me feel lighter. Each exhalation released residual tension. With each breath cycle, I became more focused on the tingling in my nostrils. The localized stimulation gradually rose to my nasal cavity and reached around my face and chin, then to my ears and the top of my head. Each breath uplifted my center of control. I felt like I was hovering over the campsite, several body-lengths high, belly parallel to the ground, arms and legs spread. My stomach tingled with delight, but it wasn't the stomach in my tent; it was the one above my body. Another inhalation later, I levitated even higher and observed the campsite from above as my belly churned. Soon, it was too overwhelming. I opened my eyes and zoomed back into my body, pain and worry gone.

I sat there in awe at my state of normalcy. It felt as though I'd shut my eyes amidst the delirium only a few minutes earlier. Now the sun blinded me, and I was renewed, resurrected from sickness into health. My head light and clear, I pried off the layers that had protected me from the previous evening's ice storm. I unzipped my tent and glanced up at the blue sky and stretched my arms in the air, elated that the illness had vanished.

I tore off my bicycle tires, handlebars, and pedals and stuffed them into a big cardboard box, lifting the aluminum frame with ease. Forty minutes later, the job was done. Packing complete. I was ready to return to South Korea with renewed vigor for life. What an amazing ride.

The cab driver, Ahmed, a middle-aged guy with a shaved head and thick, bushy eyebrows, grabbed one end of my box and grimaced as he loaded it into the trunk of his vehicle, a rusty, green compact.

"Where are you from?" I asked, in an attempt at friendly conversation.

"Harar. Have you heard of Harar?" he inquired with a squinty-eyed smile.

"Of course! Harar is supposed to have the best coffee and the sweetest mangoes in Ethiopia! Haile Selassie spent his early life there." I was excited to meet a man from a region I'd missed.

"Oh! You know a lot about my country." He focused his gaze on the road.

"Sure! I rode my bike to Aksum in one month. Ethiopia is beautiful, and I need to see more of it. Next time, I'll visit your hometown!"

"Wow! One month with only a bicycle? You must write a book!" He chuckled.

"Great idea!"

"If you do, promise to include me in your book." He took his eyes off the road to glance at me.

"Of course, Ahmed! Of course!"

Chapter 26

Return

"Any who may wish to profit alone from the knowledge given him, rather than serve others through the knowledge he has attained, is betraying knowledge and rendering it worthless."
—Haile Selassie

"An army of sheep led by a lion can defeat an army of lions led by a sheep."
—Ghanian proverb

I plopped on the floor next to my gate at the airport in Dubai. My head still pulsated from the illness. Another six hours and I'd be in South Korea again. The land of cheap saunas, fermented vegetables, and my girlfriend's warm touch awaited. I couldn't wait to get back into the classroom. Even teaching for 10 hours a day seemed like a daydream. My students would smile, ready to have fun and make new friends, while I'd encourage them along the path of self-discovery. No one would throw stones if my jokes weren't funny. Students wouldn't ask for money during lunchtime. No one would assault me with gardening tools if I gave homework. My utopia awaited.

Six hours of movies, sleep, and reading later, an air hostess passed me a card that read South Korea Quarantine Survey. I was coming from Dubai, a high-risk MERS (Middle

East Respiratory Syndrome) region, and the authorities were determined to keep the horrid virus off Korean soil.

The 10 questions that lined the survey related to fever symptoms. My thoughts backtracked eight years to when H1N1 had ravaged the peninsula. The government quarantined a group of non-Koreans, including myself, in a teacher-training ground for one week. Back then, it was fun being with several hundred other expats. I made friends and practiced my language skills with cute Korean American girls. This time I was alone and couldn't afford to miss classes.

If I lied about my illness, I'd face a fine or potential jail time. As a criminal, they'd fire me in a heartbeat. Goodbye motivated students. Goodbye four months of paid vacation. Goodbye three-day weekends.

Or I could blame it on the pen. My pen ran wild and had a mind of its own. Lies, lies, lies.

I had to tell the truth. It wasn't worth risking my life in Korea and putting others' health at risk. Headache? Yes. Nausea? Yes. Dizziness? Yes. Fever in the past three days? Big time.

My head spun and beads of sweat trickled down my cheeks as I stood in the health-inspection queue. I clenched my frigid hands together until my forearms twitched. A row of red ropes blocked the airport entrance. Two pistol-packing security guards stood with their arms crossed, scowling as if they'd never experienced a moment of joy in their lives. But I was armed with my invisible weapon. If I coughed from several meters away, my germs would drop them to their knees, collapsing the human barricade, and I could make a dash for it, blazing a trail into the Land of the Morning Calm. All the vitamin-infused fermented cabbage in the world didn't stand a chance against my battle-ax.

Stand still and look healthy! Smile, greet, and use every funny Korean phrase and proverb you can to charm your way into the country! Tell them about your love affair with kimchi and how your dream is to listen to your half-Korean babies say, "*Appa. Sa rang hey!*" *I love you, Daddy*! Make them think you are the savior who'd reverse the declining birthrate.

The line evaporated. *Look at these healthy people! Waltzing their way into the country uncontested.* I stood eye to eye with a cute Korean girl in her late twenties. She wore a white nurse's gown, surgical mask, latex gloves, white slippers with stripes that exposed child-sized toes, and, in her right hand, carried an electronic thermometer. She must've weighed half as much as the sickly man in front of her.

Here we go. Her eyes peered into mine as if scanning for deficiency. My breath shortened, my eyes widened, my hands trembled.

"Card please."

"Yes."

"I am going to take your temperature."

"Okay."

She stuck a thermometer in my ear for what seemed like a few minutes. My chest pounded as I took in a slow breath.

"You have a fever."

The pounding in my chest sped up to a rapid-fire beat.

"I do? That's strange. I feel fine now." I threw up my hands in surprise and disbelief.

This is it. Quarantine time. How am I supposed to teach classes while stuck in a government facility? My university is going to be livid. Because of me, my school's going to enact new rules about leaving the country during winter and summer vacations. From now on, my coworkers and I would be signing contracts stating, "I understand my employment will be terminated if I'm not here for the first day of classes." I'd ruin the fun for everyone.

The woman sifted through a pile of business cards while I shuddered in anticipation of unwelcome news.

"Call this number if you still have a fever after two weeks."

"Okay. Sure."

"Next!"

Free at last! I made it! Life waited for me, and I couldn't wait.

A few days later, I stood in front of a classroom of students who were leaning forward on their desks. Pencil cases open and papers in hand, their eyes sparkled on the first day. Twenty-five kids in their early twenties sat ready to learn more about global citizenship and life skills. After introducing myself and class members to each other, it was question-and-answer time.

"Why do you travel to hard places like Ethiopia?" asked a girl with oval-shaped glasses and straight, black hair.

"Great question! It's part of my global citizenship and life-skills education. The world is my teacher, and Ethiopia was my training ground for a month. Experiences become part of who I am. If I do something hard during my vacation, then my everyday life becomes simple. We'll talk about this throughout the semester."

"This sounds like a great class." She smiled while resting her fist against her chin.

"A class is as good as its students, and I'm grateful to always have *haksengbok*," I said. *Student luck.* "Luck is on my side."

The class erupted in laughter.

Luck. My favorite four-letter word. I'm such a lucky guy.

That evening, after a day of teaching and two hours of front squats, push presses, and muscle snatches, I visited a bathhouse in my neighborhood. I took a cold shower first then tiptoed into a piping-hot whirlpool of ginseng-infused water. It reminded me of my baptism at Henok's church, cleansing me of evil and the fatigue of a month on the road in Ethiopia. Two men in their late fifties sat across from me, bodies submerged up to the nose, groaning in relief. They were being relieved of the stress of sitting at desks or being on their feet for hours on end. Men responsible for sending their children to night school to compete in an educational system that prioritized rote memorization of English vocabulary words, Chinese characters, and Korean poems. With luck, their children would enter one of Seoul's most prestigious universities. These were men responsible for bringing honor to their families via a paycheck. The water baptized them into relaxation, a brief escape from the pressure that was slowly killing them. The evils of intense competition and endless craving for respect lifted for a few minutes.

I wondered what Henok would've thought of this place: a set of 10 showers, five whirlpools with variable temperature settings, three sauna rooms with the heat cranked. Drops fell from the ceiling or trickled down the walls—condensed vapor that had left its mark on every corner of the room. This was far different from the holy water Henok and I had soaked ourselves in but also similar. I was in the basement of an eight-story building surrounded by concrete walls, not in a desert oasis stepping around stones in the sand. There were lockers to store clothes, and a key bracelet wrapped around my wrist. At the desert stream, Henok and I had had the outdoors, with a few cloth sheets shielding us from potential voyeurs. Both places had their charms, but nothing beat bathing under the desert sun.

As steam rose from the pool and fogged up my glasses, I thought of the mentally ill woman at Henok's church who'd grabbed my specs and blurred my vision. Perhaps the awe of a Korean bathhouse would've snapped her back to normalcy. She'd become an electrical engineering student again, wondering at the electrical connections necessary to make this place exist. I wondered whether she'd returned to differential calculus and Ohm's Law or was still screaming at the memory of the *faranji* who'd sat in her tent.

A few meters to my left, a man and his son sat on knee-high plastic stools, both naked. Soapy water slid along the boy's back; his father's hair was white with shampoo. The man scrubbed the boy's back with a towel, pressing and kneading in a circular motion.

"Daddy's going to give you a good massage since you studied so hard last week," the father said as the child grinned.

I thought of Selam's hand-feeding. Her germs infiltrated my food and gave the wedding cuisine its unique flavor. A massage to the taste buds and display of love. So many similarities existed from one continent to the next. From massages to methods of stress relief to bathing with loved ones. We are the same in our desire for healing, in showing and displaying affection, but we express it in different ways.

I reflected on my accomplishment—cycling across Ethiopia. I'd been preparing my entire life for the trip by seeking situations that made my heart pound. Going alone to parties where I knew no one and choosing water over alcohol to work on my social skills. Playing basketball with strangers in Detroit neighborhoods where I was the only light-skinned man. Moving to New York and then Texas during my university years instead of staying close to home. Backpacking solo in Central America and Mexico after leaving my corporate job. Moving to Korea and competing as the only non-native speaker in Korean speech contests in front of auditoriums of people. Cycling across Asia's most challenging countries. Meditating for several hours a day while acknowledging the misery of aching knees and lower-back pain. Pushing my body to its limits while training twice a day in the months leading up to Ethiopia. I made it out alive thanks to 20 plus years of preparation. Ethiopia frustrated me, tested my limits of rage and fury, and showed me what humility and friendship were about. The life experience was priceless.

The warm pool of comfort made me miss everyday life in Ethiopia. I missed the coffee vendors, banana-cart pushers, shoe shiners, white-robed churchgoers, goat-herding villagers, and women with crosses tattooed on their foreheads. The shoulder-bump greetings, the gregarious smiles from men in the street and shy grins from women at food shacks, the slight bows of respect from wrinkled old men. Then there was Amharic, the tongue-popping and gasping for breath mid-sentence and rapid-fire cadence of the only African language that has its own script. Ethiopian pop music—the pounding bass lines, electronic trumpet choruses, staccato snare-drum beats, and high-pitched vocals blaring around every corner in the cities. The social spontaneity of dancing in coffee shacks, impromptu friendships, and wedding invitations. I missed glaring at mountain peaks, canyons with dried-up rivers, and steep drops that made Africa's most mountainous country so thrilling. The dry desert air, sandy terrain, and grainy gusts of hot wind. I missed pedaling uphill along switchback roads as my squeaky chain broke the morning silence and gliding downhill as my ears popped and wind smacked my helmet. I missed the children and their naughty persistence and boldness, giggling at the *faranji* and trying to unzip his bags while running alongside a crazy-looking mountain bike from the other side of the world. Mostly, I missed the tension and unpredictability. Not knowing where I'd sleep or whether a hyena or baboon lurked around the next corner. Sandstorms could let up within a few minutes or a couple of hours. When I needed a breather, shady outposts might've been plentiful or scarce. No one could predict whether political strife or cattle wars would lead villagers to use their AK-47s in a vendetta killing. I yearned for Ethiopia and her charm.

One day I'd return, and I'd appreciate her charisma and flaws the minute I stepped off the plane.

Help Me Keep Doing This

Congratulations! You made it to the end! I hope you enjoyed this book and learned something useful. This book took 41 years to write—two and a half years of editing and tweaking the manuscript, and 38 years of accumulating the experiences that prompted me to sit down and write it. This is my first book, but I hope it will not be my last. Being an independent author without the backing of a publishing house means writing is only half the battle. I don't have a big marketing budget to help people find the book. I can't hire publicists or run a commercial about my book during the next Manchester United game—not on my South Korean teacher's salary.

I have something much more important than any of that—**readers like you!** Honest reviews are the fuel that keeps independent authors like me doing this. I want to write more books and I hope you want me to also. I'd love to share more of my adventures with you. Please go to the website where you bought this book and write a line or two about your thoughts and opinions. You can also sign up for my newsletter at intrepidglobalcitizen.com to receive updates about the Intrepid Global Citizen Podcast and my upcoming books.

Thank you! Kimchi and rice are on me when you come to Seoul! Please reach out anytime.

George (georgebalarezo@gmail.com)

About the Author

George Balarezo is an adventurer, university lecturer, engineer, and author who lives in Seoul, South Korea. Accused of being a CIA spy, he went on to hike the Hindu Kush with five military escorts in Pakistan in 2011, immersed himself in Vipassana meditation in India in 2012, hitchhiked across Southern Africa in 2013, and threw his backpack aside to embark on his first tour-cycling journey in 2014 with a $180, second-hand bicycle. During his first long-distance bicycle adventure, he scavenged for water in the deserts of Uzbekistan, was pelted by summer hail on the Pamir Highway in Tajikistan and Kyrgyzstan, and learned how to fix a flat tire for the first time while savoring stale bread, butter, and tea at every meal. That first expedition led to unsupported, solo cycling journeys in Oman, Bangladesh, Turkey, Russia, Mongolia, China's Xinjiang Province, and Kenya. He recharges his adventure battery by motivating South Korean university students to step out of their comfort zones, competing in speech contests as the only non-native Korean speaker at Toastmasters' meetings, sampling fermented bean paste and silkworms in South Korea's traditional markets, and sweating it out in CrossFit gyms. He is also the host of the *Intrepid Global Citizen Podcast*, aimed at spreading peace by sharing travel stories and providing the listener with an adventure-based education.

Acknowledgments

They say it takes a village to raise a child, but it takes an even larger village to write a book. I'd like to thank my family for putting up with my escapades over the years. My mother and father now have many more gray hairs and wrinkles due to my journeys. Throughout my life, they've given me the unconditional love and support necessary for a son to go for his dreams. I inherited my father's stubbornness and my mother's energy level—a tough combination for any parent to deal with. I'd also like to show appreciation for my brother Grant, who always joins me for crazy physical training sessions when I'm getting ready for an adventure. His company makes the sweat, blood, and tears a joy no matter how hard much of the aforementioned I shed.

I'd like to thank Jinhee, who enthusiastically supports my crazy ideas and shows me what kindness and friendship are all about.

Several good friends, including Terry Stone, Travis Shaw, Curtis Chin, and Jason Ferguson, took the time to read early versions of the manuscript and provided me with invaluable suggestions.

Thanks to Ryan Anderle and James Lightfoot for providing AI-based images for the book concept.

Also, I'd like to show my appreciation to my friends at the Ann Arbor Revision Group. Thanks to Kimberly Krauss, Josie Scheider, Sarah Nassiri, Ben Nadler, Jonathan Allen, Maryann Lawrence, and Rachel Tasker for their constructive criticism.

Without your feedback and support, this book wouldn't be readable.

I'd also like to thank the members of the Los Angeles Writers Critique Group, especially organizers Gabi Loreno and Christopher Kowalchuk, for their tireless dedication to providing a supportive community for writers of all genres and levels. Waking up at 3 a.m. to attend Zoom meetings during the pandemic was a worthwhile experience, and I'd do it again in a heartbeat.

I'd like to thank Scott DeVogelaere and all the members of the Metro Detroit Writer's Workshop for reading the very first version of this manuscript. It was with you I learned that more than 90 percent of writing is editing.

Thanks to Le Bailey Senior for always supporting my crazy decisions even before I moved to South Korea in 2007.

Thank you to Tony Hester for being my best friend since elementary school and for always cheering me on during my journeys.

I'm grateful to my editor, Vincent Czyz, whose valuable feedback resulted in a polished manuscript and helped take my writing to a higher level. If you are writing a book, be sure to hire him as your editor.

I'd like to thank everyone in the Toastmasters Korea community who listened to my speeches about my adventures in a language I've been struggling with for years.

Thanks to Autumn Kim and Landis Fryer for providing feedback on the book title, subtitle, and cover pictures.

I'd like to show my appreciation to all my coworkers at my university in Seoul. It's always a pleasure spending time in an office full of kindred spirits who support one another.

Thanks to Jared Sandler for accompanying me on journeys on the Korean peninsula and listening to accounts of the trials and tribulations I experienced while away on an adventure.

Lastly, thank you to everyone in Ethiopia and across the world for their smiles, friendship, and gifts of hospitality. It is because of you that I have an unwavering positive outlook on the future of humanity. Your kindness motivates me to be a better global citizen every morning that I wake up.

Printed in the USA
CPSIA information can be obtained
at www.ICGtesting.com
CBHW021754220624
10478CB00004B/13